Call No Man Normal

BENJAMIN B. WOLMAN

Call No Man Normal

INTERNATIONAL UNIVERSITIES PRESS, INC.

New York

Copyright © 1973, International Universities Press, Inc.

Library of Congress Catalog Card Number: 79–184211
ISBN: 0–8236–0610–4

Manufactured in the United States of America

Acknowledgments

I am deeply indebted to Drs. Henry A. Brill, John Exner, Edward J. Hornick, Bernard Kalinkowitz, and J. Richard Wittenborn who read the entire manuscript, sparing neither time, effort nor enlightening critical comment. Norma Fox, the editor at International Universities Press, offered most competent help in editing the manuscript. At various stages of the work, I was assisted by Susan Knapp, Marcia Rosser, and Kathy Mankes. To all of them, my warmest thanks.

B.B.W.

Contents

vii

With the exception of organic cases, mental disorder is caused by mismanagement of people (children) by people (their parents).

B.B.W.

Preface

The purpose of this book is to introduce a series of new ideas concerning the nature of mental disorders. Although these new ideas are deeply rooted in the work of Freud, they suggest new solutions to some of the problems he either dealt with or omitted.

There are practical as well as theoretical reasons for introducing new ideas. The practical reasons are related to the present-day confusion in the classification and diagnosis of mental disorders. The Freud-Abraham classificatory system is subject to criticism and the system suggested by the American Psychiatric Association is full of inconsistencies, reflecting a distinct regressive tendency in its emphasis on symptoms rather than causes.

Small wonder that diagnosticians are faced with a maze of poorly defined and overlapping categories. Moreover, how can one make a diagnosis if one operates with theoretical constructs of Freud's theory, such as "weak ego," "repression," "anxiety," and so on, which are not related in an equivocal manner to observational data. Even more confusing are the superficial and changing categories coined *ad hoc* by the behaviorists.

The lack of clarity in psychopathology does not help in diagnosis and treatment. What indeed is mental disorder? Is it a disease? Or a fixation on a developmental stage? Or a cluster of conditioned reflexes? What are the causes of mental disorders? What are the factors that determine symptom formation?

The probing of these and related questions resulted in the development of a new conceptual system. Leaning heavily on

Freud's work, the new system introduces a distinct revision of the theory of the instinctual drives. The economic part of Freudian theory is further elaborated and new items are added to the theory of developmental stages.

These new concepts are applied to family dynamics and pathogenesis of mental disorders. A new classification system is introduced which links observable and easily diagnosed behavioral patterns to fundamental etiologic factors. This new system offers a solution to two perennial problems plaguing psychiatrists, clinical psychologists and psychoanalysts, namely the relationship between the choice of symptoms and etiology, and the relationship between personality dynamics and overt behavior.

Finally, as the title of the book indicates, the present book follows the direction indicated by Freud. Mental disorder (except in cases which are clearly organic in nature) is not a disease in the usual sense. In fact, it is not a disease at all.

All human beings experience fluctuations in mood. All human beings fight for survival, love and hate, fear and dare. Even the so-called "normal" people are not always rational, and the most disturbed schizophrenics do not act in a schizophrenic fashion all the time. Human behavior can be viewed as a continuum of love and hate directed toward (cathected into) oneself and others. In some individuals there is more love of oneself and more hostility directed toward others; in others there is more love for others and more hostility directed toward oneself; or in others there is a shifting of love and hate for oneself and others.

These three basic types of relative behavior can be found in daily life. Moreover, people are, at times, more irrational than at others. Some people are severely irrational, causing tragedies and mounting disaster.

But no one is fully adjusted or rational at all times. Hence, CALL NO MAN NORMAL.

Benjamin B. Wolman

❧ 1 ❧

Eros and Thanatos

Mental Energy

According to Freud (1938) mental processes are derivatives of physical processes. "We assume," he wrote, "as the other natural sciences have taught us to expect, that in mental life some kind of energy is at work; but we have no data which enables us to come nearer to knowledge of it by analogy with other forms of energy" (p. 14).

The postulate of the conservation of energy and its transformability into physical energy and vice-versa ("the mysterious leap from mind to body") is one of the fundamental principles of psychoanalytic theory. According to Freud (1894b): "The visceral excitation will then actually develop continuously, but only when it reaches a certain height will it be sufficient to overcome the resistance in the paths of conduction to the cerebral cortex and express itself as a psychical stimulus" (p. 108). And later on: "Once it has reached the required level, the somatic sexual excitation is continuously transmuted into psychical excitation" (p. 108).

In another paper published in the same year Freud (1894a) explained:

> Among the psychic functions there is something which should be differentiated (an amount of affect, a sum of excitation), something having all the attributes of a quantity—although we possess no means of measuring it—a something which is capable of increase, decrease, displacement and discharge, and which extends itself over the memory-traces of an idea like an electric charge over the surface of the body. We can apply this . . . in the same sense as the physicist employs the conception of a fluid electric current [p. 160].

3

The Constancy Principle

The so-called *constancy principle* was one of the earliest psychoanalytic concepts, formulated by Freud and Breuer in 1892. "The nervous system endeavors to keep constant something in its functional condition that may be described as the 'sum of excitation.' It seeks to establish the necessary precondition of health by dealing with every sensible increase of excitation along associative lines or by discharging it by an appropriate motor reaction" (p. 30). The same idea of equilibrium was repeated by Breuer in 1895 in *The Studies in Hysteria,* written jointly with Freud.

Freud's principle of constancy is parallel to Cannon's homeostasis, Goldstein's equilibration, Pavlov's equilibrium, and resembles Newton's law of inertia. Freud was particularly influenced by Fechner's principle called "the tendency toward stability," and associated disequilibrium with tension and equilibrium with relief.

According to the constancy principle, all living organisms are capable of responding or reacting to inner and outer stimuli. When an organism is stimulated, a state of disequilibrium is created. This disequilibrium is self-terminating, for every living organism tends to restore its former balance through a discharge of energy. It is a universal tendency to keep the quantity of excitation as low as possible, for an increase in excitation disrupts the inner balance of the organism.

Another application of the constancy principle, deduced from the pleasure principle and interpreted as reduction of tension, was the idea of the perfect sleep. When all tensions are removed, the infant falls blissfully asleep. Sleep is the escape from overstimulation; thus the perfect sleep is the perfect satisfaction (the Nirvana principle).

Freud believed in the principle of the conservation of physical and mental energy. Energy can be invested or cathected into various objects; it can be transformed; it can be released or accumulated. Whenever energy is invested into an object, this object becomes charged with some amount of mental energy in the same manner that bodies become charged with static electricity. Cathexis can be applied to external objects as well as to one's own organism.

Accordingly, mental processes have been viewed by Freud as *quantitative* processes of investment, discharge, accumulation and transformation of mental energy. All mental processes are energy consuming, some more, some less. When a stimulus acts upon an organism, it creates a disequilibrium perceived as tension. Tension leads to an action, which is a discharge of energy. Discharge of energy restores equilibrium; the new equilibrium is perceived as relief or relaxation.

Between the processes of tension and discharge of energy, two contradictory forces step in. One force facilitates discharge of energy which brings relief; the other prevents or postpones this discharge. The inhibitory forces, described in Freud's structural theory, were the ego and the superego. The forces that urge and facilitate discharge Freud called *drives* or *instincts*. The instincts or instinctual drives press for discharge of energy, for a lowering of the level of excitation and for a reduction in the disequilibrium and tension in the organism. Freud believed that the tendency to maintain equilibrium or homeostasis was a general tendency of living matter. Thus he regarded the instinctual drives as innate and primary biological forces.

Theory of Instincts

Instincts represent the bridge between the physical and the mental worlds. They are rooted in the body, and serve as release mechanisms. The chemophysical processes of the organism are the source of instincts. "The instincts are mythical beings, superb in their indefiniteness. In our work we cannot for a moment overlook them, and yet we are never certain that we are seeing them clearly" (Freud, 1933, p. 131). The instincts represent the demand "made upon the mind in consequence of its connection with the body." Instincts arise from sources of stimulation within the body and operate as a constant, everpresent force. One can escape an external stimulation, but one cannot escape inner stimulation caused by instinctual forces. All instincts have an impetus, a source, an object, and an aim. Impetus is the size or amount of force. The source is some excitation within the body caused by deficiency, such as thirst, hunger, or any other deprivation or disturbance of the inner balance. The aim of any instinctual activity is a discharge of energy aiming at the reduction of excitation and restoration of the inner equilibrium." All instinctual activity can be pictured as "a certain sum of energy forcing its way in a certain direction."

Instincts, believed Freud, are "an expression of the *conservative* nature of living substance." Migrations of fish and birds, heredity, and embryology bear witness to the "organic compulsion to repeat." An instinct is "a compulsion inherent in organic life to restore an earlier stage of things which the living entity has been obliged to abandon under the pressure of external, disturbing forces; that is, it is a kind of organic elasticity, or, to put it another way, the expression of the inertia inherent in organic life" (ibid., p. 47).

In the *New Introductory Lectures* Freud (1933) described instincts as follows:

> The theory of the instincts is, as it were, our mythology. The instincts are mythical beings, superb in their indefiniteness. Our first step was tentative enough. We felt we should probably not go far wrong if we started by distinguishing two main instincts, or species or groups of instincts—hunger and love . . . We are here overshadowed by the immutable biological fact that the living individual serves two purposes, self-preservation and the preservation of species . . . In accordance with this view, we introduced the "ego-instincts" and the "sexual instincts" into psychoanalysis.

An instinct differs from a stimulus in that it arises from sources of stimulation within the body, operates as a constant force, and is such that the subject cannot escape from it by flight as he can from external stimulus. An instinct may be described as having a source, an object, and an aim. The source is a state of excitation within the body, and its aim is to remove that excitation; in the course of its path from its source to the attainment of its aim the instinct becomes operative mentally. We picture it as a certain sum of energy forcing its way in a certain direction . . . The evidence of analytic experience proves conclusively that instinctual impulses from one source can join on to instinctual impulses from another and share their further vicissitudes, and that in general the satisfaction of one instinct can be substituted for the satisfaction of another [pp. 131–133].

Eros

Freud divided all instincts into *self-preservation* or *ego-instincts* and *sexual* or *libido instincts.* The sexual instincts are more flexible than the self-preservation instincts; they can be held in suspense (aim-inhibited), sublimated, diverted into new channels, and perverted; their gratification can be denied or substituted and their objects can be changed and displaced. Freud (1905a) wrote:

The popular view distinguishes between hunger and love, seeing them as representatives of the instincts that aim at self-preservation and reproduction of the species respecti ely. In associating ourselves with this very evident distinction we postulate in psychoanalysis a similar one between the self-preservative or ego-instincts on the one hand and the sexual instincts on the other; the force by which the sexual instinct is represented in the mind we call "libido"—sexual longing—and regard it as analogous to the force of hunger, or the will to power, and other such trends among the ego-tendencies [p. 217].

With the discovery of narcissism the distinction between libido and ego-instincts became untenable. The ego-instincts became a special case of the libido-cathexis, that is an investment of libido in one's own person. In 1914 Freud arrived at

a monistic interpretation of the instinctual life and believed
in *one* instinctual force, the force of love. Eros encompassed
all sexual and egoistical drives, and libido included all energies at the disposal of Eros.

The conflict that often takes place between the sexual and
self-preservation instincts was interpreted as a conflict between self-love (Narcissism) and object-love. In well-adjusted
individuals there is a balance of cathexis in oneself and cathexis in others which permits the individual to protect himself and to take care of those whom he loves. In some individuals this balance is disturbed; some develop secondary and
morbid narcissism after they have been seriously thwarted in
their development of object-cathexis. Some are unable to
take care of themselves due to insufficient narcissism or over-
adundant object-cathexis (Federn, 1952; Wolman, 1957).

With the inclusion of narcissism in the group of life or
Eros instincts, the sexual instincts became just another class
of instincts within this larger category. As Freud put it (1921,
p. 56, footnote) the erotic instincts are "the purest example"
of the instincts of life. However, in contradistinction to other
life instincts, Freud (1933) regarded the sexual instincts as
being "remarkable for their plasticity, for the facility with
which they can change their aims . . . for the ease with
which they can substitute one form of gratification for another, and for the way in which they can be held in suspense,
as has been so well illustrated by the aim inhibited instincts"
(p. 134).

Fulfillment of an instinctual urge gives pleasure. In the
Fechner-Freud conceptual system pleasure was associated
with the reestablishment of equilibrium and relief. Pleasure
was a broad concept; the pleasure arrived at from the union
of genital organs was considered the highest but certainly not
the only type of "organ pleasure." In 1933 Freud restated the
main ideas expressed in 1905:

We do not, that is to say, believe that there is a single sexual instinct, which is from the first the vehicle of the impulse towards the aim of the sexual function, that is, the union of the two sex cells. On the contrary, we see a large number of component instincts, arising from various regions of the body, which strive for satisfaction more or less independently of one another, and find this satisfaction in something that may be called "organ pleasure." The genitals are the latest of these erotogenic zones; and their organ-pleasure must certainly be called "sexual" [p. 135].

The Death Instinct

It appeared that the 1914 revision of the theory of instincts was adequate and final. Men were driven by the life instincts of Eros. Whenever the libidinal energies, activated by Eros, were directed toward oneself, they served the self-preservatory function; whenever the energies were object-directed, they were sexual.

There seemed to be no need to introduce additional concepts for hostile behavior. Conflict of interests was the cause of hostility, and hatred could be explained as an act of self-love. "In the undisguised antipathies and aversions which people feel toward strangers with whom they have to do, we may recognize the expression of self-love—of narcissism. The self-love works for the self-assertion of the individual" (Freud, 1922, p. 55).

Undoubtedly, this self-assertiveness was associated with readiness for hatred and hostile behavior. Yet, pretty soon Freud was confronted with several phenomena that evaded the self-love explanation. These phenomena were (1) man's senseless cruelty to fellow men, (2) sadism and masochism, (3) suicide, and (4) death. None of these phenomena could be interpreted by self-cathected libido. The German atrocities in Belgium during the First World War were not self-defense. Obviously the oppressors found delight in their cruelty. Cruelty, destructiveness, and death required new interpretations.

It took Freud a long time to admit to the existence of destructive instincts in men. He (1933) explained this as follows:

> To introduce it [the death instinct] into the human condition seems impious; it contradicts too many religious prejudices and social conventions. No man must be by nature good, or at least good natured. If he occasionally shows himself to be brutal, violent and cruel, these are only passing disturbances of his emotional life, mostly provoked, and perhaps only the consequence of the ill-adapted social system which he has so far made for himself [p. 142].

A complete revision of the instinct theory took place in 1920. Almost 20 years later Freud (1938) described this revision as follows:

> After long doubts and vacillations we have decided to assume the existence of only two basic instincts, Eros and the *destructive* instinct . . . The aim of the first of these basic instincts is to establish ever greater unities and to preserve them, thus—in short, to bind together; the aim of the second, on the contrary, is to undo connections and so to destroy things. We may suppose that the final aim of the destructive instinct is to reduce living things to an inorganic state. For this reason we also call it the death instinct [p. 20].

Destructiveness is primarily directed towards one's own life, it is a drive toward death. In order to protect ourselves from this self-destructive tendency we must find some external channels for aggressiveness.

All instincts, Freud (1933) believed, are "directed toward the reinstatement of an earlier state of things. We may assume that as soon as a given state of things is upset there arises an instinct to recreate it, and phenomena appear which we may call 'repetition-compulsion'" (p. 145). This basic law of constancy has been applied to the interpretation of destructiveness and death.

Freud (1933) continued as follows:

> If it is true that once in an inconceivably remote past, and in an unimaginable way, life arose out of inanimate matter, then, in accord-

ance with our hypothesis, an instinct must at that time have come
into being, whose aim it was to abolish life once more and to reestab-
lish the inorganic state of things. If in this instinct we recognize the
impulse to self-destruction of our hypothesis, then we can regard that
impulse as the manifestation of a *death instinct* [p. 147].

Accordingly, Freud divided all instincts into two types: the
erotic that try to collect "living substance into larger unities,"
and the *death* instincts that "act against this tendency and
try to bring living matter back into an inorganic condition"
(p. 147).

In another work Freud (1920) stated, "If we are to take it
as a truth that knows no exception that everything living dies
for *internal* reasons—become inorganic once again—then we
shall be compelled to say 'the goal of all life is death' and
looking backwards, that 'what was inanimate existed before
what is living' " (p. 50).

Organic life has developed out of inorganic matter. When
life originated, an instinct was born that aimed at destruction
of life and reinstatement of the inorganic state that existed
previously. The origin of life has brought about the origin of
the destructive instinct directed against life. The aim of this
instinct is death and the reestablishment of the inanimate
nature. Life and death are interwoven; construction and destruction are inseparable. No vital process can be free from
the death-instinct. The life instincts try "to collect living substance together into even larger unities," and the death instincts "act against this," and bring living matter back into
inorganic condition. "The cooperation and opposition of
these two forces produce the phenomena of life to which
death puts an end" (Freud, 1938, pp. 146–147).

In the life span of an individual Eros and Thanatos often
combine their resources, frequently fighting one another. Eating is a process of destruction with the purpose of incorporation, while the sexual act is an act of aggression that aims at
the "most intimate union."

Freud arrived at the idea of the death instinct in another way too, through study of the pathology of sexual life. In 1933 he wrote:

> It is not on account of the teaching of history and of our own experience of life that we maintain the hypothesis of a special instinct of aggression and destructiveness in man, but on account of general considerations to which we were led in trying to estimate the importance of the phenomena of *sadism* and *masochism*. . . . Both of them, sadism and masochism, are very hard to account for by the theory of libido, and especially masochism . . . For we believe that in sadism and masochism we have two admirable examples of the fusion of the two kinds of instinct, Eros and aggressiveness [p. 143].

With the introduction of the structural concepts of ego and superego, Freud's theory became more flexible and more apt to include the variety of human feelings and their combinations. One may love self or others; one's feelings may be spontaneous and impulsive, originating in the id, or controlled by reality considerations of the ego, or shaped moralistically by one's superego. Undoubtedly, a great deal of hostility toward one's parents finds its seat in the superego and turns inwardly, against one's own ego.

Thus, the destructive energy, analogous to libido, can turn either inwardly or toward the outer world. Freud (1932) states that under certain circumstances the death instinct

> turns into the destructive instinct if, with the help of special organs it is directed outwards, on to objects. The living creature preserves its own life, so to say, by destroying an extraneous one. Some portion of the death instinct, however, remains operative *within* the living being, and we have sought to trace quite a number of normal and pathological phenomena to this internalization of the destructive instinct [p. 282].

Libido and destrudo[1] are most important determinants of human behavior. According to Freud (1938):

> . . . the interaction of the two basic instincts [and the energies acti-
> vated by them] with and against each other gives rise to the whole
> variegation of the phenomena of life . . . Modifications in the propor-
> tions of the fusion between the instincts have the most noticeable re-
> sults. A surplus of sexual aggressiveness will change a lover into a sex-
> ual murderer, while a sharp diminution in the aggressive factor will
> lead to shyness or impotence [p. 21].

The balance of cathexes of libido and destrudo determines the direction of human behavior. In his last work Freud (1938) formulated this idea as follows:

> So long as that instinct operates internally, as a death instinct, it re-
> mains silent; we only come across it after it has become diverted out-
> ward as an instinct of destruction. That that diversion should occur
> seems essential for the preservation of the individual; the musculature
> is employed for the purpose. When the superego begins to be formed,
> considerable amounts of the aggressive instinct become fixated within
> the ego and operate there in a self-destructive fashion. This is one of
> the dangers to health to which mankind became subject on the path
> to cultural development. The holding back of aggressiveness is in gen-
> eral unhealthy and leads to illness. A person in a fit of rage often
> demonstrates how the transition from restrained aggressiveness to
> self-destructiveness is effected, by turning his aggressiveness against
> himself: he tears his hair or beats his face with his fists—treatment
> which he would evidently have preferred to apply to someone else
> . . . Thus it may in general be suspected that the *individual* dies of
> his internal conflicts but that the *species* dies of its unsuccessful strug-
> gle against the external world, when the latter undergoes changes of a
> kind that cannot be dealt with by the adaptations which the species
> has acquired [pp. 22–23].

[1] Some authors call destructive energy "mortido." I prefer destrudo. Freud himself did not use either term.

❧ 2 ❧

Critique
of the Instinct Theory

It has been my intent in describing Freud's instinct theory and quoting relevant passages to clarify where and on what issues I shall modify Freud's theory. I believe that I do not actually deviate from Freud, but rather suggest an avenue of approach which insofar as it corrects some of the inconsistencies and inadequacies of the master will hopefully lead to a further development of his ideas.

I see no point in quoting or analyzing the ideas of other theoreticians who, like myself, have tried to "correct" Freud. Some of them have contributed magnificent ideas. Some, I believe, have weakened rather than strengthened the foundation on which Freudian thinking rests. My aim is to continue Freud's work with only those corrections that are, I believe, dictated by empirical data and formal rules of theory formation. Thus, I shall refrain from description and analysis of the works of Freud's disciples, except in those cases where I feel that my ideas are a continuation or a development of theirs. I shall start with a critique of Freud's version of conservatism.

First, I see no reason to believe in the existence of a tendency toward *phylogenetic* conservatism, for such an assumption would contradict evolution. Were it true that organic nature tends to restore the former state of things, men would turn into anthropoids, mammals into fish, vertebrates into invertebrates, and so on. No such tendency has been observed in living nature. The assumption that organic nature tends,

14

in the span of centuries or millenia, to become inorganic is certainly unwarranted.

Conservatism in *ontogenetic* evolution does not mean that an organism goes back to its origins. Regressive tendencies are pathological. It was Freud himself who explained neurosis in terms of fixation on an earlier developmental stage and/or regression to it!

Freud could not muster much evidence for his version of conservatism. Certainly sexual instincts did not conform to his formula. Actually, Freud was aware of this and wrote in 1938:

> If we suppose that living things appeared later than inanimate ones and arose out of them, then the death instinct agrees with the formula that we have stated, to the effect that instincts tend toward a return to an earlier state. We are unable to apply the formula to Eros (the love instinct). That would be to imply that living substance had once been a unity but had subsequently been torn apart and was now tending toward reunion [p. 21].

In a footnote to this he adds: "Something of the sort has been imagined by poets, but nothing like it is known to us from the actual history of living substance."

Freud's error probably lies in the lack of precision in the use of the phrase "earlier state." It is in this way that he described the origin of life in *Beyond the Pleasure Principle:*

> The attributes of life were evoked in inanimate matter by the action of a force of whose nature we can form no conception . . . The tension which then arose in what had hitherto been an inanimate substance endeavored to equalize its potential. In this way the first instinct came into being: the instinct to return to the inanimate state . . . For a long time perhaps, living substance was thus being constantly created afresh and easily dying, till decisive external influences altered in such a way as to oblige the still surviving substance to diverge ever more widely from its original course of life and to make

ever more complicated detours before reaching its goal in death [1920, p. 50].

[Each organism] wishes to die only in its own fashion . . . The living organism struggles most energetically against events (dangers, in fact) which might help it to attain its life's goal rapidly—by a kind of short-circuit [Ibid., p. 51].

But it is precisely this which is questionable. Does any organism "wish" to die? All known organisms resist destruction by fight or flight. No organisms, except in pathological cases of suicide, to be discussed later, display the wish or desire to die. Moreover, natural death cannot be considered as an act of regression. How can death be a regression to an early state? Was any organism dead before it was born? Does birth necessarily mean resurrection?

Western philosophy and religion are full of such speculations. For instance, Hegel, Spencer, Spengler and other philosophers speculated about dialectic laws, evolution and dissolution, rise and decline, and other dichotomies. All these metaphors have little if anything to do with empirical data regarding any biological species including Homo sapiens.

Freud (1920) maintained that "the vital process of the individual leads for internal reasons to an equalization of chemical tensions, that is, to death" (p. 76). However, the assumption that equalization of chemical tensions necessarily means death is a most questionable one. In fact, death does put an end to certain biochemical processes such as breathing, digestion, oxidation, metabolism, and so on, but it does not stop decay, decomposition of cells, and other chemical changes in body chemistry. It is an unwarranted assumption that in a corpse all chemical processes come to an end. Death does not put an end to chemistry; true, it stops certain biological processes, but it does not convert organic into inorganic chemistry.

The term "death" does not apply to inorganic matter. Inorganic nature is neither dead nor alive. Living bodies may cease to live, but rocks are neither dead nor alive. Men, animals, and plants can be alive or dead, but the wind, a cloud, a piece of lead, carbon dioxide, or an entire ocean are neither dead nor alive. The concept of constancy is inapplicable to inanimate nature. There is no necessary return to a former stage in Neptune's satellites, in the separation of the moon from the earth, in the separation of Australia from Asia, in the eruptions of Vesuvius, in the formation of geological strata, in erosions, floods, draughts, or earthquakes.

Vitality or the chance for survival of organisms can be measured by the amount of energy at their disposal. An organism may be full of life and blooming, or declining, starving, or decaying. The instinct of life serves to protect life and increases vitality. Conversely, can an alleged death instinct serve to increase or protect death? The decline of life brings one closer to death, but death itself is not a process or anything else definable. Death cannot be described in a sensible way, for death is merely the zero point, the nothingness. That "someone is dead" is a negative statement: it means that someone is "not-alive." No action "serves" or "protects" death; no living organism uses an energy, instinctual or otherwise, to die, to increase, to strengthen or to protect death. There are many causes of death, but it would be improbable to assume that there is an inner, innate instinctual force that releases energy (in the same way as the Eros releases libido) to produce death.

Life can be a state of equilibrium or of disequilibrium, of action or rest, of a waking state or sleep, of tensions and reliefs. Death is neither action nor inaction, neither tension nor relief, neither equilibrium nor disequilibrium. Life is a process of oxidation, input and output, and metabolism. Sometimes it is a balanced and sometimes a disbalanced process. In accordance with the principle of constancy, there is a tendency to restore the balance of life, the balance of the living organism. No such tendency exists in corpses. The constancy principle applies to living organisms only.

Fenichel (1945) criticized Freud's conceptual work as follows:

> A death instinct would not be compatible with the approved biological concept of instinct as discussed above. The thesis of an instinct source that makes the organism react to stimuli with drives toward "instinct actions" which then change the source in an appropriate manner cannot be applied to a death instinct. The dissimulation in the cells, an objective destruction, cannot be a "source" of a destructive instinct in the same way that the chemical sensitizing of the central nervous system in regard to stimulation of the erogenous zones is the source of the sexual instinct. According to the definition, the instinct attempts to remove the somatic changes at the source of the instinct. The death instinct does not attempt to remove the dissimulation [p. 60].

One may add to Fenichel's remarks that there is no deficiency or excitation or any other disbalance in an organism hit by a car or by a bullet. Yet death may come. Death does not remove tensions nor does it develop or assure an equilibrium. Death is the dead-end of everything, of tensions and reliefs alike. Organisms die when their energies reach zero point as a result of old age, or violence to their vital centers caused by a bullet, germs or poison.

The Meaning of Death

Biology deals with a variety of phenomena of the living cells, tissues, and organisms. There is a starting point in ontogenetic history, followed by growth, development, decline, and decay. Each new life is a continuation of former lives. Although we can describe the ending of a life we cannot describe what happens subsequently. There have been several descriptions of dying organisms, but dying organisms are still alive. The vital processes of the organisms, such as metabolism, digestion, respiration, circulation, secretion, and several other processes, end with death.

Philosophers, poets, and theologians have tried to comprehend death, but whenever they spoke about death they inevitably described life. Religion imagined a hereafter as some sort of eternal life after death, as if trying to deny and obliterate the fact that men die. The hereafter was often painted as a Sleeping Beauty story with a Messiah or Prince Charming bringing Resurrection. The days and years after death were pictured as an undisturbed and peaceful life, very much resembling the deep sleep of a tired man and a dream of a pleasant reawakening. Men are afraid of the unknown, and no one can know of the nothingness called death. The natural fear of death was softened by thinking of and believing in the continuation of life. Death is indeed unbelievable; not even perceivable. Men dread death and substitute dreams for death's nothingness.

Whenever people think about those who have died, the dead ones appear in dreams and in thoughts as if they were alive. A dead love object becomes incorporated and lives, as it were, in the mind of the introjecting person. Whenever one talks about a dead person, he is described in the way one believed he was before his death. Thus poets, priests, and philosophers will describe death in terms of eternal life, indicating how peaceful the dead ones are or how much they suffer.

The idea of death has been influenced by what people have experienced in quiet, restful sleep. However, sleep is not death, nor does it resemble death. Pavlov (1928) believed that sleep is a "general inhibition" which enables the living organism to keep an equilibrium between the processes of cellular destruction and restoration. Action uses up energy; sleep restores it. Sleep preserves energy, increases the energetic reserves, strengthens vitality, and serves life. Thus it serves restoration of equilibrium in accordance with Pavlov's version of the principle of constancy.

Sleep and death represent two entirely different states of

the organism. Sleep is a state of a living organism that serves its preservation. The concept of death implies destruction of life, destruction of the living organism. The sole similarity of these two states lies in the lack of gross motility of the organism. Such a highly superficial similarity is no more enlightening than the similarity between eating and yawning; in both functions the mouth is open.

The fear of death is related to the fear of sleep. The Jewish morning prayer contains thanks to God for the restoration of the soul into the body. Children afraid of death are often afraid to fall asleep. The fear of death has caused men to compare death to a sleep from which there is no awakening. It has been, indeed, a great consolation to allay the fear of death by representing death as some sort of a deep and relaxing sleep with an expected pleasant awakening of resurrection. Greek mythology described the relaxing and peaceful hereafter in the Elysium where happy souls of deceased men wander aimlessly with no worries of the future and no memories of the past. The monotheistic religions believe in the hereafter and in resurrection perceived as a return of the soul to the body after a long and peaceful sleep which death is supposed to resemble. The "Requiem" prayer alludes to this "resting in peace" as if a dead organism were capable of "resting" peacefully.

The regressive wish to sleep is not necessarily a wish to die. The manic-depressive's wish to unite with his mother is actually a wish to sleep well, in the safest place—in the womb. It is not a wish to die (Wolman, 1957, 1960a, 1966b).

The Two Dimensions

Life and death are concepts of energy. Life contains a certain amount of energy; death contains none. Life is power; decline of life is the decline of power. Death comes when all the energy is exhausted or its source or flow is destroyed by physical violence or other noxious factors.

When there is life, energy can be used either to support or to destroy it. The instinctual force that serves and supports life is called *Eros* or love. Love or support of life can be directed toward oneself or toward others. The energy of a living organism can also be directed toward destruction of oneself or others. Life represents amounts of energy; the life instincts of love and hostility indicate the aim of this energy and the direction in which it is channeled. This bidimensional issue can be described graphically on the Cartesian coordinates as follows. The vertical dimension represents life. One can have more or less vital energy, but when he dies, his vitality has reached the zero point. The horizontal line indicates the use of energy: it can be used in the plus direction for protection of life or in the minus direction for the destruction of life. One should, therefore, distinguish how *much* available energy one has (i.e., how much life and vitality one possesses) from the *way* in which this energy is used (i.e., for or against survival).

While life or death is a matter of fact, the use of life energy requires an additional distinction. One can protect his own life or the life of someone else; one can destroy his own life or kill someone else.

Eating is done for the protection of one's own life. It is, however, most frequently accomplished at the expense of someone else's life. Every living organism needs food for survival and every living organism seeks food. Animals that fail to find food starve to death.

Food is a matter of life and death. To get food is a matter of life for the eater, and a matter of death for the one to be eaten up. Wolves and sheep are the proverbial poles of this life and death axis, but let us remember that sheep eat too. Sheep, being *herbivorous*, destroy plants by eating them. Wolves, being *carnivorous,* destroy sheep by eating them. The wolf who eats the sheep does not serve Thanatos; he eats for his own survival. The sheep who is eaten up, has not done anything to promote its own death. He simply failed in the fight for his own survival. Apparently, the greatest single destructive action, eating, does not fall in line with Freud's theory of Thanatos.

In accordance with his theory of the death instinct Freud (1933) assumed that self-destructiveness precedes object-directed destructiveness. Freud believed that masochism is older than sadism. When outward aggression is unable to find satisfaction in the external world, it may "turn back and increase the amount of self-destructiveness within." It would seem, therefore, "as though it is necessary for us to destroy some other thing or person in order not to destroy ourselves, in order to guard against the impulsion to self-destruction" (p. 105).

This assumption is a logical outcome of Freud's belief in an inner-directed death instinct, since instinctual drives are deeply rooted in biological heredity. Therefore if Freud were right, biologists should have discovered as many instances of self-destructiveness as of object-destructiveness.

Freud's theory of Thanatos implies that suicidal tendencies occur earlier than do genocidal tendencies, in both the phylogenetic and ontogenetic sense. Were this true, animals would have eaten themselves up before they ate one another, and babies would have hurt themselves before they began to suck mother's breast. Of course, one may further hypothesize that only those species which had a strong instinct for survival did in fact survive but such a hypothesis is weak in view of the rarity of suicidal behavior in nature.

There are undoubtedly cases of self-directed hostility. But, in Freud's own clinical investigation, self-directed hostility was seated in the superego. Needless to say, the superego is the last of the three systems of the mental apparatus to develop. The superego is invested with parental hostility toward the child and the child's hostility toward his parents. Both types of hostility are object-directed. They become self-directed by the introjection of parental images.

Freud (1938) believed that "when the superego begins to be formed, considerable amounts of the aggressive instinct become fixated within the ego and operate there in a self-destructive fashion. This is one of the dangers to health to which mankind became subject on the path to cultural development. The holding back of aggressiveness is in general unhealthy and leads to illness" (p. 22).

But all these assumptions are open to discussion. How can people not hold back aggressiveness? And if they do not hold back, as, for instance, in catatonic fury, are they mentally better off? And again, if this holding back is a product of cultural developments and self-directed hostility precedes object-directed hostility, the history of humanity should have begun as a history of mass-suicides. It is, however, a matter of fact, that from the earliest times men killed each other and rarely killed themselves.

We have apparently arrived at a dead end in the analysis of the death instinct. There is no doubt that organisms die. Nor can there be any doubt that organisms destroy other organisms. In some rare cases they destroy themselves.

Undoubtedly these phenomena do not fit the Eros-libido scheme. Fresh hypotheses have been necessary. I question whether Freud's Thanatos-destructive instinct hypothesis gives a satisfactory answer to this complex problem. In the following pages I shall endeavor to outline an alternative to Freud's theory of the death instinct.

But before we venture on a search for a better answer to this problem, let us explore a few preliminary questions and look into certain empirical data. First of all, what are the origins of feelings of love and hate and of life-protecting and life-destroying behavior?

Sexuality and Love

The undeniable fact is that a great part of animal and human behavior is directed not toward the survival of the individual but rather to the procreation of the species. Moreover, procreative behavior does not necessarily serve the well-being and survival of the individual. For instance, amoeba A ceases to exist as soon as it splits up into its progeny, called amoebas B and C.

Animals reproduce in a great variety of ways and manners. Paramecia reproduce by fission or by splitting into two organisms. Hydras, most jellyfish, coral polyps and other coral animals reproduce by budding. *Planaria* worms reproduce by regeneration. The water flea, Daphnius, reproduces from unfertilized eggs. Frogs can reproduce by parthenogenesis without fertilization. Some protozoa have the ability to reproduce either way, i.e., by splitting or by sexual reproduction.

Sea urchins reproduce by fertilization of eggs without the sexual partners ever having been in contact. Most female fish lay eggs in the water; the males ejaculate sperm on the eggs outside the female body. Salmon migrate great distances for the spawning procedures. Male frogs help the females to release eggs and ejaculate on the eggs outside the female body; no copulation takes place.

Nature offers a variety of sexual styles. In some species males do all the courting, displaying color and sound. But male domination is not a general rule; consider the ants and bees. Male domination is quite frequent in fish, birds and mammals; it appears to be the rule whenever males are larger and stronger. Red deer herds are most often dominated by a female leader, while Rhesus monkeys practice both hetero- and homosexuality. Some animals stay together; some do not. Lorenz (1964) calls animals "married" whenever they stay together, protect one another, and share social status.

Most animals practice some form of polygamy, polyandry and promiscuity. However, lions, wolves and most big apes stay mated all their lives; their marriages are monogamous and loyal. Most animals are neither monogamous nor loyal. Nature does not offer any guidance as to what is right and wrong in sex.

Anthropology does not offer any guidance either. Beach (1965), Malinowski (1929), Ford and Beach (1951), Mead (1949) have found innumerable patterns of sexual life, marriage, and family life.

It was quite late in evolution when procreation became interaction and required two partners. Even when it required two, it could still be performed without physical contact between them; yet some cooperation was necessary. Participation of the two included, as a rule, a certain amount of fighting. Most fights however occur *within* the same gender and rarely if ever during copulation. Courtship has often been associated with pursuit on the part of the male and a half-hearted resistance on the part of the female. The main reason that males pursue females is, according to Tinbergen (1951), that "one male can fertilize more than one female" and females play a more important role in feeding and protecting the young (p. 22).

Sexual intercourse can be performed in various ways. It would be presumptuous to assume that sexual intercourse in lower species is accompanied by any feelings whatsoever. Neuroanatomists would reject such an assumption. Insects procreate sexually; one can, however, hardly ascribe much emotionality to insects.

At a certain evolutionary stage mating becomes associated with care and protection of the male. Nature is all but compulsively systematic, and one cannot guarantee better marital behavior on higher levels of the evolutionary ladder. Male wolves care for their females, but this does not necessarily apply to anthropoid apes. Protection of the female by the male and mutual aid in the search for food becomes more frequent among primates. On the whole, sex in higher species becomes less of a rape and more of a courtship, less mechanical motion and more of an affective emotion.

On higher evolutionary levels the relationships last longer and are more tender and friendly. Marriage is not a human artifact; it is a product of evolution, and it takes on a variety of forms and patterns.

Sex produces offspring. In several species, parents take care of their offspring. Most birds make affectionate parents, although there is considerable variation in quality. There is no one universal pattern of parent-child relationship. Wolves are good fathers. Their cousin species, bears, are bad fathers; often mother bears have to protect the young ones against their own father.

Some families are composed of both parents and children. Some families do not include fathers. Human families offer a spectacular variety of types, matriarchal and patriarchal, polygamous and polyandrous, group and individual. The Lesu practice all of them (Powdermaker, 1933); the Tibetans prefer polyandry (Malinowski, 1929); most ancient Oriental tribes favored polygamy. In all the disparate multiplicity of patterns, sexual attachment usually excludes or at least mollifies hostility. Certainly this rule has a great many exceptions, yet there is the unmistaken trend toward an increased cooperation between mates and in parent-child relationships. Libido counteracts destrudo.

Apparently this evolutionary process introduced a new direction in which libido could be invested. Instead of all libido being invested or cathected in survival, in a narcissistic fashion, part of it becomes invested in others via sex, parenthood, and in nonsexual ways. One may, continuing Freud's reasoning, view this evolutionary process as follows. In the beginning there was only selfish love, love being defined as the urge to life. At a certain evolutionary stage this love Eros branched off; while part of the libido energy, activated and released by Eros, remained and will always remain self-directed, part of it became invested in procreation and in care for others. The feelings of affection, kindness, care, tenderness and loyalty originated in sex.

In the spirit of monistic transitionism one can view the development from physical into mental, from general biochemical energy into its psychological derivative, libido, and from sexual urge toward kindness, affection, and sublime love, sung by poets.

A profound transition takes place through the ages of phylogenetic evolution, through the stages of ontogenetic, individual development, and through everyday life experiences of higher organisms. In human beings libido is originally self-invested, narcissistic, but part of it can easily be diverted into object-cathexis; biochemical energy can be transformed into any other kind, be it physical or psychological, and the object-directed libido can be sexual or desexualized. When it is sexual, it has its impetus, source, object, and aim. Freud (1905) pointed out the evolutionary aspect of sexuality in both the phylogenetic and ontogenetic sense, stressing the transition from one erotogenic zone to another.

The lower stages do not disappear in evolution. They persist in many ways, usually subordinated to the higher level. For example, the oral zone, the mouth, always remains an erotogenic zone, albeit subordinated to and incorporated in the adult genital sexuality.

On a higher evolutionary level (history is but a part of the evolution of the human species), sexuality becomes refined, combined with admiration and void of hostile elements. Here is how Freud (1921) described it:

> When we are in love a considerable amount of narcissistic libido overflows on to the object. It is even obvious, in many forms of love choice, that the object serves a substitute for some unattained ego ideal of our own . . .
>
> If the sexual overestimation and the being in love increase even

further . . . the tendencies whose trend is toward direct sexual satisfaction may now be pushed back entirely . . . the ego becomes more
and more unassuming and modest, and the object more and more
sublime and precious, until at last it gets possession of the entire
self-love of the ego, whose self-sacrifice thus follows as a natural consequence . . . Traits of humility, of the limitation of narcissism, and
of self-injury occur in every case of being in love [pp. 74–75].

Unfortunately, forcefulness has often been confused with
hostility and called aggressiveness. When a man holds a
woman tightly in a love embrace, he is *not* aggressive but
desirous and forceful. When a woman hugs and kisses passion-
ately, this is not aggressiveness. Both love and hate require
energy; both can be weak or forceful. But love is love and
hate is hate. In lower ontogenetic levels sex can be combined
with hostile behavior. Rape, sadism, prostitution and other
types of sexual behavior void of love are cases in point. But
one must not say then that every intercourse contains aggressiveness interpreted as hostility. Intercourse can be weak or
forceful and can be pure love in either case.

Hartmann (1949, p. 17) has assumed that like the libidinal
discharge, "aggressive discharge per se may be experienced
as pleasurable," and need not necessarily be in fusion with it.
The outbursts of rage "follow patterns of discharge specifically related to the oral and anal phases of pregenital
development."

Hartmann has also discussed the contrast between the plasticity of libido as compared to the rigidity of aggression. A
further analysis of aggression is impossible without a thorough discussion of ideas pertaining to love and hate.

✃ 3 ✃

Lust for Life

The theory of behavior proposed here is a set of working hypotheses designed to give what I believe to be a more likely explanation of observable facts. A theory is neither true nor false in the empirical sense; it merely binds empirical facts together into a coherent system.

A theory must meet certain methodological requirements (Nagel, 1961; Wolman, 1960b). It must be (1) free of inner contradictions (immanent truth), (2) in agreement with the body of established empirical data and open to empirical test (transcendent truth), and (3) methodologically useful and competitive, that is, more conducive to explanation and prediction of empirical data than any other theory that covers the same area of research.

It seems that the causal principle offers the best link between empirical data and theory. Causation binds empirical data in temporal sequences and the causal continuum permits one to present events or actions to be viewed in such a way that each event can be seen as a total or partial *effect* of antedating events and, at the same time, as a total or partial cause of future events. In such a causal chain, the present events will be *explained* by an answer to the question, "Why did it happen?" The future events are predicted by the answer to the question, "What will be the outcome of the present events?"

The doubts in regard to the meaning of temporal sequences that perplex modern physics, especially quantum

29

mechanics, need not worry the psychologist. Psychology
deals with living organisms, and life has its well-defined starting point and a very deadly deadline. The life span of an
organism unmistakably follows the sequences of beginning by
hatching or birth, then growth and phasic changes, and ultimately death, either natural or caused by physical, chemical
or other factors. Every life process contains definite temporal
sequences. The march of life is measurable in lunar or solar
years, in a series of clearly distinguishable sequences of "before" and "after."

A radical empiricist who shuns the causal principle must
stick to bare facts and take his chances over and over again. A
somewhat less radical empiricist (I shall call him "empirico-
realist") trusts causation and, all other factors being equal,
sits down to his dinner placing good faith in the predictable
effect food will have on his hunger. At best, a radical empiricist relies on probability calculus and figures out with a
certain level of confidence that food does satisfy hunger. An
empirico-realist sees in probability calculus a useful though
unprecise application of the causal principle, and does not
shy away from predicting an individual case without the calculus.

Thus an empirico-realistic psychologist tries not only to
describe but also to *explain* hostile behavior, overt and covert
alike. He may relate it to a general principle of constancy as
Freud did, or he may seek organic roots of hostile impulses as
Hartmann proposed. This is not to say that he cannot look
for other interpretations. No matter what the content of
theoretical constructs is, the general principle of causation
allows for a fairly consistent logical structure.

The principle of causation is most likely to offer definite
methodological advantages in psychology. I have discussed
elsewhere the content and application of this principle to
physical science (Wolman, 1938) and behavioral sciences
(Wolman, 1946). It suffices to state here that any theory of

motivation, whether Pavlov's, Hull's or Freud's, is inescapably coined in terms of the causal principle and thereby links present empirical data to past and future data in a necessary and temporal sequence. Such a sequence is the essence of the causal principle (cf. Planck, 1933). Pavlov, Freud, Hull, Piaget and many other productive research workers in psychology have proven by their works the usefulness of the deterministic approach to the study of psychological data.

The Problem of Reductionism

Before introducing a theory of hostile motivation and action, one has also to consider, albeit briefly, the relationship between the organism and those of its functions that can hardly be called organic. One may call this issue the mind-body issue.

Although the mind-body controversy continues unabated, a dualistic approach would render any psychological inquiry impossible. There are, however, several proposals to bridge over the mind-body gulf and a great variety of reductionistic systems. Despite all the theoretical differences, neither Freud nor Pavlov nor any other serious student of human life could dismiss the fact that all life processes are processes of matter and energy. Since Einstein's famous formula $E = mc^2$ matter and energy have been viewed in a continuum. Such a continuum has also been proposed for mind and matter; it has been named "the principle of monistic transitionism" (Wolman, 1965a). Monistic transitionism implies evolutionary continuity; it states that at a certain level of evolution, some inorganic matter turned into organic matter and, at a later stage, some organic matter developed mental functions. Human life is a series of somatopsychic and psychosomatic processes, and the transition from one into the other bears witness to the monistic continuity of nature.

Freud's model, which resembles a psychohydraulic model

of instinct with its reservoir and accumulation of energy, fits well into a monistic theoretical framework. Freud's theoretical reductionism is not radical; it is a hoped-for reductionism that assumes transition from body to mind and vice-versa. Living organisms are seen as reservoirs of physicochemical and mental energies. It is assumed that mental energy, phylogenetically, is a derivative of physical energy. In higher organisms there is a continuous *transition* (Freud referred to it as a "mysterious leap") from physical to mental and vice-versa.

Let us call the mechanism that activates the discharge of mental energy, drive (or instinctual drive). A theory of drives must fit into a general theory of behavior (principle of immanent truth) and must explain well-established empirical data (principle of transcendent truth), while at the same time being methodologically useful.

A theory of drives must be related to several psychological issues, such as the issue of (1) innate, unconditioned, unlearned reflexes, (2) conditioned reflexes, (3) cathexis of mental energy. Concerning the first issue, inherited reflexes, I would agree with the ethologist Thorpe (1956, p. 407 ff.) that carnivorous animals do not "know" their victims nor do they inherit hostile attitudes. All behavior is a combination of inherited, behavioral tendencies and conditioning. But even these two factors do not explain the totality of behavior.

The term "heredity" includes several separate elements. The first group of factors is the physicochemical constitution. This constitution, however, is not an inflexible entity. It undergoes profound changes in one's lifetime. Every living organism undergoes the process of growth and maturation. This process is typical for each species. For mammals it is conception, intrauterine life, birth, childhood, adulthood, old age, and death. In insects it is egg, larva, cocoon, adult insect. In human beings these stages are more distinct, more involved and subdivided.

The two basic elements, the constitution at the onset of life and the biologically determined developmental stages are not the sole determinants of behavior. No organism lives in a vacuum. Intrauterine or intraoval life is rich in exogenous influences: the young organism takes in food and is exposed to certain temperatures, air pressures and several other non-heredity factors that must, inevitably, affect his development. A newborn mammal is an organism that has had a long life history and was exposed in his intrauterine life to a variety of factors. His biophysical and biochemical makeup is a product of genes (genosomatogenic) and environment (ecosomatogenic) factors.

The same applies to postnatal life. The neonate is endowed with a certain constitution produced by genes and exogenous factors. His growth process depends on his endogenous constitution and the developmental laws typical for his species. In this growth process the young organism is exposed to a variety of ecosomatogenic factors, such as nutrition, water, temperature, physical and social environment. The physical growth and survival of an organism depends on the way in which he copes with all the exogenous factors. Whether the organism will grow strong and healthy or starve to death will depend on how much food is available and how much competition he has.

Let us use the word "behavior" to describe the totality of interaction between an organism and its physical and social environment. This behavior is the subject matter of psychology. Behavior is unmistakenly determined by certain bodily organs, such as the glandular, autonomous-nerve and central-nerve systems. As far as we know, all three systems are inherited, yet their structure and function can be altered by exogenous factors such as injury, poisoning, disease, nutrition, and glandular conditions.

Furthermore, nonphysical elements of interaction can also affect the function and, eventually, also the physicochemical

structure of bodily organs. Psychosomatic disorders start in
interaction with other individuals, but eventually they cause
physical harm to the affected organs.

Interaction leads to conditioning. Conditioning, be it simple or of a high order, involves neurophysiological processes.
Each time an unconditioned stimulus elicits an unconditioned
response, some amount of mental energy moves from one
place to another. What the biophysical counterpart of this
motion is, I do not know, but I am willing to accept Pavlov's
laws of excitation, inhibition, irradiation, concentration and
induction as a reasonable working hypotheses. But what happens when appetites and preferences are established?

Now we are no longer talking about conditioning. No new
paths are broken; no new couplings formed. But the dog
develops a preference for a particular type of food, and a
child loves a particular woman. A certain amount of energy
(call it libido) is invested in these objects, food and mother.
No new, conditioned reflex is formed, but a certain unconditioned pattern is preferred over others due to an investment
of energy.

This investment of energy, *cathexis,* is one of the most
important discoveries made by Freud. Behavioral powers
cannot, therefore, be presented as a combination of heredity
and learning. An additional process, the process of cathexis,
must be accounted for. In this process developmental stages
merge with interactional factors. A child is prone to go
through the oral and anal stages, but how well he goes
through them depends on the cathexes of mental energy,
largely determined by the child's interaction with his environment. A theory of motivation or of instinctual drives must
be related to all of these factors.

Conservation and Self-Preservation

Instincts, wrote Freud (1920), are "an expression of the
conservative nature of living substance" (p. 47). Conservation

of the living substance as a living substance means *conserva-tion of life* and Thanatos does not serve this goal. Following Freud's main idea, I believe I am being more consistent than Freud was in this regard, for I postulate that *all* instincts are an expression of the conservative nature of living sub-stance and hence serve conservation of life. Certainly there could not be any conservation of life in destruction or in the death instinct.

The discussion seems to border on tautology. What one should do at this point is to state the empirical fact that all living organisms act in a way that clearly indicates the ten-dency to *preserve their own life*. When organisms take in oxygen, water, and nutritive materials, it is in the service of self-preservation. Deprivation of these essentials puts an end to their existence. All organisms protect themselves against threats to their life whether the threats come from cold, heat, storms, or other organisms. Self-preservation is neither a myth nor a hypothesis; it is the most general and best known empirical fact pertaining to living matter.

The various functions that serve self-preservation may be divided into intake of oxygen, food, and water, flight, fight, and so on. One may call oxygen, food, and water "needs," defining "need" as a condition for survival. However, since the term "need" has several connotations, it might be advis-able to call oxygen, water, and other things necessary for survival "vital needs" or "biological needs."

It is obvious that deprivation of one of these or other bio-logical needs, defined as conditions for survival, motivates the organism to act in a way that leads toward the satisfaction of these needs. In other words, the most basic motive of living nature is self-preservation. The self-preserving actions are, as a rule, typical for each biological species and are determined by the heredity, anatomy, and physiology of each organism, by its age and physical fitness, by physical and social environment, and also by intelligence, learning, and other factors. It would be, therefore, impractical to assume that there are certain rigid, inflexible, inherited behavioral patterns called "instincts" or "propensities," or any other name.

On the other hand, there is some degree of consistency and uniformity in the way organisms go about their need fulfillment. Thus, there is nothing methodologically wrong in developing personality models that include drives or instincts or whatever one prefers to call these *theoretical constructs* that explain motivation. That which is *empirically* perceivable, is the behavior of the organism, and what *explains* it is a set of constructs and concepts that bind the empirical data into a coherent theoretical system.

The observable behavior of all living organisms is obviously *conservative* in the sense of the conservation or preservation of life. This overall tendency described by Charles Darwin as the "fight for survival," can be conceptualized in terms of an overall instinct or drive or complex of unconditioned reflexes. It may correspond to Pavlov's instinct of life. Pavlov (1928) wrote: "All life is nothing other than the realization of one purpose, viz; the preservation of life itself, the tireless labor of which may be called the general *instinct of life* . . ." (p. 277). And further on: "Life is beautiful and strong only to him who during his whole existence strives toward the always desirable but ever inaccessible goal . . . All life, all its improvement and progress, all its culture are effected through the reflex of purpose, are realized only by those who strive to put into life a purpose" (p. 279).

The functions of such a general instinctual drive for life can be presented in the following manner. Each organism has at a certain time a certain quantity of energy. The fact that matter, in accordance with Einstein's formula $E = mc^2$ is a peculiar accumulation of energy, need not bother us in the present context. This energy is discharged, in accordance with the principle of equilibrium, whenever the organism is exposed to internal or external stimuli.

This tendency of living matter to restore equilibrium has been elevated to a most general biological law of homeostasis by Cannon, Goldstein, Pavlov and Freud. The only qualification to be made at this point is that the homeostatic principle, whether in Pavlov's, Goldstein's, or Freud's version, is a universal law of living matter.

The point that I am trying to make is that this homeostasis or constancy of equilibration principle is not merely a tendency to restore an earlier state of things, but it is *directed toward survival.*

Such a broad hypothesis must be checked against available empirical data.

My hypothesis reads as follows: *All living matter is endowed with biochemical energy derived from the universal energy that, in turn, as explained by Einstein, is a derivative of matter. At a certain evolutionary level this biochemical energy is transformed into mental energy. This mental energy serves survival. The apparatus of discharge, call it drive, instinct, or instinctual force, reflects the most universal urge to stay alive. It is the "Lust for Life," the wonderful craving of all living matter to live.*

The process of life is a process of oxidation, digestion, incorporation, metabolism and so on. The higher the species stands on the evolutionary ladder, the more complex its life processes are. Ultimately, all action or behavior of an organism is an aggressive-defensive process, for each organism either devours other organisms or protects itself by fight or flight against being devoured.

Since organisms cannot survive without the intake of food, life in nature can be presented as a continuous struggle aimed at the destruction of the prey by the predator or of the predator by the prey. One has to be hopelessly naive to present the "natural state" as a peaceful paradise. The brutal facts of life have been described by a poet in a strikingly animalistic manner. The prey animal turns down the plea for mercy and says to his prey:

"Nein
Du bist mein,
Denn ich bin gross
Und du bist klein!" [1]

Brutality, cruelty and destructiveness have always horrified
men. At the beginning it was the brutality of others, but as
men progressed, their own brutality became frightening.

There have been several unscientific and scientific explanations of hostile behavior and of its conscious and unconscious
motives. Men have always been aware of and concerned with
the problems of hatred, destruction and death. All religions
have good and bad gods, the good ones protecting the lives
of the believers, the bad ones torturing and killing unbeliev-
ers. The ancient Egyptians had Set, the Greeks had Ares, the
Romans had Mars, the Jews had Satan, the Persians had Ahri-
man and so on. This dualism between God and Satan, good
and evil, creativeness and destructiveness, light and darkness,
and life and death has preoccupied the minds of men and has
found expression in religion, philosophy, literature and art.

Men have always feared the influence of bad gods and spirits and ascribed to them the power to induce human beings
to evil behavior, to hostile deeds and feelings. Zoroaster and
the Manicheists internalized the struggle of the good and bad
gods. They believed that the fight between the forces of light
and darkness is raging in every human heart and man alone
carries the responsibility for the victory or defeat of the gods.

In Judaism and Christianity man is the subject of struggle
between the good God of love and the bad God of hate, Satan. However, it is the good God who is believed to be the
Stronger one and who controls life and death. Fear of hostility and death has made men believe in a God of justice, responsible for the lost Paradise in the past and for the future
Redemption. Human life has always been harsh, and Judaism

---

[1] Translation: "No, you are mine, for I am big and you are little!"

and Christianity have offered hope and consolation to those who could not win otherwise. The victory of right over wrong and peace on earth was promised at the end of the individual's life and at the end of human history.

Charles Darwin presented the issue of good and bad in a new light. All living creatures fight for survival. The concepts of good and evil are man-made value judgments. Biology has no part in them. Survival of the fittest is the law of nature and the natural state is neither Ovid's nor Jean Jacques Rousseau's golden era of peace and brotherhood, but rather Hobbes' *Bellum omnium contra omnes* (war of all against all). Value judgements are a human perogative; nature knows none of them.

It was under Darwin's influence that modern psychology became interested in how organisms live and act and stay alive. MacDougall, Watson, Sechenov and Pavlov were Darwin's disciples. So was Freud. Life and death became the subject matter of psychology. Psychology gave up the discussion of how men were *supposed* to feel, think, and act. Instead psychology began to study how men *do* feel, think and act and how they live and fight for survival. The issues of life and death are unescapably connected with love and hate. There are obvious reasons for such a combination in human minds, for love means support of life and hatred leads to its destruction. God creates; Satan destroys. Those who love and create are called good; those who hate and destroy are called evil. Freud's theory of Eros and Thanatos closely corresponds to this antinomy of life and love versus death and hatred.

The difficulty with this otherwise plausible set of concepts lies in lack of clarity with regard to intraindividual and interindividual motives. Freud's death instinct is primarily suicidal in relation to the narcissistic direction of libido. Certainly, in the phylo- and ontogenetic development, libido is primarily narcissistic. Is destrudo also self-directed and thus a death promoting energy?

Freud's own reasoning does not support the idea of this kind of death instinct. Reading Freud strengthens the belief that object-destrudo or fight for survival is the sole source of hostility.

> From the earliest times it was muscular strength which decided who owned things or whose will shall prevail. Muscular strength was soon supplemented by the use of tools; the winner was the one who had the better weapons or who used them the more skillfully. From the moment at which weapons were introduced, intellectual superiority already began to replace brute muscular strength; but the final purpose of the fight remained the same [1932, pp. 274–275].

The killing of enemies has had two advantages: a dead enemy could not fight back and his ill fate deterred others. An enemy's life could be spared whenever he could be forced into slave labor or when his broken might represented no threat to the victor. In times when physical forces counted most, men were killed, but women and children were included in the spoil.

The original state of things was domination by whoever had the greater might, either through physical violence or violence supported by intellect. Primitive men did not hate themselves; they loved themselves and hated their enemies. "Thou shalt love thy neighbor as thyself," says the Scripture. There was never any doubt in regard to self-love, but the love for one's neighbor has always been the stupendous task. It seems that at the onset of prehistory man's libido was self-directed and destrudo object-directed. There was no death instinct, but there was plenty of fighting for survival.

Thus, the following hypothetical system is introduced: In accordance with Freud's personality model, living organisms carry a certain amount of energy. This energy is activated by threat to one's life. The built-in release apparatus, the force that opens the valves of the hydraulic model, is called instinctual drive.

Obviously this force activates energies in the direction of survival. Thus it should be named "Lust for Life." At a certain evolutionary level part of this energy became invested in procreation or the preservation of the life of the species as if life of one individual continued through this offspring. From that time on the "Lust for Life" drive split into Ares and Eros, the War and Love drives respectively.

Life and death of a single organism are terms that indicate the viability of the organism. There are degrees of viability. An organism can be forceful, full of energy, vivacious, most capable of providing food for itself and well prepared for self-defense. Or it may be sick, declining, and dwindling to nothing. When the vital energies become exhausted and vitality reaches the zero point the organism dies. Lack of "Lust for Life" does not point to self-destructive tendencies; it is precisely what it is, namely a decline in the zest for life. An organism that has lost its urge to live may give up the fight for survival and die.

As long as an organism is alive, its energies can be used in two directions, either toward the promotion of life or toward its destruction. The instinctual force, "Lust for Life," divides into two arms, the one that serves promotion of life is *Eros* or love. Love can be directed toward oneself or toward others. The other arm serves destruction and may be called Ares.[2] Ares, too, can be directed toward oneself or toward others. Life and death deal with *quantities* of energy. The instincts of love and hostility deal with the *direction* in which the mental energy is used by Eros and Ares.

The entire issue can be presented graphically on the Cartesian coordinates as follows. The vertical line represents life; energy is marked plus and lack of energy is marked zero. An organism is alive as long as its energies are above the zero point. The horizontal dimension represents the direction in

[2] The Greek god of war.

which the vital energies are used: the plus sign indicates Eros
or promotion of life and the minus sign indicates Ares or destruction.

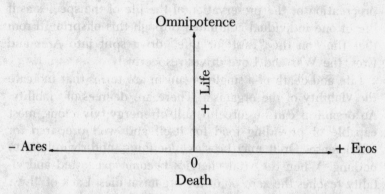

There is but one general, universal drive, the "Lust for
Life." There is, for organisms, only general biochemical energy. But the energy can be transformed into mental energy
in a transitionistic fashion and the discharge of energy can go
in either direction. It is Eros and libido whenever it supports
life; libido can be invested in oneself or in others, in a sexual
or a desexualized way. Whenever there is a threat to life, the
self-directed Eros is accompanied by the object-directed *Ares*.

Ares is the name for the destructive arm of the universal
"Lust for Life" drive, and serves the same purpose of survival
as Eros does. However, should an immortal and omnipotent
creature exist whose life could never have been threatened,
such a creature would be pure Eros; such a creature would
have had no use for Ares.

But all living organisms, including human beings, live under the threat of inanimate and animate nature. To face this
threat, "Lust for Life" turns not into Eros, but into Ares.
Eros and Ares are two channels of the same drive of "Lust
for Life"; activated in two different types of situations, they
serve basically the same goal, the survival of the individual,
and, in some situations, survival of the species.

It seems that Ares is not only a more primitive and phylogenetically earlier drive than Eros, but as a rule it is more powerful than Eros. Pavlov's dogs did not copulate when their skin was burned, but they salivated even when he burnt their skin (Pavlov, 1928, p. 228). Apparently the cortical food center is stronger than the skin center, and the sex center is weaker than the skin center. When Pavlov tried to crush the dog's bones, even salivation stopped. Hungry dogs can bear minor wounds, but bone breaking means death, and in face of death all energy is mobilized for self-defense.

Hungry, thirsty, sick, and wounded organisms act in an aggressive and destructive manner. It seems that whenever the supply of libido is used up, the organism works on destrudo. Libido seems to be a "higher" fuel, destrudo a "lower" one; when there is no threat to life, a balanced love for oneself and for others may suffice for survival. In emergencies the destrudo takes over. In danger and anger men act with what seems to be added energy, the latent energy of destrudo.

Eros and Ares are the two basic releasers of mental energy. Ares, like Eros, has an impetus, source, object, and aim. The impetus is the amount of destructive energy (destrudo) that is discharged. Its source is a threat to one's own life. The aim of Ares is the complete or partial destruction of enemies. The object can be oneself or any other organism.

Ares, the instinct of hostility, fits well into the definition of instinct given by Fenichel (1945) that reads: "The instinct attempts to remove the somatic changes at the source of the instinct" (p. 60). The somatic changes in Ares are an accelerated heart beat, perspiration, trembling, contraction of muscles, baring of teeth, growling and so on. The threat of annihilation is the main cause of the somatic changes. The hostile action, which is a discharge of destrudo aiming at the destruction of the threatening object, restores the inner balance (analogous with the actions of Eros). The threat may be related to an inner stimulus of hunger or an outer stimulus that jeopardizes one's life, prevents satisfaction of hunger, prevents escape, or any other combination of hostile stimuli.

Pavlov (1928, p. 255 ff.) believed that hostile behavior is a *guarding reaction* against real or threatened injury. Several experimental studies on frustration (Dollard et al., 1939; Lawson, 1965) stressed the fact that frustrated individuals tend to become hostile. It seems as though adverse life conditions act as releasers of hostile actions, be it as a scapegoat mechanism (Allport, 1954), antisocial actions in migratory groups (Wolman, 1949a), or any other hostility (Redl and Wineman, 1952).

Fear and Hostility

Aggressive behavior originates in the fear that one's life is in some way being threatened. No one hates unless he fears. Immortals do not have to fight for survival; omniscient and omnipotent beings need not compete with anyone. A perfect being does not hate. Buddha did not hate. Nor did Jesus; he could easily forgive his enemies, for he believed in His Resurrection. A self-assured mother does not hate a cranky infant. Only the perfect and immortal being can forgive all his enemies because he does not fear them.

But animals and human beings fear death and hate their enemies because enemies inflict injury which may kill them. The strongest fear is the mortal fear, the fear to perish, the fear of losing what all men have: life.

Various types and degrees of fear may be distinguished. One may agree with O. Rank's birth trauma theory, or J. B. Watson's loss of support and frightening noise theory, or any other theory as to the origin of fear. It is, however, rather obvious that regardless of how fears begin, the ultimate in fear is *the fear of death*. All other fears are apparent derivatives or degrees of the arch-fear of death.

Types of Hostility

One can distinguish several types of hostility. The first two categories are "wolf versus sheep" and "sheep versus wolf."

The first is aggressive, the second defensive, and both are directly related to self-protection. In the first, the *aggressive* type, the wolf acts in a hostile manner toward the sheep by virtue of its intention to eat it. No feeling of hate is involved in eating unless the sheep resists. Men who eat chicken do not hate chickens but nonetheless destroy them. The instinctual source of aggressive hostility is the threat of starvation. Hungry beasts attack.

The second type of hostility is *defensive;* it is usually combined with hate. Defensive hostility is aimed at the destruction of a deadly menace. It leads sheep to fight against wolves and man to fight against floods and predatory animals. It is reflected in a child's fight against another child who hits him or takes away his toy. Defensive hostility aims at the destruction of the forces that jeopardize survival. One may defend himself by fight or flight, but he hates in either case.

Other types of hostility serve survival in a less efficient manner. The third type, *panic,* implies an impulsive, unplanned, often useless effort to escape danger. People caught in fire may storm locked doors instead of seeking rational exit. There is neither consideration nor mutual help in panic; goats chased by wolves fight one another, overcrowding and blocking the narrow escape passages. The fourth type of hostility, *terror,* can be seen in the mortally wounded animal who attacks indiscriminately. Because no gain can be expected from turning blindly against everything, terror must be considered as pure Ares gone wild in the face of lethal danger.

Hostile actions can be repressed or displaced, just as libidinal actions are. Hate can be displaced from the menacing object to some other object and turned into scapegoatism. Destrudo may turn not against the real cause of damage but against one's own ego in a self-defeating or self-destructive manner. Destrudo can be combined with libido and turned into sadism. When rationalized, it assumes the proportions of

fanaticism and chauvinism, which when sufficiently kindled
result in war.

Ares, like Eros, can undergo innumerable changes. It starts
as a defense against dangers, combined with self-directed
Eros. But it may become hate without danger, and cruelty
without gain, or cruelty combined with sexual pleasure, or
hate for oneself. As mentioned above, discharge of the aggressive energy (destrudo) is as pleasurable as any discharge
of instinctual energy.

Consider the story of the Vandals. After looting the treasures of Rome, they demolished whatever they could not
carry away with them. During the First World War the
Germans plundered, tortured and murdered the Belgians
without apparent reasons. Destrudo can be acted out for the
sheer pleasure of vandalism.

Lorenz (1964) once said that "the presence of an outlet for
an external aggression is necessary to prevent intramarital
fighting" (p. 73). The history of persecutions and wars, especially the history of Nazi Germany, bear unmistakable witness to the brutal force of Ares. Although Ares starts as a
self-defensive device, it may become a goal in itself. Men
may derive great satisfaction from a display of violent force.
The discharge of destructive energy create a feeling of power, thus magnifying one's self-confidence. Screaming at and
hitting someone make one feel strong and thus enhance faith
in one's own vitality.

❧ 4 ❧

Freud's Theory
of Neurosis and Psychosis

Freud's main contention was that mental disorders do not spring out of unknown chemical agents, but are a result of fixation and regression of one's personality, especially of its unconscious layers.

In his first major work, *The Interpretation of Dreams*, Freud (1900) introduced a new theory of unconscious motivation. He discovered that unacceptable wishes may become *repressed* and stored, as it were, in the unconscious. These memories would reappear in the conscious in a variety of disguises, most typically, the dream. Severe unconscious conflicts may give rise to morbid symptoms. According to Freud, a neurotic or a psychotic is not a malevolent individual nor a victim of a paralyzing disease; he is a man caught in a web of inner conflicts, most of which he is unaware of.

The treatment of mental disorders could not be patterned after the medical practice of administering drugs or performing surgery on the patient. That is, the traditional therapeutic relationship in which the physician is active, giving, helping and ordering, and the patient is passive, receiving and obeying, is of no avail in psychoanalysis. In psychoanalysis, the patient cannot hide behind the façade of the sick role and put the entire responsibility on the therapist. In traditional medicine the patient is supposed to obey doctor's orders; in psychoanalysis, there are two parties that enter an agreement of cooperation. The psychoanalyst promises to put

47

his entire skill, knowledge, and experience at the disposal of the patient, but without the patient's cooperation, psychoanalytic treatment is rendered impossible. The patient agrees to the fundamental rule of "free association," that is, to say whatever comes to his mind without holding back even what seems to him to be irrelevant, embarrassing, or painful. In short, the patient shares the responsibility for the treatment and participates actively in it.

A psychoanalyst does not "cure" a patient in the traditional medical sense. He neither prescribes medication nor does he "treat" him in the traditional sense. The psychoanalyst adheres to the rule of "evenly hovering attention"; his permissive and rather passive behavior permits the patient to relive past experiences in transference and to resolve his inner conflicts. The patient is more active than the analyst; he leans on the analyst and, so to speak, uses the analyst as a target for reliving his immature emotional experiences. Ultimately, by leaning on the analyst, the patient grows up, and as a mature adult no longer requires this kind of crutch.

Psychoanalytic technique is a method of enabling people who are entangled in their infantile conflicts to resolve these conflicts and become more mature. Since conflicts creating mental disorder are unconscious, psychoanalysis helps patients to elevate these conflicts from the unconscious to consciousness, where they can be dealt with.

Freud introduced a personality model (the so-called "structural theory") composed of the id, ego, and superego. The inherited instinctual forces of love (Eros) and hate (Thanatos) are seated in the *id*, the "boiling cauldron" of all human impulses. The id follows blindly the principle of immediate gratification of needs, regardless of consequences (the "pleasure principle"). The newborn child's personality is comprised of the id only, but as the child grows a shell develops and turns into the protective and controlling part of the personality, called ego. The id is entirely unconscious and wholly irrational in its pursuit of immediate gratification; the *ego* is an outgrowth of the id. It pursues pleasure, but not at all costs. Acting as guardian of the system, the ego's main task is survival under optimal conditions. The ego controls the unconscious impulses and guides the entire behavior toward an optimal adjustment to life.

Standing at the extreme opposite of that instinctual reservoir represented by the id, is the *superego*. The superego develops as a result of introjection of parental images and an identification with their "do's" and "don't's." The superego represents one's guilty conscience and the internalized voices of parents, teachers, and other authority figures whose moral standards the individual has accepted.

The ego of well-adjusted individuals exercises control over the organism. It satisfies the *animalistic* demands of the id, but it does so in a way that does not invite adverse repercussions. The ego also takes into consideration the *moralistic* demands of the superego provided that they are not too exaggerated. The ego keeps a reasonable balance between the conflicting demands of the id and the superego, and acts in a realistic fashion, anticipating the consequences of its actions.

A weak ego is a sign of mental disorder. A state of *anxiety* arises when the ego is pressured by the id or the superego. Mental symptoms result from the morbid efforts of the ego to retain its control against undue inner pressures. As long as the ego is still in charge of the entire system, the disorder is mild and called *neurosis*. A psychosis begins to develop when the ego fails to control the system, and a flood of unconscious impulses originating in the id or the superego sweeps over the conscious state.

After Freud, no one could any longer draw a sharp line dividing normal from abnormal behavior. The term abnormal psychology is apparently a heritage of the past, for every human being may fall prey to inner tensions, and no one is perfect or immune from mental disorder.

*A mentally healthy person is, therefore, a person whose id,
ego, and superego are in a sort of delicate balance, with a distinct ego supremacy. Disturbed individuals are those whose
personality structure is unbalanced. A balanced or an unbalanced state of personality is a matter of degree, and no human being is always well balanced.* Freud's concepts rendered obsolete the "normal versus abnormal" and "healthy
versus sick" dichotomies, presenting mental health as a continuum of successes and failures in adjustment to life, and
mental disorder as regression to infantile modes of behavior.

Regression

"Regression," Freud wrote as early as 1900, "plays a no
less important part in the theory of the formation of neurotic
symptoms than it does in that of dreams" (p. 548). Not all
human beings pass through and outgrow successfully the
developmental stages. Quite often, parts of the libido or its
component impulses become arrested at an early phase of
development. Freud called this arrest in personality development *fixation*. When certain portions of the libido become
fixated at a certain point, the entire libido may one day *regress*
to the point of fixation. Under stressful circumstances the
fixations may become quite substantial, and a weakened libido is less capable of overcoming external obstacles and
proceeding smoothly to the next stage. Regression to an early
developmental stage is the core of every neurosis and psychosis.

There are two types of regressions of the libido: one is a
regression to a stage where early love objects (e.g., breasts,
mother) are again of transcendent importance; the other is a
regression to an early developmental stage (i.e., oral, anal).

The danger of regression under stress depends on the
strength of past fixations and the severity and duration of the
stress. The fixation of libido is the predisposing factor, while
actual *frustration* is the precipitating factor. However, not

every stress situation and frustration is pathogenic, that is, producing disorder. Everyday life is full of adverse, painful, and threatening events that do not affect an individual's mental health and turn him into a neurotic or psychotic.

Anxiety

The ego's reaction to external threats is called *fear*. When the ego is exposed to threats from within, that is, coming from the id or the superego, its reaction to such a threat is called *anxiety*.

The term anxiety as used by Freud had several connotations. Originally Freud believed that anxiety was the result of blocking of sexual impulses. The combination of unsatisfied libido and undischarged excitation was supposed to be the cause of anxiety-neuroses, and the thwarted libido was believed to be transformed into a state of anxiety.

Three years after having presented the structural theory in 1923, Freud introduced a new theory of anxiety. The new theory did not discard the old one but reduced the scope of its meaning to particular cases. According to this new theory (1926), anxiety originates from the infant's inability to master the overflow of excitations. A neonate is usually exposed to more stimulation than he can possibly master. Excessive stimulation may become traumatic, and hence create the painful feeling of *primary anxiety*.

Rank (1929) assumed that the birth-trauma is the prototype of all anxiety states. Separation from mother is another severe anxiety-producing factor. Castration fears, guilt feelings, fear of abandonment, and rejection are the most frequently experienced anxiety-producing situations. The feeling of helplessness is one of the most frequent symptoms of neurotic disturbance; it is especially typical of traumatic neuroses. Also, the inability to control one's own excitation (whether aggressive or sexual) may create a state of anxiety.

Freud's early theory of anxiety became incorporated in the

new and more broadly conceived theory. Since the satisfaction of instinctual demands may create a dangerous situation, the ego must control the instinctual impulses. A strong ego accomplishes this task easily, but a weak ego has to invest more energies in an anticathectic effort to ward off the unconscious impulses.

Anxiety is "a specific state of unpleasure accompanied by motor discharge along definite pathways," Freud wrote in 1926. Ultimately, the three types of anxiety-producing situations in childhood can be put together and reduced to one fundamental cause, namely, loss of the love object. Thus, being left alone, being in the dark, and finding a strange person in place of the mother are the main anxiety-producing situations which reflect the *feeling of loss of the loved person*. In other words, anxiety is a reaction to the absence of, or separation from, the love object. This feeling of loss is experienced in the birth-trauma, in weaning, and later on in castration fear. In all these situations, loss of support causes increased tension, and an economic disturbance demanding some discharge of energy.

The infant longs for the sight of the mother because he knows from experience that she gratifies all his needs without delay. The situation which the infant appraises as "danger" and against which he desires reassurance is therefore one of not being gratified, of an *increase of tension arising from nongratification of his needs*—a situation against which he is powerless (Freud, 1930).

A strong ego can cope with danger, but a weak ego reacts with anxiety. When the ego is threatened by external reality, it develops *reality-anxiety*. When the superego attacks the ego, feelings of guilt and inferiority, called moral anxiety, ensue. When the id's pressures threaten to break through the ego controls, neurotic anxiety develops.

Reality-anxiety is a reaction of the ego to a danger from without. Anxiety-preparedness may develop in one of the two following manners: either an old danger-signaling experience called "anxiety development" is re-experienced, or a past danger, having a paralyzing effect on the individual, is re-experienced.

Neurotic anxiety manifests itself in three ways. The first is anxiety-neurosis, typically felt as an overall apprehension and a sense of oncoming doom. Anxiety neurosis is usually caused by the existence of undischarged excitation when blocked libido energy is transformed into an anxiety state.

Neurotic anxiety is manifested also in hysteria and in other neuroses. Certain ideas attached to libido become repressed and distorted, as a result of which the energy, whether libidinal or destructive, turns into a state of anxiety.

The earliest neuroses are phobias and obsessions. The fear of one's own libidinal destructive impulses is externalized and transformed into a fear of threats from without; thus the neurotic anxiety is experienced as objective reality-anxiety. The threat from within is perceived as an external threat. The fear of one's own libido or death instinct from which there is no flight is disguised and perceived as an alleged external danger that can, supposedly, be warded off by obsessive behavior.

Moral anxiety is a reaction of the ego to unduly harsh superego pressure. It is experienced as feelings of guilt, shame, inferiority, and inadequacy. A real threat to the organism evokes fear but does not necessarily produce anxiety; however, anxiety can easily be produced by inner tension that is experienced as a threat from without. Freud (1932) wrote:

> What is it that is actually dangerous and actually feared in such a danger situation? It is clearly not the objective injury, which need have absolutely no importance psychologically, but it is something which is set up in the mind by it. Birth, for example, our prototype for the state of anxiety, can hardly in itself be regarded as an injury, although it may involve a risk of injury. The fundamental thing about birth, as about every danger situation, is that it evokes in mental experience a condition of tense excitation which is felt as pain and which cannot be mastered by discharge . . . The operation of the

pleasure principle does not guarantee us against objective injury but
only against a particular injury to our mental economy . . . The magnitude of the excitation turns an impression into a traumatic factor
which paralyzes the operation of the pleasure principle and gives
significance to the danger situation [p. 130].

Defense Mechanisms of the Ego

The term "defense mechanism" was introduced by Freud
in 1894. In 1936 Anna Freud described defense mechanisms
in detail. Defense mechanisms are methods used by the ego
in fighting off the instinctual outbursts of the id and the attacks of the superego. A strong ego does not typically use
defense mechanisms, but when it is unable to cope with id
and superego pressures, it may resort to the use of these
mechanisms. Therefore, all defense mechanisms, except sublimation, indicate an inner conflict and a state of anxiety.

The main defense mechanism is *repression*. Repression is
an unconscious exclusion from the consciousness of objectionable impulses, memories, and ideas. The ego, as it were,
pushes the objectionable material down into the unconscious
and acts as if the objectionable material were nonexistent.

The ego uses its energy to maintain the repressed material
forever (anticathexes). Whenever a repressed wish or idea
comes close to the surface and attempts to re-enter consciousness, the ego's main defense mechanism is applied in
order to push the undesirable wish back into the unconscious.
Thus by applying powerful anticathexes and by keeping close
surveillance over the repressed material the ego prevents the
unconscious from becoming conscious. This preventive action, called *resistance*, is merely a continuation of repression.

The mechanism of *regression* is applied to fight off Oedipal
desires and castration fears. When the mechanism of regression is used, the genital organization of the phallic stage is
wholly or partially turned back to the earlier anal-sadistic

stage, or to an even earlier stage. Regression is always a going back related to past fixations; it may be limited to a certain erotogenic zone (such as a regression to orality), or it may be an overall regression to primary narcissism.

A successful and normal defense against instinctual wishes is called *sublimation*. Sublimation is a cathexis of instinctual energy into a substitute aim or object or both; it is a channeling of the instinctual demands into a new desire or idea and a desexualized cathexis of libido or destrudo.

Rationalization is another important defense mechanism. It is an effort to distort reality in order to protect one's self-esteem. In its attempt to mediate between the id and reality, the weak ego ascribes rationality to the irrational demands of the id. The ego displays a "pretended regard" for reality, while the id has actually abandoned it. Rationalization is fallacious reasoning that misrepresents irrational motivation in an effort to make it appear rational. A strong ego can cope with failures and frustrations, but a weak ego would rather distort the truth than admit defeat. Rationalization is used as a cover-up for mistakes, misjudgments, and failures: it tries to justify behavior by reasons that are made to sound rational.

A common type of rationalization is known as "sour grapes," taking its name from the fable about the fox who, upon failing to get the grapes he desired, consoled himself by calling them "sour." People rationalize in the same way; it takes a mature personality with a strong ego to admit that not all desirable grapes are also attainable. A neurotic tends to make himself believe that sweet grapes are sour rather than admit that he has failed.

The defense mechanism of *undoing* represents a far-reaching loss of contact with reality. Undoing is a fallacious belief that one can undo or nullify previous actions that make one feel guilty. A strong ego admits to past blunders, and a mature individual assumes responsibility for his behavior. A weak ego fears the superego's reproaches and acts in accordance with a belief that wishing to nullify the past deeds can effect such nullification. The mechanism of undoing is a patent distortion of truth; it is a kind of magic. Freud pictured the ego as trying to "blow away" not only the consequences of an event, but the fact that the event itself ever took place.

Sometimes the weak ego rejects not the past but the present; the defense mechanism called *denial* is involved in such a rejection. When its actual current life becomes too painful to accept or too difficult to cope with, the infantile ego withdraws from reality, breaking away from the truth, and refusing to acknowledge the existence of painful facts. Memory and perceptions prevent an unlimited escape from reality; but in some pathological cases the hard-pressed ego gives up reality-testing and simply denies facts. Some persons go so far as to deny the loss of beloved ones by acting as if the latter were still around.

The desire to swallow the love object and to identify with it is called *introjection*. Introjection expresses the primitive and ambivalent attitude that combines love and destruction in a cannibalistic incorporation of the love object, and in identification with the object incorporated. When certain adults are unable to develop more mature object relationships, their weak egos regress to the oral defense mechanism of introjection. Neurotic identification with the love object becomes the only possible object relationship.

Projection is a defense mechanism diametrically opposed to introjection. It is an externalization of wishes that leads to paranoid distortion of reality. The primitive, archaic ego draws a line between "something to be swallowed," which is pleasurable, and "something to be spit out," which is unpleasurable. What was "inside" was believed to be a part of the ego, and what was spit out becomes an alien body. When the weak ego harbors desires and feelings that invite the superego's harsh disapproval, the ego may ascribe them to the outer world. Forbidden homosexual impulses are a case in point, for most homosexuals "project" their homosexual urges and believe that other people of the same sex desire them. Neurotic and psychotic individuals, who cannot admit their own hostility will frequently ascribe it to others in delusions of persecution.

A strong ego is in control of the entire system; it satisfies some of the id cravings, while it postpones or modifies others and flatly rejects and suppresses those demands which it deems unacceptable. A weak ego resorts to the use of defense mechanisms against impulses. One of these defenses is the development of an attitude diametrically opposed to the id desires. For instance, an individual with strong homosexual impulses may crusade against homosexuality. An individual who hates his father and is very unhappy about it may develop a ritual of affection directed toward his father; an individual torn by an impulse to be dirty may develop compulsive cleanliness. This formation of opposite attitudes aimed at warding off the id impulses is called *reaction formation*.

The defense mechanism of *isolation* consists of an "interposition" of a refractory period in which nothing more is allowed to happen, no perception registered, and no action performed. Most often isolation develops after an unpleasant experience, when the ego, unable to face pain or humiliation, stops functioning for a while. Isolation is often present in compulsion neuroses. This defense mechanism separates an emotional content from the idea into which the emotion was cathected, thus splitting an emotional experience into two separate parts. In cases of the so-called "split ego" or "dual personality," part of an experience is kept separate from the rest of one's ego.

In *displacement* there is a shift of emotion, symbolic meaning, or fantasy from the person or object toward which it was originally directed, to another person or object. It involves the discharge of aroused emotions toward neutral or less dangerous objects. A child who has been spanked may kick another child or break his toys. Sometimes a minor situation may act as a trigger that releases pent-up emotions in a (displaced) flurry of anger that appears to be all out of proportion to the immediate incident.

The defense mechanism of displacement may have some adjustive value because it enables the individual to discharge dangerous emotional tensions without recognizing the person at whom such feelings were originally directed, thereby avoiding the risk of loss of love and possible retaliation.

Through the process of symbolic association or spread, displacement may become extremely complex and deviant. Destructive criticism and gossip are frequently disguised methods of expressing hostility.

The Neuroses

Mental health was viewed by Freud (1938) as a precarious balance between the id, ego and superego, and between the total personality and the outer world. This balance can be easily upset, and "there is scarcely any condition generally recognized as normal in which it would not be possible to demonstrate neurotic traits" (p. 81).

Neurosis is a *quantitative disharmony* between the various parts, forces, and areas of personality. It is always a disorder of the ego. Insofar as the weak or poorly organized ego is unable to cope with inner and outer pressures, the precipitating cause of neurosis is either that reality has become "intolerably painful," or that the instinctual pressure of the id has become unusually intensified.

In the infantile stages of development the ego struggles through difficult situations, warding off some of the instinctual demands by *repression,* and some of the demands of external reality by *denial.* Both defense mechanisms are usually unsuccessful. Actually, the ego is called upon to master the sexual excitations before it has grown sufficiently to be able to do so. When the ego's development has lagged behind the development of the libido, or when the libido has not safely passed the developmental phases, or when the superego is either underdeveloped or overgrown, the stage is set for a mental disorder.

Freud's medical education and practice led him to assume two types of neurosis: the "actual" neuroses and the psychoneuroses. Accordingly he claimed that the actual neuroses, such as hypochondria, anxiety neurosis, and neurasthenia, were caused by physiological aspects of abnormal sexual life, while the psychoneuroses, such as conversion hysteria, paranoia, obsessions, phobias, and hallucinations, were a result of repressed memories of traumatic sexual experiences in the past (Freud, 1894, 1896, 1898).

For a while Freud adhered to the organic interpretation of behavior disorders. In the early stages of his work he saw as the main difference between anxiety neurosis and neurasthenia the "accumulation of excitation" in the former, and the "impoverishment of excitation" in the latter (Freud, 1894b, p. 114). Freud believed that the source of anxiety was the "accumulation of excitation" caused by sexual abstention. In other words, blocked sexual energy turned into anxiety states. On the other hand, he believed that excessive masturbation led to "impoverishment of excitation" thereby producing neurasthenia which was experienced as lack of zest, lack of ambition, and general fatigue.

Only gradually did Freud become aware of the fact that some mental disorders are of a purely psychological origin. In these disorders, called *psychoneuroses*, the symptoms "arose through the psychical mechanism of (unconscious) defense, that is, in an attempt to repress an incompatible idea . . . in distressing opposition to the patient's ego" (1896, p. 162). Thus, for example, obsession is caused by a trauma connected with active sexual behavior in childhood; obsessions aim at substituting irrelevant thoughts for painful memories of past transgressions. "The ego," wrote Freud (1915–1916) "breaks away from the incompatible ideas" (p. 48). A passive participation in forbidden sexual activities may lead to *conversion hysteria,* a neurosis in which past traumas are converted into a "bodily form of expression." In the two Encyclopedia articles Freud (1923a) repeated his distinction between actual neuroses caused by abnormalities in present sexual behavior, and psychoneuroses caused by past traumatic events.

According to Freud, the neurotic is incapable of enjoyment or of achievement—the former because his libido is attached to no real object; the latter because so much of the energy which would otherwise be at his disposal is expended in maintaining the libido under repression, and in warding off its attempts to assert itself. He would be well if the conflict between his ego and his libido came to an end, and if his ego again had the libido at its disposal (Freud, 1915–1916, pp. 394–395).

Neuroses can offer the individual certain types of "gain." Some neurotic symptoms offer a *primary gain,* that is, an alleviation of the state of anxiety. Anxiety, being a state of tension between the ego and the id, or the ego and the superego, is painfully experienced as apprehension, as feelings of inadequacy, fatigue, depression in general, and a diffuse state of discomfort that accompanies almost every neurosis.

Apparently, neurotic symptoms are a morbid way of escape from the painful anxiety state. A splitting headache that imitates physical illness is one way out; it is easier to assume that one is physically ill than to be torn by an inner conflict that demands making a decision. The physical symptom, referred to by Freud as *conversion,* may alleviate the patient's guilt feelings and thereby justify his procrastination. In such a case this conversion or psychosomatic symptom serves as a primary gain; it is, indeed, an escape from the frying pan into the fire.

Some neurotic symptoms provide *secondary gain,* as for example, loss of memory, morose moods, or self-inflicted pain, which serves to protect the individual against social disapproval and wins sympathy. Secondary gain is actually an escape into illness, a means of avoiding responsibility.

All mental disorder represents regression to an earlier developmental stage. According to Freud, the time and nature of fixation determine the nature of a given mental disorder. Abraham (1924) suggested the following timetable of libido development and pathogenesis.

TABLE 1

Stages of Libidinal Organization	Stages in Development of Object Love	Dominant Point of Fixation
1. Early oral (sucking)	Autoeroticism (no object, preambivalent)	Certain types of schizophrenia (stupor)
2. Late oral-sadistic (cannibalistic) stage	Narcissism: total incorporation of the object	Manic-depressive disorders (addiction, morbid impulses)
3. Early anal-sadistic stage	Partial love with incorporation	Paranoia, certain pregenital conversion neuroses
4. Late anal-sadistic stage	Partial love	Compulsion neurosis, other pregenital conversion neuroses
5. Early genital (phallic) stage	Object love, limited by the predominant castration complex	Hysteria
6. Final genital stage	Love (postambivalent)	Normality

° This table follows Fenichel's modifications (Fenichel, 1945, p. 101.)

Development of Symptoms

The maintenance of certain internal barriers or controls is a *sine qua non* of normality. Lowering of these barriers with a subsequent pressing forward of unconscious material takes place in sleep and is a necessary precondition for the formation of dreams. In dreams all of us behave like psychotics. But if, in the waking state, unconscious becomes conscious and thinking, speaking, and acting processes are seriously regressed to include condensations, displacements, secondary elaborations, and other unconscious elements, then the individual has regressed into psychosis.

The term "neurosis" was used by Freud to describe both neuroses and psychoses. In 1924 Freud drew a clear-cut line between neurosis and psychosis. He wrote:

> *Neurosis is the result of a conflict between the ego and its id, whereas psychosis is the analogous outcome of a similar disturbance in the relation between the ego and its environment (outer world)* . . .
>
> The transference neuroses originate from the ego's refusing to accept a powerful instinctual impulse existing in its id, and denying its motor discharge, or disputing the object toward which it is aimed. The ego then defends itself against the impulse by the mechanism of repression; the repressed impulse struggles against this fate, and finds ways which the ego cannot control to create for itself substitutive gratification (a symptom), which is forced upon the ego in the form of a compromise; the ego finds its unity menaced and injured by this interloper, pursues against the symptom, just as it fended off the original instinctual impulse, and all this together produces the clinical picture of a neurosis . . .
>
> Melancholia is the model of this group, and we should put in a claim for the name of "narcissistic psychoneuroses" for these disorders . . . A narcissistic neurosis (corresponds) to that between ego and superego, and a psychosis to that between ego and outer world. To be sure, we can hardly say at a glance whether this really represents new knowledge or is merely an addition to our list of formulas; but I think that after all its capacity for application must give us courage to keep in mind this dissection of the mental apparatus that I have proposed, namely, into ego, superego and id [1924, pp. 149 ff.].

Schizophrenia

According to Freud there are two phases in schizophrenia.

First, loss of reality, i.e., the ego has lost its ability for object cathexis. The second is restitution, or striving toward recapturing reality. In neurosis reality is circumvented by a fantasy; in psychosis its is replaced by delusion and hallucination.

Manic-depressive psychotics oscillate between the joy and happiness resulting from the all-approving superego and the tortures of guilt feelings and depression that appear when the superego becomes sadistic.

> The superego becomes over-severe, abuses, humiliates, and ill-treats his unfortunate ego, threatens it with the severest punishments, reproaches it for long-forgotten actions which were at the time regarded quite lightly, and behaves as though it had spent the whole interval in amassing complaints and was only waiting for its present increase in strength to bring them forward and to condemn the ego on their account. The superego has the ego at its mercy and applies the most severe moral standards to it; indeed it represents the whole demands of morality and we see all at once that our moral sense of guilt is the expression of the tension between the ego and superego [1932, pp. 87–88].

In latent schizophrenia, the ego is at the mercy of a severe and punitive superego. The introjected parental images assume a despotic control over the patient's mental apparatus until the hard-pressed ego may give up the struggle and submerge the unconscious in a psychotic breakdown.

❧ 5 ❧
Developmental Stages
and Personality Types

Libidinal Types

Further discussion of normal and abnormal behavior (I use the term behavior in a broad connotation that includes overt and covert, conscious and unconscious processes) may benefit by relating Freud's clinical data and theoretical concepts to empirical categories developed in experimental research in social psychology (Wolman, 1949a, 1958). Freud's paper on "Libidinal Types" (1931) has inspired my thinking in this direction, leading to an elaborate system of observable personality types somewhat isomorphic to Freud's three libidinal types, namely the erotic, obsessional, and narcissistic.

Freud distinguished three normal personality types related to the balance of libidinal cathexes. "Experience shows," Freud wrote, "that all these types can exist without any neurosis" (1931, p. 219). However, Freud remarked, should people of the erotic type "fall ill, they will develop hysteria just as those of the obsessional type will develop obsessional neurosis . . . People of the narcissistic type . . . are peculiarly disposed to psychosis, and they also present essential preconditions for criminality" (1931, p. 220). This transition from normal to disturbed personality types merits special attention. My observational and experimental studies in overt patterns of interaction have led me to distinguish three personality types roughly corresponding to Freud's libidinal types, namely erotic-mutual, obsessional-vectorial, and narcissistic-instrumental, to be explained in detail further on. A quote from

64

the above-mentioned paper of Freud's might serve as an opening:

> The *erotic* type is easily characterized. Erotics are persons whose main interest—the relatively largest amount of their libido—is focused on love. Loving, but above all being loved, is for them the most important thing in life. They are governed by the dread of loss of love, and this makes them peculiarly dependent on those who may withold their love from them. Even in its pure form this type is a very common one. Variations occur according as it is blended with another type and as the element of aggression in it is strong or weak. From the social and cultural standpoint this type represents the elementary instinctual claims of the id, to which the other psychical agencies have become docile.
>
> The second type is that which I have termed the *obsessional*—a name which may at first seem rather strange; its distinctive characteristic is the supremacy exercised by the super-ego, which is segregated from the ego with great accompanying tension. Persons of this type are governed by anxiety of conscience instead of an outer dependence; they develop a high degree of self-reliance, and from the social standpoint they are the true upholders of civilization, for the most part in a conservative spirit.
>
> The characteristics of the third type, justly called the *narcissistic*, are in the main negatively described. There is no tension between the ego and super-ego—indeed, starting from this type one would hardly have arrived at the notion of a super-ego; there is no preponderance of erotic needs; the main interest is focused on self-preservation; the type is independent and not easily overawed. The ego has a considerable amount of aggression available, one manifestation of this being a proneness to activity; where love is in question, loving is preferred to being loved. People of this type impress others as being "personalities"; it is on them that their fellow-men are specially likely to lean; they readily assume the role of the leader, give a fresh stimulus to cultural development or break down existing conditions [pp. 248–249].

These three libidinal types are not necessarily related to fixations on a particular developmental stage. They do repre-

sent, however, significant differences in the balance of cathexes and interindividual relations. Freud's "erotic" type is
bound on giving and receiving love; people of the "obsessive" type apparently cathect large amounts of libido in others if they are "upholders" of civilization; the third type, the
"narcissistic," is self-explanatory.

Power and Acceptance

In observing overt behavior one cannot overlook two fundamental patterns. The first is the fact that everyone struggles for survival and in this struggle some people are forceful
and strong, while others are weak and helpless. The second
fact is that some individuals use whatever power they have
for helping others in cooperation and friendliness, while others act in a competitive, destructive and hostile manner.

Apparently we are dealing here with *two* dimensions of
behavior. The first is the strong-weak or *power* dimension.
The amount of *power* an individual has indicates how well he
can protect life and satisfy his own needs and the needs of
others. Whoever can satisfy needs and protect life is strong;
whoever cannot is weak. Obviously, power is related to vitality and ability to survive, and the dimension of power includes all levels and degrees of one's ability to satisfy needs,
from omnipotence at the top to a complete decline of power
and death at the bottom.

The second dimension, called *acceptance*, describes the
way in which the available amount of power is used. One
may use his power to satisfy the *needs of others* or to *prevent*
their satisfaction. One may be friendly or hostile. The terms
"friendly" and "hostile" do not indicate the amount of power
but the *direction* in which it is used. *Thus power may be
defined as the ability to satisfy needs, and acceptance as the
willingness to do so.* A strong individual *can* satisfy needs, the
most basic of which for the living organism is to stay alive.

As mentioned before, there are degrees of power, the lowest point, the point of zero power, being death.

The term acceptance is isomorphic to Freud's libido and destrudo cathexes. For whoever has power may use it *for* or *against* the satisfaction of others' needs. Whenever he uses his power *for* the satisfaction of others' needs, he is friendly. Whenever he uses it *against* the satisfaction of others' needs, he is destructive and hostile. In the first case it is object cathexis of the libido; in the second, the destrudo is object cathected.

Apparently, the terms "friendly" and "hostile" describe one's attitude toward other people; A., for example, may be friendly or hostile toward B. These terms can also be used in regard to oneself. For example, A. may like or hate himself. Whenever the terms "friendly" and "hostile" are used to indicate one's attitude toward others, it is *interindividual cathexis* of libido or destrudo respectively. Whenever we speak of one's attitude towards oneself, it is *intraindividual cathexis*, to be explained below.

One can be friendly and strong, friendly and weak, hostile and strong, or hostile and weak. In a sociopsychological study of classroom relationships, teachers viewed by students as strong and friendly had the best classroom discipline, whereas weak and hostile teachers could not control their pupils (Wolman, 1949b).

The term aggressiveness indicates both hostility and forcefulness; one may be a weak enemy or a strong friend, and *forcefulness* does not necessarily indicate hostility. A forceful, decisive, competent surgeon saves the lives of his patients, and he is, in regard to them, strong and friendly.

Four Types of Behavior

Interindividual relationships may be divided into four observable patterns, depending upon the aims of the participants. I call them H (hostile), I (instrumental), M (mutual), and V (vectorial).

Whenever an individual seeks to harm or destroy the other participant(s) in the encounter, he displays *hostility*. Whenever he wants to use him, to gain benefits, to have his own needs satisfied, this is *instrumentalism*. Whenever his aim is to satisfy both himself and his partner(s), in a give and take relationship, this is *mutualism*. Whenever his aim is to satisfy the needs of others without expecting anything in return, this is *vectorialism*.

One's attitude toward others is not always simple and clearcut. Often behavior is ambiguous or even ambivalent. Ideally, antisocial behavior is pure hostility, the infant's attitude toward his mother is exploitative, parasitic, and instrumental; marital partners usually seek mutual gratification, and mother's attitude toward her infant is vectorial. An infant is *weak*, he has nothing to give; he must be instrumental, he must receive supplies from without, or he will not survive. Gradually, as he grows, develops and learns, he acquires strength and becomes capable of giving. Sexual and nonsexual friendships by definition involve a give and take or mutual relationship. A fully mature adult is capable of giving vectorial love and care to his children without asking anything in return. A normal and well-adjusted individual combines all four attitudes in a balanced manner. He is reasonably hostile whenever attacked (defensive type of hostility), reasonably instrumental in livelihood-procuring activities, reasonably mutual in sex and marriage, and reasonably vectorial in regard to his children, to those who need his help, and to those things he believes in. He is neither an angel nor an animal, but a balanced human being.

There seem to be definite though not rigidly circumscribed developmental stages from the onset of life toward a balanced maturity.

Interindividual Cathexis

Before I describe the developmental stages of interindividual behavior, I would like to compare it to Freud's conceptual system. Freud's model of personality includes topography, that is, the mental strata (unconscious, preconscious, and conscious), dynamics of the driving forces (libido and destrudo), and the structure of mental apparatus (id, ego, superego). Yet Freud's model does not do justice to the problems of social relations as do the neoanalytic schools (Horney, Sullivan, etc.). I suggest therefore some modification in Freud's concept of cathexis in the hope that such a modification will increase the understanding of social relations.

Freud described the individual who cathects his libido in others but he did not attempt to explain what happens to the one who receives the cathected libido. When a mother loves her child, her libido is cathected in the image of the child; the loving mother "gives love" to her child and some amount of emotional energy, libido, is given away. Freud dealt with the giving mother—but did not study what happened to the receiving child. Does the child "receive" the love that is "given" him? What happens to the child whose mother does not love him? And what happens when the mother demands love from her child?

The sociologically oriented psychoanalyst Karen Horney stressed *the need to be loved*. When a child feels loved and accepted, he experiences the feeling of *safety*. When a child feels rejected, *basic anxiety* develops. Human activities are guided by both pleasure related to satisfaction of basic needs and safety related to human relationships. According to Horney (1939) people would rather renounce pleasure than safety. Instead of promoting Freudian love, sexual or aim-inhibited, Horney introduced the concepts of protection and safety; in place of Freud's active cathexis of libido, that is, the need to give love, she emphasized the need to be loved.

H. S. Sullivan went even further in his thinking. His theory is rightly called a theory of interpersonal relations. According to Sullivan (1953) personality can never be isolated from the complexity of interpersonal relations in which the person lives. Sullivan stressed the concept of *empathy*, described by him as a kind of "emotional contagion or communion" between a child and his parental figures. Thus, the infant shows a curious relationship or connection with the significant adult, ordinarily the mother. When the feeding mother is upset, the infant may develop feeding difficulty and indigestion.

Freud dealt with the person who invests his libido in others: I suggest broadening the concept and studying the cathected person and the *interindividual cathexis*. The concept of interindividual cathexis is merely a theoretical concept and there are no neurological counterparts to it. It may, however, resemble Pavlov's explanation of reflex. According to Pavlov (1928) an external stimulus is "transformed into a nervous process and transmitted along a circuitous route (from the peripheral endings of the centripetal nerve, along its fibers to the apparatus of the central nervous system, and out along the centrifugal path until, reaching one or another organ, it excites its activity)" (p. 121). Pavlov's description can be explained in terms of cathexis of physical energy; the external stimulus transmits a part of its energetic load in the peripheral endings of the centripetal nerve, cathects or charges this nerve ending, and through the circuitous route it cathects the nerve center.

One may but speculate about the interindividual cathexis of mental energy, for there is no empirical proof of cathexis of mental energy, nor can one be sure that a cathexis of mental energy follows the same rules as the cathexis of physical energy. The term "interindividual cathexis" is thus introduced as a theoretical construct and not as an empirical fact.

This new construct can serve as a bridge between psychoanalytic studies of personality and observable social interaction. As described in Chapter 1, the objective of instrumental relationships is to receive libidinal cathexes from others. The individual's own libido is self-cathected and he expects the libido of others to be object-cathected into him. All neonates are instrumental and narcissistic and want to be loved. An infant's attitude is instrumental, for he wishes to receive cathexes and to become a libido-cathected object. The same applies to any other instrumental relationship.

The objective of mutual relationships is the give and take, that is, to receive libidinal cathexes as well as to give them to others. As mentioned above satisfactory sexual relations are mutual. Nonsexual friendship is also mutual for each partner desires to object-cathect his desexualized libido in his partner and expects the same from his partner.

A disbalance in interindividual libido and destrudo cathexes, caused by faulty interaction between the individual and his environment, creates a disbalance of libido and destrudo in *oneself.* Since this kind of disbalance leads to behavior disorders, it is reasonable to assume that faulty social relations may be the main cause underlying such disorders. If these faulty social relationships start early in childhood, the damage caused to one's personality can be quite serious.

There is neither a clearcut criterion nor a precise and wholly objective yardstick for the measurement of cathectic disbalances. All efforts of quantification of libido and destrudo are doomed to fail because libido and destrudo are not empirical data but theoretical constructs However, an isomorphic theoretical framework derived from descriptive data may open new vistas in the direction of precise and quantitative diagnostic techniques based on overt interactional behavior.

Intrauterine Life

Studies of pregnancy in human females describe a peculiar relationship between the mother's body and the new organ-

ism. With the fertilization of the egg by sperm and the formation of a zygote, throughout the stages of embryo, fetus,
and birth, and until the umbilical cord is cut, the two organisms of the mother and child share metabolic, cardiovascular,
circulatory, gastrointestinal and respiratory processes. These
processes, unless disturbed, are not communicated to the
higher cortical centers and they are therefore wholly *involuntary* and *unconscious*. Typically the mother does not
"know" that her circulatory system supplies oxygen to the
fetus, or that the amount of amino acids in her body determines the chemistry of her infant's body.

The as-yet-unborn infant knows even less. Although one
may hypothesize some rudimentary stimulus-response mechanism quite early in the prenatal life, the intrauterine development of the nervous system excludes the possibility of
awareness and of conscious processes in the fetus. Whatever
mental life exists prior to birth, it is totally unconscious. One
may therefore safely conclude that whatever transpires between the mother's organism and the new organism is entirely and completely unconscious, in mother and child alike.

The objective facts are clear: the mother's body offers an
unconditional and unreserved support to the new organism.
Though the mother does all that unconsciously, she assumes a
supportive and even *subservient* attitude toward her own
child. Her body becomes, as it were, a servant of her child.

The zygote, and in the later stages the embryo and the
fetus, receive priority treatment necessary for their survival.
Oxygen, iron, calcium, and whatever else is necessary for survival is unconditionally supplied to the new organism. This
supply is continuous, often at the expense of the mother's
well-being. Even when, for instance, the maternal body
suffers from iron deficiency, iron is still given away to the
fetus, even to the point where the supply may be depleted.
The maternal organism supplies water, oxygen, food, housing

and physical protection at no charge and at the risk of harming itself.

Intrauterine life is parasitic from its inception. The unborn organism acts in utter disrespect for its mother's health and well-being, taking whatever it needs and offering nothing in return.

This "give" (mothers being vectorial) and "take" (infants being instrumental) relationship is apparently necessary for the survival of the infant and, in most cases, it is not harmful to the mother. Pregnancy is not a disease but a state of increased efforts necessary for the development of the child. Mature women can assume this burden, but the maternal attitude of giving has its natural limit, namely the survival of the mother herself.

Abnormal, damaging and painful pregnancies evoke self-defensive reactions and are often abruptly terminated by the expulsion of the noxious fetus in abortive motions. Abortions can be either involuntary or voluntary. Mothers who after taking thalidomide feared that their babies might be born deformed sought to rid themselves of the embryo. Many unwed pregnant women who fear ostracism, or married mothers who are worried about social, economic, or psychological burdens may seek abortions.

A natural limit to the intrauterine parasitism is imposed by the size of the fetus. Should the fetus keep growing inside the uterus, both mother and child might be killed. At a certain point, the pressures from the growing fetus cause severe pains to which the mother responds with cramps. Subsequently the bag of water opens up, labor begins, and the mother's body expels the infant. The mother must do this or perish: thus birth is her desperate attempt to survive. Yet birth does not bring the parasitic relationship to an end. The human neonate, as Carmichael (1954) pointed out, is poorly prepared for extrauterine life. Compared to the proverbial guinea pigs, human infants are born immature and, unless cared for with kindness and love, they may not survive.

From the beginning of the intra- and later extrauterine life, the new organism is a taker. One may hypothesize that all the available libido of the neonate is self-cathected, and all his destrudo is directed against the outer world for self-defense.

Developmental Stages

Human development is a product of several factors, some of them rooted in genetically transmitted maturational tendencies and some dependent upon interaction with the physical and social environment. These two clusters of factors are not closed entities nor are they mutually exclusive. Consider the development of seeds into trees. Certainly a seed of oak will never develop into a maple tree, but the seed kept in acid will never develop at all. An insect egg turns under favorable conditions into a larva, then a cocoon, and ultimately becomes an adult insect, but whether it will develop at all and how well it will develop depends upon a variety of environmental factors.

The higher the species, the longer and more complex is the process of growth and maturation. In humans, birth is the beginning of a prolonged maturational process that leads from a wholly parasitic beginning toward a nonparasitic maturity. Maturity includes the ability to support oneself economically, to perform sexually, to assume parental responsibility, and to cooperate with one's social environment.

Several factors have to be accounted for in this long maturational process. First, there are the hereditary factors that determine the basic phases of growth from infancy, through childhood and puberty, to adulthood. Freud's developmental stages can be viewed in this light. All children *tend* to go through the oral, anal, urethral-phallic, latency and pubertal stages; these stages are *biologically* determined. Certainly

Kardiner (1939, 1945) had a point in relating personality differences to child-rearing practices. Studies by Whiting and Child (1953) and others have shed additional light on the impact of sociocultural factors upon the child's growth and development. The tendency to pass through certain developmental stages is universal as demonstrated by the work of many researchers, including Piaget (1954) and Gesell (1933). This research basically affirms Freud's concept of psychosexual developmental phases. However, it is apparent that the way in which a child passes through the developmental stages and the resulting degree of fixation and regression depends largely on what the individual child inherited and the child's interaction with his particular environment. When a child is exposed to a friendly, wholesome and affectionate environment, his libido, initially self-directed, is lured into object cathexes. In an overdemanding environment, there is a danger of object hypercathexis and self-hypocathexis (Federn, 1952; Wolman, 1957, 1966a). In a rejecting and hostile environment, object cathexis of destrudo is encouraged.

According to the principle of survival of the fittest, the survival prognosis for an infant who is unable to take advantage of his environment is rather poor. To take everything and to give nothing in return—that is instrumentalism, the survival device of the weak. An infant who voraciously grabs his mother's breast or the bottle of milk displays more vitality than the infant who lacks enthusiasm for milk. At this stage of life, there is no love for anyone except for oneself. The narcissistic, parasitic self-love is a prerequisite for survival. As mentioned above, in neonates the entire libido is self-cathected in primary narcissism and all destrudo is ready for discharge in self-defense through primary hostility.

Whereas everything is supplied in intrauterine life, life after birth becomes a matter of sink or swim. A threat to life, be it a physical threat or a disruption of narcissistic supplies, elicits an immediate discharge of the destrudo.

Threat produces *fear;* fear is the alarm bell of the organism. Fear produces either fight or flight or both. Those who have no fear cannot be hostile. If absolute security were possible, fights and wars would disappear. People fight either as greedy aggressors who fear they may die unless they devour someone, or as defenders who fear death inflicted by aggressors. Those who fear, hate and those who hate, fear.

In neonates, neither reaction is tempered by any significant control apparatus. There is no need to reiterate here the Hartmann, Kris, and Loewenstein (1946) theory of ego; if there is any rudimentary ego, it is too weak to inhibit wild outbursts of destrudo. Fear in infants means panic; fight means furious rage. In autistic children and in catatonic adult schizophrenics (Wolman, 1966a, 1968, 1969) there is no calculated evasion of risk or planned escape, nor is there a goal-directed attack on enemies; instead, there is blind panic or wild rage, often senseless and indiscriminate.

Under normal circumstances, libido becomes gradually and to a great extent object cathected. In the normal adult libido is distributed between self and object cathexes which enables him both to take care of himself and to be friendly to others.

There are, however, no developmental stages of destrudo. Destrudo is archaic, primordial, primary. There can be no developmental stages in destrudo analogous to Freud's developmental stages of libido, because destrudo cannot progress. Destrudo serves self-defense and survival; when object love fails, part of frustrated libido turns into secondary narcissistic love, and part into destrudo. Probably destrudo and libido are, as it were, two types of mental energy, two kinds of fuel that are transformable into each other. In states of emergency, severe deprivation, lack of sleep and exhaustion, the destrudo takes over. It is as if hate is called into play when love cannot help. Destrudo is the more primitive energy of the organism, always present, leading to outbursts of rage in animals and to temper tantrums in infants.

In states of serious regression, destrudo is the sole drive of the organism. In normal states, destrudo is partially fused with libido, partially suppressed by the ego, partially sublimated. An uninhibited, object-directed destrudo is genocidal and a menace to others; in cases where destrudo is self-directed, it becomes suicidal.

Kittens raised for four months together with rats did not kill the latter, but 85 per cent of the kittens raised by mothers who killed rats did likewise (Kuo, 1930). According to Freudian theory, kittens and infants are initially endowed with self-hate, which may eventually turn outward. The fact is that all infants are object-destructive. Their oral love is a fusion of object-libido and object-destrudo with the predominance of destrudo. At the anal stage libido object-cathexis becomes somewhat stronger (Abraham's "tenderness"). The possessive-protective love of the phallic stage represents an additional gain of libido over destrudo. In normal development, binding and neutralizing of the destrudo takes place.

Regression is a reverse process. People who failed to grow up are aggressive. Manic-depressive and schizophrenic psychotics display excessive destructiveness. According to Anna Freud (1949):

> The pathological aggressiveness stems not from the aggressive tendencies themselves but from the lack of fusion between them and libidinal (erotic) urges. The pathological factor is found in the realm of erotic, emotional development which has been no help through adverse external or internal conditions . . . Owing to the defects on the emotional side, the aggressive urges are not brought into the fusion and thereby bound and partially neutralized, but remain free and seek expression in the forms of pure, unadulterated independent destructiveness [pp. 41–42].

The Oral Stage

At the oral-cannibalistic stage, libido and destrudo are not fully separated. In the infant, to quote from Freud's (1905a)

Three Essays, "the sexual activity is not yet separated from
the taking of nourishment . . . The object of the one activity
is also that of the other; the sexual aim then consists in the
incorporation of the object into one's own body . . ." (p. 197).

It is not the cannibal's intention to die; rather he kills for
food and eats for survival. There is no drive-to-die at the oral
stage, but there is a lot of object destructiveness for one's
own survival. Incorporation does not mean decrease or decline, but self-aggrandizement.

Freud (1938) wrote in the *Outline* as follows:

> The first organ to make its appearance as an erotogenic zone and to
> make libidinal demands upon the mind is, from the time of birth
> onward, the mouth. To begin with, all mental activity is centered
> upon the task of providing satisfaction for the needs of that zone. In
> the first instance, of course, the latter serves the purposes of
> self-preservation by means of nourishment; but physiology should not
> be confused with psychology. The baby's obstinate persistence in
> sucking gives evidence at an early stage of a need for satisfaction
> which, although it originates from and is stimulated by the taking of
> nourishment, nevertheless seeks to obtain pleasure independently of
> nourishment, and for that reason may and should be described as "sex-
> ual" [p. 28].

Although sadistic impulses begin to occur sporadically during the oral phase along with the appearance of the teeth
(Freud, 1938), aggressiveness does not originate with the development of teeth.

Normal parents or parental substitutes usually relate to an
infant in a vectorial way, feeding him in a kind, protective,
and loving manner. The infant is a taker, putting into his
mouth whatever is given to him; hence the name, the *oral*
stage. Characteristic of the oral stage is a "devouring affection" toward the love objects and a love which is "cannibalistic."

In terms of the power and acceptance theory, the oral stage is an early form of *instrumentalism*. It is an interindividual relationship in which the desire to be helped (to get) is combined with considerable fear and hostility. The "weak" infant needs food and must receive it at any cost. When refused, all four forms of hostility (i.e., aggressive, defensive, panic, and horror) are promptly elicited.

The Anal Stage

Abraham (1924) called attention to two stages in the anal-sadistic phase. In the former of these, the destructive tendencies to annihilate and to get rid of things have the upper hand, while in the latter, those tendencies predominate which are friendly to the object and seek to possess things and hold them fast. Somewhat toward the middle of this phase, a consideration for the love object appears; this consideration is a forerunner of a later relation of love towards the object.

A similar division was introduced in the oral phase. The early stage was referred to as "oral incorporative," while the second stage was believed to be oral-sadistic. I believe that the destrudo is present at all times, and that it serves Ares and not Thanatos.

It is my belief that hostility never disappears entirely. At the prenatal and neonatal stage, the infant's lust for life is motivated chiefly by Ares. At these early stages, hostility, not love, is the choice means of survival. The neonate has nothing to give yet. He has a long way to go, through the oral-cannibalistic, anal-retentive, phallic-possessive, latent-aim inhibited, pubertal-genital, toward the mature love (mutual) and self-sacrificing love of parenthood (vectorial). In order to give, one must have something to give. The progress toward adulthood is a gradual victory of power over weakness and of love over hate.

The entire oral stage is instrumental and hostile. The more primitive the personality, the more it is driven by hostility. Weakness produces fear, and fear is a Siamese twin of hostility.

The anal stage is characterized not only by toilet training but also by walking and talking behavior. The erect position and walking around permit the child to use hands and manipulate objects to a much greater extent than he could have done in the oral stage. The child can explore distant places, disappear from mother's sight, and reach into new areas hitherto forbidden. What an increase of power!

The beginning of speech is another source of everincreasing power. To be able to comprehend and be comprehended, to call and be called to, to exchange wishes and demands—all this gives the infant a new feeling of power. Perhaps infants hallucinate power, but the toddlers who babble nonstop obviously enjoy their torrent of talk. With the increased mastery of words, they flood their environment with a tidal wave of questions *(Fragenwut)* to which they do not necessarily expect an answer.

Another source of power lies in toilet training. At the anal stage, unless the mother is sadistic and resorts to enemas, she is often at the mercy of the child. The mother can seat the child on the toilet, but thereafter she relinquishes her control. Mother may refuse food to her child, but feces are the child's indisputable possession, the prototype of money and of any future property.

Feces can be retained for "future use" or future regulation of pleasure. One can give generously, withhold love, or use delayed giving for building up of pleasure. This "reality principle" or ability to postpone gratification will play a tremendous role in sex and its sublimation.

By the same token, control of bowels may be used as a regulator of hate. Extortion of concessions and dictatorship are derivatives of the anal-retentive attitudes. In face-to-face relationships, anal retentiveness may be acted out in revengeful, cold, domineering attitudes, as well as in withholding of affection, ignoring and rejecting.

Anal-sadistic impulses can be acted out in active-expulsive ways. The smell of feces is offensive, and spiteful elimination on mother's new rug is a hostile act. The language describing elimination is meant to be offensive; one shows hostile disrespect by applying it in conversation. Anal-expulsive actions such as elimination, flatulence, or their verbal equivalents are repulsive and aimed at hurting those toward whom they are directed.

The anal phase still belongs to the instrumental pattern of interaction. It is a kind of advanced instrumentalism, where one does not devour immediately, but keeps for future use. Adults with strong oral fixations are selfish and inclined to take advantage of others. Anally fixated individuals are somewhat kinder; they do not destroy their slaves, but care for them in order to get more out of them. Abraham's (1924) "tenderness" is merely a higher level of instrumentalism.

Instrumentals cannot tolerate frustration. They turn hostile whenever their wishes are not satisfied. Oral instrumentalism operates on the "pleasure principle" and demands immediate gratification; anal instrumentalism can postpone gratification in accordance with the "reality principle," which is a definite sign of progress.

The Phallic Stage

The phallic stage has been described by Freud (1938) as the beginning of the organization of libido. "In the earlier phases, the separate component instincts set about their pursuit of pleasure independent of one another; in the phallic stage there are the first signs of an organization which subordinates the other trends to the primacy of the genitals and signifies the beginning of a coordination of the general pursuit of pleasure into the sexual function" (p. 30).

At the phallic stage, object love is channeled into genital desires directed toward the parent of the opposite sex, and becomes, for the first time, the dominating force, stronger than destrudo. At the oral stage, the cannibalistic object relationship (unfortunately called cannibalistic "love") is dominated by destrudo. Infants eat, and eating is destruction. When one says, "I love chicken," he really does not love it; he merely "loves" to eat it, and by eating it he performs an act of destruction. There is no object love at the oral stage; the only love is self-love, that is, self-directed libido.

There are some modest beginnings of love at the anal stage, but love, defined as behavior aimed at the protection of life, does not exist even at that stage. Abraham's "tenderness" is, at best, a delay in destruction or in expulsion for the sake of a greater pleasure at a later stage. A child "keeps" feces to derive increased pleasure later on; he "keeps" a candy bar for the sake of more enjoyable munchings at a later stage. Both the oral and anal phases reflect the instrumental attitude.

The anal "keeping for a future use" is, however, a forerunner of love, of keeping for protection. To keep someone in order to protect him implies love and caring, which is basically what we mean by "love."

Love is necessarily possessive. It is not easy to take care of remote objects or people. One can take care of his house, garden, treasures and beloved persons; one can protect them from harm and defend them whenever necessary. Hugging, kissing, and caressing are pleasurable for both the one who hugs and the one who is being hugged. The infant has learned to derive pleasure from being hugged and taken care of. Mother's affectionate embraces and kind words were reassuring and comforting. When mother held him tightly in her arms, he felt loved and happy. Whenever he felt lonely or hurt, he ran to mother for comfort. Although the desire for physical proximity is instinctive, it is further reinforced by conditioning. Affection and praise are a kind of additional stratum superimposed upon the innate tendencies of physical proximity.

Possessiveness hinges on physical proximity. The first love which one experiences is the narcissistic love for oneself. The infant loves to take in, to incorporate, and to serve and aggrandize himself by this intake. He loves what he can hold and holds on to what he loves to have. Ultimately, all this is instrumental self-love. The mouth is the opening through which he can possess things that will become part of himself through incorporation. Later on he holds on tightly to his favorite toys, to the doll or piece of rag he sleeps with, or to any other treasure. Physical proximity gives him the feeling of security and comfort. To let things go or to part from objects is tantamount to losing them.

It takes years of growth and learning before the child will be in a position to return some of the love that has been bestowed upon him by his parents. The greater the amount of vectorial, desexualized libidinal cathexis which the child has received from his parents, the more libido he will have at his disposal for object cathexis. Children who enjoyed parental love are more prone to give love to others; children who suffered love deprivation may remain love-hungry addicts who forever must seek love and approval from others.

Cathexis and conditioning are intertwined in this developmental process. In daily interaction with other children, the child clings to his own possessions while trying to take hold of the attractive toys his playmates display. The playground, the sandbox, the backyard and the nursery school all serve to teach the child mutuality, for children are instrumental-minded and selfish. They will typically engage in numerous frustrating confrontations until, with the guidance given by adults, they learn to give in order to receive, and to share in order to enjoy, thus taking the first steps in the direction of *mutualism.*

The phallic phase is witness to the origin of possessiveness and jealousy. Given the nature of the nuclear family the child's security is rooted in the one-to-one relationship. Everyone else, be it the other parent or the siblings, is viewed as a competitor whose very presence threatens the child's possession of and belonging to the beloved parent.

To possess and to be possessed are the fundamental elements of sexual love. Thus, promiscuity is ultimately a form of regression to a prephallic stage of development. Those who engage in this kind of behavior use and are used but they do not belong nor do they possess. Never fully satisfied, they may continue their regressive manoeuvers *ad infinitum.* Mature men and women, as long as they love one another, don't need anyone else.

The oedipal love for mother leads to ambivalent feelings toward the chief competitor, the father. During the phallic period, the child derives pleasure and security from protecting the beloved parent (Eros) and wishes to destroy the competing one (Ares). Hence, both Eros and Ares serve the child's needs.

The father is usually the main provider and satisfier of material needs. Whenever father is strong (capable of satisfying needs) and friendly (willing to do so), the child wishes him to be even stronger and friendlier, but this wish gives rise to a profound conflict—between the desire to protect and destroy, to love and to hate.

The oedipal conflict signals the future cooperation and competition among adult members of the same sex. Under normal circumstances, the oedipal conflict leads to inhibition of love and hate. Hate can be inhibited either by love or by fear, or by a combination of both. The strong and friendly father evokes fear by his strength, and love by his kindness. A fusion of love and fear gives rise to the feeling of *awe* and thereby leads to development of the superego.

Freud believed that Thanatos would eventuate in one's

own destruction unless it were diverted into overt hostility against the outer world. Part of this hostility, directed against the restricting and prohibiting parents, becomes incorporated in the superego and channeled against one's own ego, that is, against oneself. It is my contention that the destrudo serves survival and that it is initially directed against threats from without. The question is, how can one's destrudo become directed towards oneself in a defiance of the universal law of struggle for survival?

Apparently, such a reversal of direction occurs only when one treats oneself as a hostile object. Here Freud's structural theory of id, ego and superego is helpful in offering an explanation for this reversal. The original *situs* of the destrudo is the id, the "boiling cauldron" of all innate energy. The destrudo, anchored in the id, is object-directed, in the service of the fundamental law of struggle for survival. The destrudo is also invested in the ego. The difference between the id-seated and the ego-seated destrudo hinges upon topographic (conscious-unconscious) and structural (id-ego-superego) factors. The outbursts of the id-located destrudo are blind, immediate, uncoordinated, and often useless and senseless. Id operates on the so-called "pleasure principle," the principle of immediate discharge of energy. Such a blind discharge of destrudo usually corresponds to what was described above as the "panic" and "terror" types of hostility. Basically, all hostility serves survival, but panic and terror are the irrational, primary expressions of the fight for survival.

The fight for survival is better served by a more rational, controlled and goal-directed hostility. The ego, operating on the "reality principle," delays and controls destrudo reactions. Instead of reacting with an outburst of the panic or terror variety, the ego exercises judgement. The reality principle is not an antipleasure rule; rather it is a rule given to pursuit of pleasure at minimum risk. Whereas the id is prone to fight at the slightest provocation the ego fights to win. Thus, the ego-seated discharges of destrudo are aggressive or defensive or both, always aiming at the well-being of the organism.

Introjection of the image of the parent of the same sex, a mechanism resembling patricide and mourning, puts an end to the oedipal wish to kill the father. Yet, according to the principle of preservation of energy, rather than disappear, the undischarged hostility is stored in the superego. This stored-up hostility originally intended for the parent, is often directed against oneself. Viewed within the context of Freud's structural theory, the superego may be said to "attack" the ego. The superego, reflecting parental criticism, pursues the line of censoring and rebuking the ego.

Such self-directed hostility is a normal procedure. Balanced individuals are capable of self-criticism and experience guilt feelings whenever they act in a manner offensive to their own convictions. The ego finds a reasonable balance between the moral demands of the superego, the instinctual demands of the id, and the conditions of the outer world.

Following Freud's line of reasoning, I assume that energy, not only from the libido but from the destrudo as well, is invested in the ego. Since the ego is the guardian of the system, the destrudo, anchored in the ego, continues its defensive-aggressive functions, guarding the individual against being attacked by others and facilitating his aggressive behavior toward the world. Ego-anchored destrudo is object-directed, always ready to strike against the enemy. The ego, as the protector of life, operates as it were on two channels: it uses both love and hate for the protection of one's own life.

With the formation of the superego, a part of the destrudo becomes invested therein. The superego is formed through the introjection of both parental prohibitions and the idealized parental image. The former carries some elements of destrudo; the latter includes elements of libido. When the superego is first set up, it is invested with some of the child's aggressiveness against his parents. This hate can hardly find satisfactory outlets; normal children do not kill nor do they attack the parent of the same sex. Thus, the thwarted destrudo turns inwardly, against the ego, creating feelings of guilt.

Some degree of self-directed hostility is necessary for balanced behavior. Such self-hostility in its conscious form manifests itself as self-criticism; in its unconscious form it is experienced as guilt feeling. Whenever one's behavior clashes with one's social norms rooted in the superego, self-criticism or guilt feeling or both ensue. Irrational, exaggerated, self-destructive self-hate is regressive and pathological, it will be discussed in the following chapters.

The Latency Period

During the time that Freud lived, the latency period was the period of life when inhibitory forces acted upon the child's libido and destrudo. The child was turning away from the parent of the opposite sex and becoming antagonistic to the opposite sex in general. He still loved the parent of the opposite sex, but his love became desexualized and aim-inhibited.

Freud's formulations require a cultural-historical adjustment. In a society based upon rather stable interindividual relationships, such as was true of Vienna at the beginning of this century, boys renounced mothers as love objects and girls renounced fathers. Boys played with boys, girls with girls; boys played cops and robbers; girls played house. Boys avoided girls and girls avoided boys. Eros became aim-inhibited, love de-emotionalized, and groups were formed based on hierarchic social structure, tight and exclusive of the opposite sex.

Though the basic rules of latency apply also to contemporary societies, much has changed. There is, today, much less inhibition and practically no delay in sexual information compared to that existing in Freud's times. Thus, it seems that the time span of the latency period has shrunk, and not all children go through this phase in the way Freud described it. There is no doubt that the differences in child rearing strongly affect developmental problems and the ultimate personality structure.

The main change, however, is caused by the decline in parental authority. At the beginning of our century, family ties were quite strong, and family life in Catholic and Jewish Vienna was quite conservative. Today, in the United States and in most European countries, family organization has undergone profound changes that have undoubtedly affected human feelings and actions.

The concept of latency is related to two significant changes in the child's personality: identification through introjection, and the aim-inhibition of impulses. Under normal conditions, children faced with parental punishment renounce the parent of the opposite sex as a sexual love object. The little boy does not stop loving his mother; he only ceases to desire her sexually. His love for her has become aim-inhibited and partly sublimated. According to the principle of preservation of energy, the libidinal energy can be blocked, recathected, sublimated and "neutralized" (Hartmann, 1955) but it cannot disappear. Thus even in normal development the unconscious and conscious memories of mother's looks and affection play a significant role in the choice of a love object. Some degree of expectancy of mothering is implicit in a man's love for his wife; it becomes pathological when it dominates the choice of a love object or makes the man expect his wife to be a copy of his mother. Exaggerated and infantile demands are often a product of childhood experiences that becloud the husband-wife relationship. Viewing people not as they really are but as mere reflections of childhood memories is the essence of transference. Transference occurs in the psychoanalytic or in any other relationship where past power and acceptance relationships cast shadows on the present ones. A satisfactory resolution of the oedipal involvement permits reasonable marital choice and a rational husband-wife relationship, based on the *here and now*, realistic appraisal of oneself and the marital partner. Some residues of the past remain forever, for the Oedipus complex is never completely resolved, either in men or in women. An overt incestuous desire for a parent has been observed in psychotics (Bychowski, 1952; Wolman, 1966a), and an unconscious repressed oedipal conflict forms the core of most neurotic disorders. The degree to which the Oedipus conflict is resolved may serve as one of the indicators of personality adjustment.

Present-day family dynamics hardly facilitate such an adjustment. In a great many families, father's authority has declined to such an extent that he is hardly a figure to inspire fear in his sons. The chances are that contemporary boys and girls may fear mother more than father. Therefore it may not be easy for the male child to identify with the father, a situation which may be responsible for the steady increase in incidence of male homosexuality. At the same time one may speculate about the apparent decline of feminine traits in females, who either identify with the domineering mother or, if they identify with the weak father, will also tend toward homosexuality.

In the not too distant past the nature of the latency period was determined by the degree to which there was acceptance of parental authority. The more the child accepted parental admonitions, restrictions and prohibitions, the stronger was his superego. It seems that in our times, and probably in this country more than elsewhere, parental authority has declined to such an extent as to affect the strength of the superego. The apparent increase in delinquency and hyperinstrumental types, to be described later, bears witness to this effect.

The developmental theories of Freud, Piaget, Gesell, Erikson and others require some sociocultural correction. These theories certainly hold true for those cultural groups where parental authority and especially father's authority survived two world wars, social upheavals, mass communication, and rapid social mobility. In these more conservative and traditional social groups, latency is still the period of aim-inhibited love for the parent of the opposite sex and aim-inhibited hate for the parent of the same sex. The future will tell to what extent developmental stages will be affected by sociocultural changes (cf. Kardiner, 1939, 1945; Erikson, 1963; Whiting and Child, 1953). The fact is that in some primitive tribes, such as the Marquesans and Trobrianders, where there is little if any cultural restraint, sex is practiced in preadolescent years and the concept of latency is inapplicable to their developmental years.

Sociopsychological studies of that age group (Caplan and Lebovici, 1969), pointed to the unisexual structure of interindividual relations. These relations, being more instrumental than mutual, reflect the tendency of children at this stage to associate with other children of their own sex and thereby strengthen sex-role identifications. Boys who have at least to some extent identified with their fathers and renounced their mothers as love objects tend to identify with other boys and to reject all girls. The dyads, triads, and larger groups and cliques are usually composed of children of one sex only.

The spontaneous organizations of children at this age tend to be hierarchic. The hierarchic systems are based on a submissive attitude toward those who dominate and a domineering attitude toward those who are on a lower level of the social ladder. In terms of the power and acceptance theory, in hierarchical systems one relates in a friendly-submissive way to those who have more power, and in a hostile-domineering way to those who have less power. It is indeed a "pecking order"; one yields to the stronger and takes advantage of the weaker. One's submission to the stronger is a form of instrumentalism which may lead to mutualism, for one tries to please the strong ones, hoping that they will reciprocate. This was the essence of the feudal system, based on the vassal's subservience to his senior.

Hierarchy, be it feudal or otherwise, is domineering and exploiting. The seniors were not "friendly" to their vassals; nor did the vassals serve their seniors out of pure love. It was a somewhat modified form of instrumentalism in which both parties did as little as possible for the well-being of their partners.

Children, at the middle childhood or latency stages, are far from having achieved self-sacrificing vectorialism. They are hardly capable of a genuine give-and-take mutualism. Wolman's (1951) study of spontaneous groups and Piaget's (1932) classic study of moral judgment in children point to the lack of genuine compassion, sympathy and consideration at this age. Children seek friends not in order to help but to be helped. Whenever they reciprocate, it is not because of their heart's innermost desire, but because otherwise they would lose their friends. Be that as it may, this unwilling reciprocation is a step forward toward mutuality.

Instrumental attitudes easily lead to hostile behavior. The feudal lords were inclined to punish disobedient vassals. Children at this age tend to take advantage, ridicule, ostracize and bully the weaker members of their group. Hostility among competing leaders and competing groups breaks out frequently. Intolerance against children who differ in race, religion, social status or even neighborhood is a daily occurrence. Ten-year-olds are anything but considerate and magnanimous.

Their newly developed identification with like-sexed members of the peer group helps to strengthen their superegos. Now they know what is right; right is what the leader says is right. Such authoritarian thinking is not conducive to tolerance and, as would be expected, most children at this age are far from tolerant. Group hostility for the "right" cause against "wrong" people is a typical phenomenon. Ares, supported by the self-righteous superego, practices scapegoating.

Adolescence

I am not at all sure that personality structure is shaped in the latency period or at any other phase of life. Even inherited features, such as blood chemistry, endocrinological constitution, and neurological structure can be altered through psychological changes, poisoning, infectious diseases, brain injuries, etc. Russian studies in interoceptive conditioning prove beyond doubt that human nature can be changed at any stage of life. It can be modified either from the somatic or the psychic end of the somatopsychic entity that the human organism is (Bykov, 1957; Wolman, 1965a).

Adolescence is believed to be a period of transition, though it is no more transitional than any other growth period. Somatic changes that constitute puberty, such as physical growth, endocrine development and secondary sexual signs are no more revolutionary than the transition from zygote to embryo, from fetus to neonate, from babbling to talking. As any other growth period, adolescence introduces new psychological elements.

The biological changes in adolescence seriously affect the balance of the intra- and interindividual cathexes. Puberty is, undoubtedly, a period of substantial changes, for it is at this point that the adolescent becomes capable of reproduction and ultimately attains biological adulthood. In several primitive societies puberty rites lead to the onset of the three most significant functions of adulthood, namely breadwinning, marriage, and participation in community life. In civilized societies physical maturity antedates psychological and cultural maturity, creating a situation that breeds conflict. When one is physically as tall as one's parents, and physically capable of becoming a parent, but is yet unable to assume responsibility in any of the three above-mentioned functions of adulthood, a conflict in one's social role is inevitable.

This culturally conditioned conflict affects behavioral patterns related to love and hate. The increase in sexual excitability is apparently accompanied by an increased frequency of sexual behavior. Kinsey et al. (1948) maintained that the highest incidence of all types of sexual activities, including intercourse and masturbation, takes place in males in their early teens.

One may have serious doubts concerning the accuracy of Kinsey's data, for volunteers hardly represent a fair cross-section of the population. Let us, however, for the sake of argument, assume that Kinsey was right; the fact of high frequency of sexual behavior could be interpreted not as an increase in sexual urge, but also as a decline in self-control.

The upsurge of sexual arousal and activity in adolescence as compared to the latency period is dependent both on physiology and psychology. Insofar as the physiological aspect is obvious, there is no need to explain it in the context of the present volume. However the psychological aspects are quite complex.

In cases where the Oedipus complex was successfully resolved, the latency period should bring a considerable decline in masturbatory and other sexual interests and activities. The onset of puberty brings a biologically determined upsurge in sexual impulses. Libidinal desires become disinhibited, blunt, open. Masturbation increases and there is a stronger interest in the opposite sex. Boys become "girl-crazy" and girls become "boy-crazy." This definite increase in instinctual drives is not accompanied by a comparable increase in the strength of the control apparatus, that is, the ego and superego. The analogy might be that of a car whose power is greatly increased without there being a proportionate increase in brakes. In cultures that impose restraint and facilitate the growth of the superego, youths try to control their impulses; in more lenient cultures there is a definite increase in a variety of sexual activities. In later teens, with further maturation and growth of the control apparatus, especially the ego, young people may become more selective in sexual choice and more cautious in relationships with other people. Hence the alleged decline in sexuality (Wolman, 1972).

In the early teens crushes seem to develop in an almost casual way. Teenagers "fall in love" with practically any new person of the opposite sex. In most cases, however, a definite pattern develops, based on past oedipal involvements.

Normally, a girl loves and adores her father, but the father, while being kind and forceful, is inaccessible. He belongs to another woman, notably the mother. Under normal circumstances the girl renounces the father as a potential lover and comes to terms with the mother.

There are, however, normal residues of the oedipal conflict that influence the sexual choice and the course of the girl's future life. The idealized image of the father may loom large and color the choice of the lover-husband. Girls fall easily in love with and want to be married to men who are "father-figures" to them, who are older, settled, established, powerful and protective. A strong and kind man is the idol of feminine dreams; it is always the "father-figure," or an "improved edition," an idealized father.

Some residue of resentment against the mother is inevitable and perhaps necessary for future adjustment. It usually spreads into relationships with other women who are perceived as competitors with whom one has to come to terms. Women compete with each other for looks, wealth, social status, conspicuous consumption, marital choice, children's success in school and anything else.

The resolution of the oedipal conflict in women often leads to the desire for having children. In Victorian times in Vienna, motherhood was the *only* socially acceptable pattern for women. Today women participate in practically all aspects of economic, cultural and political life, and marriage and motherhood do not constitute the sole vehicle for feminine energies. Many women successfully combine professional careers with family duties. Female patients often report dreams indicative of conflict in this area; fear of being a woman may lead to a reaction formation and consequent desire to renounce all other avenues except motherhood (Rheingold, 1964).

The psychosocial adjustment of young men presents no less a problem. A reasonably adjusted adolescent boy associates with boys. He feels at ease with boys with whom he identifies and also competes; his aim-inhibited resentment against his father is channeled into a spirit of competitiveness against all men. But with the onset of puberty, he is attracted to a great many of them. He associates, however, with boys only, and chooses one girl at a time for whom he feels a strong attraction. In the majority of cases this choice is temporary, for adolescents are notorious for their rapid change of romantic attachments. The memories of mother's looks, behavior and feelings will affect their choice; in normal cases the conscious and unconscious memories do not becloud the vision and do not prevent seeing the chosen girl the way she really is.

The increase in libidinal energy is not accompanied by a proportionate increase in ego maturity. In most cases libidinal strivings accompany a decline in superego controls. Parental authority is badly shattered at this age. The very fact of physical growth makes teenagers as tall as their parents; thus they don't have to look up to them any more (Blos, 1962; Erikson, 1963).

This development also affects the destrudo. Teenagers are notorious for violence. Some of them rampage in a frenzy of vandalism on public beaches, while others destroy human property and lives, instigated by ill-conceived patriotic, political or religious chauvinism.

Individual vandalism bears witness to inadequate ego and superego development. It is typical for the psychopathic, hyperinstrumental personality which will be discussed in the next chapters. It seems, however, that certain cultures foster this narcissistic, psychopathic, hyperinstrumental type of behavior.

Teenagers, as a rule, do not exercise much self-control. They are often carried away by their impulses and are notorious for poor judgment and inadequate anticipation of the consequences of their behavior. I do not think that adolescents, as an age group, are more malicious and destructive than other people, but their aggressiveness is a result of increased power and lack of adequate control.

Control of impulses, especially the aretic ones, depends on both the ego and superego. The "reality principle" is a function of the ego; it means anticipation of consequences. It provides one with a sensible fear of retaliation. Thus, one may refrain from hostile behavior out of fear of the consequences. Superego controls are dependent on moralistic rather than realistic factors. The superego is the carrier of "do's and "don'ts" planted by parents, teachers, preachers and culture at large. The superego reacts with attacks on the ego, punishing it for real or imagined transgressions of a culturally unacceptable nature.

Too lenient an attitude on the part of parents, teachers or society at large does not offer much support to either the ego or the superego. In a family where everything is permitted, the child is unable to develop a proper sense of reality because there are no real consequences to his misdeeds. If this overly permissive attitude is shared by the culture and transmitted through the media, the sense of responsibility for one's behavior becomes badly impaired.

Today's younger generation, presumably brought up in an

atmosphere of liberalism, which on further scrutiny may more closely resemble moral abdication and nihilism, has very few inhibitions, one ramification of which is an alarmingly high rate of juvenile delinquency.

Mass violence, such as in Nazi Germany, was probably a result of a collectively corrupt superego. Youth seeks and needs identification. Without ideals it is likely to become disorganized, especially when individual responsibility is removed and a monstrous destructive power takes the place of the individual superego (Wolman, 1972).

Adulthood

Whereas an infant is carried by its mother, a child led by the hand, an adolescent guided by parents and teachers—more often by his peers—an adult makes his own decisions and is held responsible for his deeds. He may seek advice and help in certain areas, while himself offering service to others in areas of his own competence. Childhood is dependence, adulthood is interdependence. An adult earns his living in interaction with his environment, forms his family group, and participates in his society at large.

The two main drives, Eros and Ares, motivate adult life, but do not exercise unlimited powers. Human behavior cannot be wholly interpreted by the economy of inter- and intraindividual cathexes of libido and destrudo. To gain a full picture of adult behavior, one must invoke Freud's topographic and structural theory and discover how much and to what extent the unconscious libidinal and destructive impulses affect one's behavior. An angry infant strikes, but an angry adult may react in a variety of fashions and thereby postpone, suppress, displace or sublimate his impulses. Normal adulthood is a state of balance between the instinctual demands of the id and the cultural demands of the superego. It is a balance of inter- and intracathexes of libido and destrudo, controlled by the ego and superego. It serves to mediate among hostile, instrumental, mutual and vectorial patterns of social relations.

Adult Sex

The higher the level of personality development, the more pronounced are the emotional aspects in a man-woman relationship. During deep emotional involvement, affection, loyalty and devotion may take precedence over the physiological aspects of sex. "When we are in love," wrote Freud (1921), "a considerable amount of narcissistic libido overflows on to the object. It is even obvious in many forms of love choice, that the object serves as a substitute for some unattained ego ideal of our own . . ."

Human sexuality has changed significantly in the course of evolution. Borrowing from the tree analogy once again, sexuality may be likened to it as follows: the roots are within the province of physiology, but trunk, branches and leaves go beyond physiology and reach out toward mutual relationships based on consideration, kindness and loyalty. In desexualized love, the neutralized libidinal energy may be channeled into artistic and other creative outlets. To assume that in normal adults sexual relations are primarily a matter of genital organs is, therefore, as erroneous as to believe that the roots are the entire tree.

The same reasoning applies to the destrudo. Destrudo does not disappear in adulthood, for both love and hate are normal human emotions. Yet, no society can tolerate uncontrolled outbursts of destrudo. Intrasocietal violence disrupts the social organization. All societies, even the most primitive ones, impose restraints and typically do not allow fighting which will lead inevitably to self-destruction. "Thou shalt not kill" is a self-preservatory device of human civilization.

But this rule may be applied as narrowly as "don't kill the members of your clan, but go ahead and kill everyone else," or as broadly as "Don't kill anyone at all." Furthermore, it can be applied on the ego level, such as "Don't kill because you will be punished," or on the superego level, such as "Don't kill because it is wrong."

Western civilization, which has combined the two approaches, threatens the potential killer with both the electric chair and guilt feelings. The emphasis varies from one cultural group to another; it also varies in individual families, depending upon parental authority and on the particular set of values and interrelationships.

Generally speaking, our society tries to discourage violence, but is not too consistent in this policy. While adults are expected to leave the protection of order to the police and solve their differences in courts or by means of arbitration, the mass communication media publicize violence with a tinge of admiration for the heroic villain.

The ego plays a larger role than the superego in inhibiting violence. In most cases the fear of retaliation, rather than moral scruples, prevents violence. The "Thou shalt not kill" commandment can be practiced on three levels. The lowest is the ego level: "Don't kill because you may be risking your own life." On the superego level it reads: "You have no right to kill others even when you feel like doing it." The third level is the level of love: "When you truly love, you don't feel like killing. You protect your love object."

Destrudo serves Ares, the god of war. People fight (1) because they are frightened; (2) in order to eat; (3) when they become panic-stricken; (4) in retaliation against attack. People fight for all four reasons or for their symbolic derivatives such as freedom, glory, self-aggrandizement, possession, pride, honor, hurt feelings, etc. Personal survival rather than the death of someone else is the driving force in hostile behavior.

People with predominantly instrumental tendencies are prone to hate those who refuse to be used. In people with mutual tendencies, the lack of reciprocity elicits hostile feelings. Hostility is rare in vectorial relationships; a loving mother loves her children even when they are ungrateful.

When hate pours out without direction, when people fight just to kill, when destrudo goes wild and does not serve one's own survival, it is clearly pathological. Pure and wholly irrational hate represents a severe regression, perhaps below the neonate level. When there is regression to pure hate, survival is jeopardized.

No human group has ever practiced complete restraint from hostility although Isaiah and Jesus called for a vectorial love and allowed no hate. Civilized societies sanction some degree of hostility in self-defense. They also permit competition, provided it is not too ruthless and is based on fair play.

Parenthood

In those species where vectorialism exists, it originates in female biology which is designed to serve the not-yet-born child. Vectorialism starts with the egg-hatching species, where some amount of care and protection of the eggs is practiced. Infant care is by no means universal or uniform. Although many mammals and most birds take good care of their little ones, there are various types of mothering in nature and many exceptions to the rule. Most mammals feed their offspring, protect then against enemies and nurture them until they are maturationally capable of independence.

The higher up on the evolutionary ladder, the longer the period of postnatal mothering. This behavior applies also to the evolution of the human species. In primitive tribes and in prehistorical and early historical societies, child care terminates with puberty rites. In contemporary culture, child care extends far beyond physical puberty, well into late teens and early twenties, often creating severe psychological problems. Sometimes mothering overextends in time and intensity, turning into pathological interactional patterns to be described in the following chapters.

Normally, mothering offers the best possible outlet for vectorialism. Mothers need no less to *give* milk to infants than infants need to *get* it. Mothers are *par excellence* vectorial; infants are naturally instrumental.

Fatherly love is less frequently observed than motherly love. Greek mythology tells of the god Kronos who ate his own children; his wife Gea hid their son Zeus who later became the king of the gods. History is replete with cases of competition and hostility between fathers and sons.

The animal world represents a variety of fatherly patterns. Wolves, for example, are model fathers, while bears are not. Storks and cranes and penguins are protective fathers. In most human societies fathers provide food and physical protection for their offspring, even if this requires some degree of self-sacrifice.

The beginning of a new life is not always accompanied by a great parental love. Many mothers feel less than loving toward their children who as a consequence do not receive vectorial love. Unwed, teenage, and unhappily married mothers do not necessarily love their children. There are mothers (and fathers) who are instrumental toward their children and who take every possible advantage of their parental position. There are alarming statistics of the number of parents who exploit their children physically, sexually, and emotionally, as will be described later.

As emphasized earlier, the prerequisite for vectorial love is the ability to give. Mother's organism can supply embryo's physical needs, but the mother must be a mature person to be able to offer emotional and nurturant sustenance to her child without demanding anything in return. Immature, insecure, and frustrated mothers "sacrifice" themselves for their children, and let the world know at what price. It is not uncommon for such parents to demand from their children the love they failed to receive from their own parents or their marital partners.

Typology

No human being is always the same, nor does he act consistently all the time. Nevertheless, one can distinguish fairly permanent behavioral patterns that permit the grouping of people into distinct personality types.

The origin of these behavioral patterns cannot be reduced to mere fixation. Fixation is but one of the factors that shape behavioral tendencies; heredity, sociocultural factors, and the particular life history of an individual may far outweigh the import of fixations.

The importance of heredity can hardly be overestimated, but even the best seed will not grow without fertile soil. Although individual differences may be related to a particular constellation of genes, genetics operates with trillions and quintillions of possible combinations. Even within relatively homogeneous races the prediction of personality traits is a hopeless task. Students of personality types may therefore assume a random distribution of hereditary traits and link typological differences to environmental factors, especially to the impact of early childhood environment. If there are broadly conceived personality types, they are related to the way children with randomly diversified dispositions are treated by their respective parents. The persistent types of child-rearing have been described by Benedict (1934), Kardiner (1939, 1945), Linton (1956), Opler (1965), and others.

I am not suggesting that the intrafamilial interaction unequivocally determines one's psychological development, for no family represents a clear-cut interactional pattern. Only the most extreme cases demonstrate the devastating effect of family on personality development. Disturbed family life demonstrates with sufficient clarity the main point of this book, namely that disbalance of interindividual libido and destrudo cathexes is the main cause of behavior disorders. Insofar as disbalance is not an absolute, the more severe is the disbalance, the more severe will be the disorder. Moreover, since destrudo is the more archaic drive, disturbed behavior, being *regressive,* must include more destrudo. The greater the amount of overt and vehement hostility in the family, the more severe will be the disorder in the offspring.

Certainly most families represent a combination of various interactional patterns with a considerable admixture of overt or covert hostility. Not all children are, however, affected in the same way. In my studies of family interaction (Wolman, 1957, 1961, 1965b, 1970), I have found an exasperating variety of patterns and offshoots of patterns. Sometimes the very same father who seduced or raped the oldest daughter related in a wholesome and fatherly way to the second daughter. Or a mother who used one child as a target for her love or hate or both may relate in a more friendly and understanding fashion to another child. Moreover, the other significant members of the family such as siblings, grandparents, uncles, aunts or cousins may affect the child's personality in a host of compensating or decompensating ways. Add to this, friends and neighbors, teachers and schoolmates, and all other life experiences such as wealth, parental occupation, ethnic and religious affiliations, and one arrives at a bewildering multitude of factors influencing an individual's personality.

It seems however that certain familial structures favor one interactional pattern over another, depending on the personalities of the parents and a host of other variables. Some intrafamilial interactions favor *narcissistic* defenses in a particular child, fostering the prevalence of *instrumental* attitudes in his behavior. Other family interactions foster *erotic* cravings in a child, making him prone to falling easily in love and preferring *mutual* attitudes. There are also families where the *obsessive* need to please and to be of help is fostered, leading to the formation of *vectorial* tendencies.

The instrumental, mutual and vectorial behavioral patterns are not neurotic styles; they are common patterns of behavior, but they are neither closed nor discrete categories. They resemble Weber's "ideal types," for in real life people may interact in all three ways, most often with a considerable and always present admixture of hostility. When the behavior patterns become rigid and extreme, the behavior becomes maladjustive and disturbed, as will be described in the following chapters.

So-called "normal" individuals display behavioral tendencies that enable even untrained observers to notice that some people tend to act in a *narcissistic, instrumental* way, while others act in a *vectorial, obsessive* way, while still others are overconcerned with love and being loved, that is, the *mutual* type of relations.

The idea of personality types is not new. Spranger (1928), for example, distinguished six personality types based on cultural preferences such as religion, politics, money, esthetics, science and sociability. Kretschmer (1925) observed the schizothymic type, which corresponds to Freud's obsessional and my vectorial type, and the cyclothymic, which corresponds to Freud's erotic and my mutual type. Unfortunately, Kretschmer linked the psychological types to alleged bodily types.

Levels of Maturity

There are also *levels* of behavior related to an overall mental maturity. Levels of maturity cannot be linked to a particular developmental stage; people are not oral or anal characters. Traumatic experiences in early childhood may prevent normal growth, but this does not necessarily imply that there will be a total fixation on a particular developmental stage. Let us assume, for example, that severe noxious factors acted upon a child during the anal stage. It is likely that certain, but only certain, unresolved anal conflicts will lead to fixations, but these fixations will affect the development in the urethral and phallic phases; thus the child will retain not only anal, but also urethral and phallic distortions. The fact that his troubles started at the anal stage may be of lesser import for his personality than the additional personality distortions in the later stages. Therefore the time of the initial traumatic experiences is but a partial factor in future personality development and must be viewed within the overall context of hereditary predisposition, earlier and subsequent experiences.

No human being is perfect, and every human being follows his particular pattern of mental development. Handicaps, road blocks, and adversities affect various people in different ways and to different extents. The nonorganic behavior or mental disorders are not diseases but excessive degrees of immaturity and personality disbalances. There is apparently no sharp line dividing normal and abnormal behavior, for hardly anyone is always "abnormal" and certainly no one is always "normal."

But what, precisely, is mental disorder? And what causes it?

✖ 6 ✖
The Nature and Classification
of Mental Disorders

Models and Observables

According to Freud a mentally healthy person is one whose id, ego and superego exist in a state of balance under the ego's unquestionable leadership. Those individuals whose personality structure is disbalanced suffer from mental disorders or behavior disorders (I use these two terms interchangeably).

Freud's theory of personality includes a series of logical constructs and models used for the interpretation of human behavior. For instance, irrational, uninhibited and aggressive behavior can be interpreted as related to the pleasure principle and primary processes, and thus ordered to the unconscious (topographic theory), destructive impulses (economic theory) and the id (structural theory).

However, in clinical practice and empirical research although one can think in terms of theoretical constructs and models, one needs *observational terms* for the assessment of factual data, diagnostic work, and scientific and professional communication. Such terms as "weak ego," "anxiety" and "fusion of the ego and superego" are nonempirical terms which do not describe any aspects of observable behavior.

There appears to be a dire need for some kind of *conceptual bridge* between Freud's theoretical framework and observable human behavior, which will permit the presentation of behavior disorders in a language of empirical data. First, one must search for an empirical definition of disturbed behavior and then relate it to Freud's or to any other sufficiently flexible and heuristic personality model. Such an empirical definition, to be universally valid, must be coded in terms of the fundamental needs and functions common to all human beings in all cultures.

Mental Health and Culture

It is a widespread belief that contemporary culture is one of the main causes of mental disorder. There are those who speculate that a return to natural life would lead to a disappearance of mental troubles. This belief is related to the ideas of the French philosopher, Jean Jacques Rousseau (1712–1778). Rousseau was highly critical of civilization and advocated return to an idealized primitive social order. Combining the call for "naturalism" with the most progressive ideas of his time, his directive to go "back to nature" influenced a great many minds. The French Revolution proclaimed the ideals of freedom, equality and brotherhood. These ideas have become associated with Rousseau's theory, which assumed that in some prehistorical time there existed a perfect and "natural" social order.

Historians and anthropologists could not, however, locate such a "natural" social order where men lived happily in peace, freedom, equality and brotherhood. The Biblical story of paradise and the ancient Greek and Roman legends of the "Golden Era" have not been corroborated by empirical studies. Anthropologists idealize neither the past nor the present primitive societies. Despite the profusion of patterns appearing in primitive communities, none corresponds to the myth of the ideal community of men who allegedly lived in a "natural" order. In short, Rousseau's lost paradise was never found.

Freud, who accepted Darwin's theory of evolution and not Rousseau's call of "back to nature," did not discuss the problem with sufficient clarity. Freud (1938) wrote: "We must not forget, therefore, to include the influence of civilization among the determinants of neuroses. It is easy, as we can see, for a barbarian to be healthy; for a civilized man the task is a hard one. The desire for a powerful and uninhibited ego may seem to us unintelligible, but, as is shown by the times we live in, it is in the profoundest sense antagonistic to civilization" (pp. 84–85).

Freud realized that, in point of fact, there was no way back. No society can survive without regulation of the two most basic human impulses: sex and aggression. If neurosis is the price to be paid for civilization, the price must be paid, or society will slide back into the abyss of savagery (Freud, 1930).

One must not underestimate the fact that all societies, even the most primitive ones, impose restrictions. The very presence of another organism limits one's freedom and may cause frustrations. Thus barbarian cultures and wild animals are not entirely uninhibited in the presence of strong adversaries, and they impose various restraints on their members. In contemporary western civilization the tendency has been to make those restrictions just and fair for all members of a society. Whenever possible, self-restraint is advocated. Does a democratic society necessarily create more inner conflict than a primitive horde?

Erich Fromm (1947) counterposed culture to nature. According to Fromm, animals are a part of nature and live in accordance with nature. Man, however, "while mastering nature, separates himself—or rather his group—as not being identical with nature" (1941, p. 33). Primitive man, through his worship of sun and moon, land and sea, still felt "as part of the world around him." This feeling of unity with the universe, contends Fromm, was lost in modern times, starting with the Reformation.

One may doubt whether such a unity with nature is more than an artifact. Empirical scientists have no way of finding out whether a chimpanzee, deer, zebra, fish, or a spider lives more in "harmony" with nature than do human beings, and may wonder why nest-building by birds and hole-digging by moles guarantees unity with nature, while human house-building separates man from nature.

Each culture poses different problems and creates its own dilemmas. At this point we cannot definitively say which fosters a higher degree and greater severity of mental disorders. Sociological and anthropological studies indicate that certain cultures produce certain symptoms (Linton, 1956) and that specific disorders may be more frequent in one cultural group than in another (Eaton and Weil, 1954). It is likely, for example, that hysteria which was prevalent during the Middle Ages and the Victorian era, may have been related to the severe restrictions in sexual life. There is some speculation that the apparent increase in schizophrenia and antisocial, psychopathic behavior peculiar to our times, is in part a function of stimulus bombardment especially true of modern industrial technologies.

Mental disorders are as old as humanity. Ancient Judea and ancient Athens witnessed mental cases that could be classified as depressive psychosis and schizophrenia (Zilboorg and Henry, 1941). In medieval times, thousands of mental patients roamed the streets and market places, many of them accused of witchcraft and consequently persecuted. Many primitive societies neglect or kill the insane.

> Psychotics of the catatonic variety, who can't take care of themselves, are usually just allowed to die. . . . Now and then there will be some very devoted relative, perhaps a son, or a wife, who will try to take care of such a psychotic, but, since there are no real facilities for ministering to them, even these caretakers finally get bored, and the psychotic is allowed to 'pass out.' The violent psychotics, particularly those in the manic phase of the manic-depressive cycle, are as a rule just too much of a nuisance for the group. Hence,

in practically all societies there are handy rationalizations for getting rid of them . . . [Linton, 1956, p. 82].

It is difficult to determine whether a given economic system, or type of government, or a kind of religion is more
conducive to mental health than another. For instance, there
is no evidence that Catholics are more or less mentally
healthy than Protestants, Jews, Buddhists, Confucianists, or
Shintoists. Nor are we able to state conclusively that the
technological society is mentally unhealthy and that the
primitive cultures of idealized shepherds offer a haven and
protection against mental disorder. There is no evidence
that the strict Spartan upbringing was more conducive to
mental disorder than the liberal Athenian education or vice
versa.

Some cultural patterns may impose more hardships than
others and thereby jeopardize the individual's emotional balance, his chances for success and his social adjustment. Let us
consider minority groups which have been exposed to segre-
gation and prejudice. The individuals concerned are exposed
to disadvantageous conditions which allegedly affect adversely their mental health. We must, however, remark that
there is no evidence that the victims of discrimination fall
prey to mental disorder, that the Jews were more mentally
disturbed than the Nazis, or that the Albigenses were more
disturbed than their Inquisitors. Perhaps mental disorder in
those who practice prejudice is far more advanced than in
their victims. However, there is a limit to the amount of
suffering each individual can take. Some individuals develop
earlier mental symptoms than others exposed to the same
degree of stress.

It appears that whenever within a certain culture regressive processes take place, there is a concomitant increase in
the incidence of mental disorder. Social upheavals, wars, catastrophic events, uprooting of population, migration and loss
of status, decline in parental authority and public morality

and loosening of cultural prohibitions that lead to a socio-psychological phenomenon of *deculturation* all seem to militate against the individual's mental health. These processes arrange themselves in the category of culture dissolution and regression to lower cultural levels. Deculturation, that is, *the regressive process in cultural development,* is a highly important factor in producing disorder.

In Search of a Definition

According to Freud, mental disorder is not a disease in the technical sense of the word, but a process of regression to an infantile developmental phase. Regressions are related to traumatic experiences in early childhood. The mentally disturbed adult is one who grew up physically and intellectually but remained immature or even infantile in his personality makeup. Severely neurotic, and to a much larger degree psychotic patients are individuals whose personality structure never developed properly or regressed to infantilism. Mentally disturbed individuals are unable to cope with life in a rational adult manner. Typically, they face difficulties in sexual life; they are unrealistic, often aggressive, frequently withdrawn and frightened; they cannot tolerate frustrations, nor are their emotions adjustive. Mentally disturbed people are often their own worst enemies, acting in self-defeating, self-destructive modes of behavior, but they definitely suffer, for their lives are frequently a chain of painful disappointments, frustrations, and miseries. With Freud the study of mental disorder ceased to be an area exclusive to medicine; the nervous system could no longer be regarded as the sole focus of study; and human personality was seen within the context of a broader perspective.

Today the field of psychopathology is undergoing a third revolution. Formerly psychopathology had been a legitimate branch of medicine; with Freud it became a legitimate branch of psychology as well. Today the social sciences study

the impact of interindividual relations upon mental health
and mental disorders. Physicians, who have been the pioneers
in this field, are now joined by psychologists and social
scientists in a mutual effort to bring greater knowledge to the
understanding of behavior disorders.

The Average and the Normal

A study of mental disorder must start, as does any other
study, with a definition of its subject matter. Mental disorder
includes a great variety of behavioral patterns, such as delusions and hallucinations, disturbances in speech and reasoning, antisocial behavior, moodiness, depressions, sexual aber-
rations, somatic disorders, and the like. This spectrum of disorder is generally regarded as abnormal behavior.

Let us try to distinguish such behavior from normal behavior. The term "normal" is often used to indicate the wholesome, complete, adequate, and perfect, while the term "abnormal" points to the imperfect, deficient, and inadequate.
Accordingly, a complete organism is normal; a deficient organism is abnormal.

Insofar as absence of something does not explain anything,
negative definitions cannot convey optimal information. One
may define health as the absence of sickness and define sickness as the absence of health, but this is obviously a circular
definition. Nor is the concept of completeness very useful
either. Let us consider dental health. According to this
definition, dentally normal individuals are those whose teeth
are perfect, i.e., no defects whatsoever. Thus, the only normal individuals are the few perfect ones, and the vast majority of people should be called "dentally sick."

Such a definition, applied to the field of mental health
would necessarily reduce the number of mentally normal
people to zero, for one may doubt the existence of ideal and
absolutely perfect individuals. According to such a definition,
practically all people would be regarded as mentally disturbed.

The Socioeconomic Bias

At the present time there is a tendency to overinclude and to classify as mentally ill anyone who appears to have difficulties in adjusting to the circumstances of his life. A recent study of mental health in Manhattan (Srole et al., 1962) found only 18.5 per cent of the population free from mental symptoms. Over 36 per cent of the people suffered from mild symptoms, about 22 per cent from moderate symptoms, and 23.4 per cent were diagnosed as severely impaired. In short, 81½ per cent of the total population was found to have some sort of mental symptoms.

According to Srole and his associates mental disorder appears to be correlated with socioeconomic status; that is, 47.3 per cent of the lower classes were found to have mental impairment as compared to 12.5 per cent of the upper classes. This is not a new finding. Several research workers, among them the sociologist Hollingshead and psychiatrist Redlich (1958) related mental health to socioeconomic factors, claiming that the lower classes suffer from a higher degree of severe mental cases.

However, despite the correlations, an evidence of cause and effect connection between economic factors and mental disorder is yet to be demonstrated. There is no proof that poor countries have a higher incidence of mental disorder than affluent ones. The United States has the highest rate of income per capita, but this does not necessarily coincide with the lowest rate for mental disorder. Periods of economic prosperity or economic recession do not correlate with respective decreases or increases in the incidence of mental disorder. In Freud's time, mental disorders were believed to be an upper-class phenomenon; today they are believed to belong to the life patterns of the lower classes. Neither hypothesis has ever been experimentally validated.

The Bias of Pain and Pleasure

Success in life depends upon a variety of factors, such as IQ, special abilities, opportunities, and so on. Certainly men-

tal health is not the sole determinant in one's success or
failure in economic, social and personal life. The quasi-
hedonistic value system of this culture has significantly
influenced our concepts of mental health. There appears to
be a cultural concensus that deprivation leads to mental distress. Thus poor people are expected to be mentally disturbed
by virtue of their impoverished state. Many a parent has been
made to feel that to discipline the children imposes deprivations which will lead to emotional disturbance. In point of fact,
recent thinking suggests that the lack of parental discipline
and the generally overly permissive culture are largely responsible for alienated, frustrated and violent youth.

The permissive philosophy has generally been attributed to
Freud, although he never suggested license; in fact, he recommended restraint, for he believed that a child who was
never frustrated would be unable to perceive reality and
would be consigned to living in an unreal dream world.

Pain and pleasure are not valid criteria respectively of
mental disorder or mental health. Mental disorder may cause
little if any pain; in some cases it may even become pleasurable. Seriously regressed schizophrenics are usually less sensitive to pain than normal people are; some of them inflict
upon themselves injuries and burns that would cause unbearable pain to anyone else. Depressive psychotics tend to
perpetuate their suffering, and in a state of manic bliss they
appear to be ecstatically happy. It would also appear that
sexual deviants are obtaining certain enjoyment from their
abnormal conduct. Drug addicts report feelings of tremendous
euphoria when they are in their transported states. It is not
uncommon for hospitalized patients to prefer the comforts of a
mental hospital to the hardships of open life. Conversely, good
mental health does not guarantee happiness. Failure or loss
of a loved one will be as painful for the mentally healthy
person (probably, more so) as it is for the disturbed indi-

vidual. No one is immune to humiliation, rejection, economic hardships, war, famine, and revolution.

Thus normal individuals react with pain and pleasure to the happenings of life and rarely go to extremes. As long as the emotional ups and downs are reasonably balanced, the sensitivity to pain and pleasure as such does not affect their adjustment to circumstances.

Statistical Bias

The term "mentally healthy" is often used synonymously with the terms "usual" and "average." The concept "average" may mean the most frequent, as it does in the case of height, weight, or intelligence. It may also indicate the majority of cases, the usual, or the center of the curve of distribution. Mentally normal people are often believed to be the average, the usual, the majority of cases.

This simple explanation is open to criticism. People are tall, short, and any other size between these extremes. Does this mean that tall men are abnormal? Or that short people are abnormal? It is customary to classify the mentally retarded as abnormal individuals, while the gifted, talented and creative individuals are not included in the category of abnormality. Thus it appears that we tend to reserve the concept of abnormality for those conditions which have a culturally determined negative valence.

The nature of the driving forces in human beings is a controversial issue, but the struggle for survival, for self-realization, for success and satisfaction, is probably the common denominator of all human motivation. Mental patients are usually unable to use their resources in that struggle; either they give up the struggle, defeat themselves, or try to destroy themselves. In most cases one's achievements are proportional to one's inherited and acquired potentialities and to environmental factors, but this does not apply to mentally disturbed individuals.

In milder cases of mental disorder, one's accomplishments usually fall short of what might be reasonably expected. A bright student ridden by emotional disorder may fail in his studies, and a brilliant man may miss the opportunities of advancement in life. The inability to actualize one's mental and physical potential is one of the outstanding signs of mental disorder. All other factors being equal, the greater the discrepancy between promise and fulfillment, the more severe is the disorder.

There are however cases of gifted individuals who function well in their professional lives as scholars, scientists and creative artists, while unable to act in a balanced and rational manner in their personal lives and interindividual relations. Apparently, their poorly integrated personality structure permits adequate functioning in the conflict-free ego spheres (cf. Hartmann, 1937), but they fail in conflict-laden areas.

Emotional Balance

The second criterion of mental health is emotional balance. All living organisms act in accordance with the law of *homeostasis*. Pavlov, Freud, Goldstein and others introduced similar principles, calling them equilibrium, constancy, or equipotentiality respectively. Although these terms are not identical, all of them convey the idea that whenever an organism is exposed to stimulation that disturbs its equilibrium, a reaction takes place in the direction of restoration of the initial state. This applies to all functions of the organism including emotional life.

Human beings react to life situations with joy and sorrow, pleasure and pain, elation and depression. The reactions of healthy individuals are typically in accordance with the nature and magnitude of the presenting stimuli. Normally we react with pleasure and joy to situations that enhance our well-being. Happiness is generally attained when one's wishes come true, while grief is the reaction to failure or loss.

There are, however, some people who react with sorrow to victory and seem to obtain certain satisfactions or secondary gain from defeat. Their emotional reaction is *inappropriate.* Some of these people appear to bring misery upon themselves, while others cannot find satisfaction in success. They are unable to appreciate what they have and are constantly looking for "greener pastures," but no pasture is ever green enough. Disturbed people often perpetuate their misery, and will refrain from any constructive efforts to alleviate it. Such people by defying their own efforts, avoiding pleasure and seeking pain, become their own worst enemies. In some extreme cases of schizophrenia, to be discussed later, the normal pain-pleasure reaction is reversed and even nonexistent.

Normal emotional reaction is *proportionate* to the stimulus. Let us consider the case of a man who has lost money. Assuming that he is emotionally well balanced, his reaction will be *appropriate* to the fact of loss and *proportionate* to its magnitude and to the ensuing financial hardship. The more money lost, the greater the degree of upset; if the loss is only a small fraction of his possessions, his worry will be mild and of short duration. A well-balanced individual will do whatever is possible to regain the loss and to prevent the recurrence of losses in the future. A rational, balanced and mentally healthy individual reacts with disappointment to failure; his reaction is proportionate to the damage incurred, and his actions lead to reduction or alleviation of past troubles, and prevention of future ones. In short, normal emotional behavior is *appropriate, proportionate,* and *adjustive.*

A less normal and less well-balanced individual will react differently. His behavior is likely to be inappropriate. Some individuals cannot take frustration and are thrown into despair whenever they meet hardships or suffer a loss. Disturbed individuals are inclined to exaggerate and see doom in the face of even mild frustrations. Some individuals blame themselves for being misfits; some blame others for their troubles.

Self-accusations or accusations against others cannot restore a lost object or person. Disturbed individuals tend to
persist in mourning and perpetuating their depressed or
aggressive moods instead of compensating for past losses and
preventing future misfortunes. Because their emotional balance cannot be easily restored, the depressed or agitated anxiety states are likely to occur again and again. The failure in
coping with hardships often leads to increasing irritability,
each new frustration adding to the difficulty in restoring
emotional balance. It becomes apparent that mental disorder
is a dynamic process with a distinct tendency for deterioration.

In psychosis, the ability to face frustration and to act in a
constructive fashion may be lost altogether. The slightest
frustration may throw the individual off and cause uncontrollable emotional outbursts. Some psychotics are in a state
of perpetual fury, continuous panic, or unbearable tension
and depression. The criterion of emotional balance can therefore be applied toward the distinction of severity of the disorder.

Cognitive Functions

The third criterion of mental health is related to the va-
lidity of cognitive functions. Survival is dependent on the
perception of things as they are. An erroneous perception, an
oversight of danger, an inability to distinguish fantasy from
reality seriously jeopardize one's existence. A realistic perception of what is going on in the outer world and in one's
own life increases one's chances for survival and helps in optimal adjustment.

In most mental disorders the perception of the outer world
is disturbed, but not as a result of some malfunction of the
sensory organs as is the case in sight or hearing impairments.
Nor is the reduced ability to perceive, compare and reason a
function of mental deficiency as is true of the retarded. The

mental apparatus is, in most cases of mental disorder, fully or partly preserved, but it seems that the mentally disturbed individual is unable to properly utilize his mental capacities because of a malfunction in the realm of feelings.

Freud called the ability to see things as they are "reality testing." The neonate, said Freud (1938, p. 42), is unable to distinguish inner from outer stimuli. Internal events, feelings and perceptions that stem from within are confused with sensory perceptions emanating from without. In other words, "me" and "not-me" are not yet clearly separated. Gradually, by checking out their perceptions and manipulating the perceived objects, infants learn to "test reality," that is, to distinguish between the inner and outer stimuli, between their own feelings and the external world, between fantasy and fact. There is no reality testing in sleep; in dreams we experience our own wishes and fears as if they were true objective facts, independent of ourselves. The state of psychosis can be likened to the dream state in that there is an inability to distinguish the products of the imagination from true happenings.

Sullivan (1953) suggested another distinction. He believed that the earliest stage in human life is the "prototaxic" mode, that is, a state of unconscious, diffused and indistinguishable experiences. In the next stage, the "parataxic," the individual perceives the world as a series of experiences, arranged in a nonlogical order; he looks upon himself as if he were the center of the universe. In the third stage, the "syntaxic," the individual develops the ability to check his perceptions against the perceptions of others and validates them through the consensus of the group. This *consensual validation* is actually one of the methods by which reality can be tested; the individual confronts his own experiences against the experiences of other individuals.

The more one is disturbed, the poorer is his contact with reality. Everyone makes an occasional perceptual error but,

as a rule, we are accurate and capable of correcting our er-
rors. In mentally disturbed individuals this ability is impaired
or nonexistent.

Neurotics, or people who suffer from mild mental disorder,
typically have an exaggerated notion of their own status and
importance, or underestimate their resources and status.
These feelings of omnipotence and inadequacy are frequent
symptoms of mental disorder, in that how people feel and
think about themselves is an area in which wish and reality
can be badly confused.

The situation can become quite serious when the picture
of the outer world is distorted. An individual who consistently misconstrues or misinterprets what he perceives is said
to be *delusional*. For example, when a mentally disturbed
individual flees a policeman who simply wants to check his
driver's license, in fear that the policeman will arrest him for
a noncommitted crime, or when he ascribes hostile feeling to
his friends who are loyal and trustworthy, his reality testing
is practically nonexistent. Whereas delusions are distorted
perceptions, hallucinations are creations out of nothingness.
Hallucination is perception without external stimulation,
such as, for instance, seeing ghosts or hearing voices. A hallu-
cinating patient is unable to distinguish his inner fears,
wishes and dreams from the outer world. His ability for reality testing is lost, and neither reasoning nor explanation can
restore it.

The question of cultural influences must be raised in connection with the problem of correct perception of reality.
History and anthropology provide several instances of culturally acceptable erroneous perceptions of the world. In such
cultures, myth and truth are confused, and wish and dream
often taken for reality. "With us a person would be neurotic
or psychotic who talked by the hour with his deceased grand-
father, whereas such a communication with ancestors is a
recognized pattern in some Indian tribes" (Horney, 1937).

Obviously it is not easy to engage in satisfactory reality testing if everyone else appears to accept delusion. When ghosts, voices, spirits, and witches form well-entrenched patterns of culture, reality testing is undoubtedly minimized. Certainly one's doubts cannot be "consensually validated." Accordingly, it cannot be said that whoever believed in witchcraft in the Middle Ages was mentally sick. But even at that time, if one believed that he himself had turned into stone or that his genuine friends hated him, it could be said of him that he was mentally disturbed. Thus reality testing within cultural limitations has always been an important criterion of mental disorder.

Social Adjustment

Men live in societies. They interact with one another in cooperation and competition, love and hate, peace and war. The term "social life" denotes both the friendly or cooperative and the hostile or competitive aspects of human interaction.

Cooperation, friendliness, and love aim at the protection of the life of the person (or object) towards whom they have been directed. We tend to help, protect, care for and support the life of those whom we like or love.

A group or society where mutual respect, consideration, cooperation, and friendliness prevail certainly has better chances for survival than a society where lack of consideration prevails, and a "cut-throat competition" and hate of all against all is the rule. The latter society is likely to find itself in the throes of constant battle and will probably annihilate itself, if it is not destroyed by enemies who exploit the internal dissension.

There are no ideal societies. Every social group has its share of the constructive, life-preserving and cooperative factors, as well as of the disruptive, destructive and antisocial forces. However, when the forces of hate prevail, life and society perish. No society can afford a free display of hostile and disruptive forces. If these forces are innate in men, they must be checked; if they are learned patterns of behavior, they must be unlearned at least to a point where they do not threaten the survival of men. There is a great diversity in the prohibitive actions of social groups; some are more, some less restrictive; some limit their "thou shalt not kill" restraint to the members of their own group only. The Judeo-Christian civilization believes in the sanctity of human life, but even the most primitive societies did not tolerate unlimited intra-group hatred and belligerence.

Thus, the fourth and last criterion of mental health is *social adjustment,* that is, the ability to cooperate with other individuals. Mentally healthy individuals are capable of living on friendly terms with other members of their group. They are capable of cooperation and are willing to enter into social relations based on mutual respect, agreement and responsibility. Normal adults accept and make commitments which they can honor. They may disagree with associates and understand why others may disagree with them. They may occasionally feel hostile, but their actions are generally kept under rational control. They may, however, fight in self-defense, and in a manner approved by their cultural group.

Mental patients are usually socially maladjusted and, as a rule, they find it difficult to relate to other individuals. They are typically afraid and suspicious of other people, often shying away from them and withdrawing into seclusion. Concomitant with a hatred for others there is a fear of their own hostile impulses. In severe cases the hostility breaks through, and in a catatonic fury mental patients may attack everything and everybody.

The severity of social maladjustment usually corresponds to the severity of mental disorder, although it is not a simple one-to-one relationship. Uncontrollable hostility is, however, a definite sign of serious disturbance.

Social adjustment must not be confused with conformity. The former is the ability for a peaceful and friendly interaction with other individuals, while the latter implies unconditional acceptance of certain social norms and mores. Were conformity identical with social adjustment, all ethnic, religious, and political minorities could be considered maladjusted. Every inventor, original scientist, creative writer, political reformer and nonconformist, and all pioneers of social, religious, or scientific progress could be branded as maladjusted.

It must be emphasized that dissent is not to be confused with maladjustment. Depending on the circumstances, it may be that the conformists rather than the nonconformists are the maladjusted ones. Social adjustment does not abolish differences of opinion; on the contrary, it implies the ability to cope with these differences in a friendly and realistic manner. Those who are afraid to be different and cannot tolerate differences of opinion are for the most part insecure and immature individuals.

Social adjustment hinges on the four previously described patterns of social interaction: hostile, instrumental, mutual, and vectorial. Mature individuals, in self-defense, express their hostility; they are instrumental in their breadwinning functions; they are mutual in friendships and love relationships; they are vectorial toward their children and toward those needing their help. Some mature individuals are more instrumental, more mutual, or more vectorial than others. Mature behavior is not perfect behavior; it is rational and balanced, corresponding to Freud's model of id-ego-superego, with the rational ego keeping a reasonable balance between the animalistic demands of the id, the moralistic commandments of the superego, and realistic pursuit of practical goals.

Man is not a solitary creature. He requires the complex fabric of ties, links and interactions which comprise interpersonal relations. A serious disbalance in human relations is a highly important indicator of adjustment to life. Mentally disturbed individuals overdo in their instrumental, mutual or vectorial attitudes; some of them fear people, some hate people, and practically all of them interact with their environment in a highly unsatisfactory way. As will be explained later, interactional patterns offer invaluable diagnostic clues.

Irrational Behavior or Mental Disease?

Mental disorder leads to *irrational behavior,* whether it involves erroneous perception, exaggerated emotionality, or avoidance of one's friends. Schizophrenics, for instance, display all three symptoms. They are, to some extent, victims of whatever factors have caused their disorder, but they are not merely passive, bedridden, helpless victims. Schizophrenia is not a disease of the brain or vasomotor system; schizophrenia is an irrational life style. Mental symptoms are hardly coincidental; they usually serve a purpose, that is, either a search for something or an escape from something. They represent morbid, irrational ways of coping or failing to cope with life.

The sick role is a passive role; one succumbs to pneumonia, typhoid fever, smallpox, thrombosis, or fracture of bones. One does not succumb in the same sense to obsessive-compulsive neurosis, sexual frigidity, severe depression or schizophrenia. One *has* pneumonia, but one *is* an obsessive neurotic.

Physical health and physical disease can be presented as a continuum terminating at a definite point. The deadline of physical disease is death; the severity of any physical disease is measured not by symptoms but by its distance from death. A simple cold, indigestion, or diarrhea can be more spectacular than a severe disease such as cancer in its inception, yet cancer is a serious disease because it is frequently fatal.

Health and sickness are states of an organism. Good health

means good chances for survival while poor health and disease point to a danger to life. No one is perfectly healthy, nor is anyone absolutely normal. Mental normality and abnormality are a matter of degree. The more realistic one's perceptions, the more balanced one's emotionality, and the more satisfactory his interaction with other people, the more one can be regarded as normal. Less well-balanced people are disturbed; at its most incapacitating the disturbance renders the individual totally helpless.

Etiology

The study of mental disorders aims at helping those who need help. Logic would seem to dictate that we begin with a search for the causes of mental disorders, for the knowledge of causes may help in curing existing ills and preventing new ones.

Mental disorders are either inherited, acquired, or caused by a combination of both. If they are inherited, they are transmitted through the genes. Those mental disorders which are not inherited are acquired through interaction with either the physical or the social environment. Thus mental disorders can be divided into three large categories related to their origins. Those that originate in the organism through heredity or through interaction with the physical environment (injuries, poisons, and so on) are *somatogenic* (soma means body). The inherited disorders are *genosomatogenic*, for they are caused by genes; the physically acquired mental disorders are *ecosomatogenic*, for they are caused by interaction with the environment, the ecos. All other disorders stem from faulty interindividual relations, i.e., they are psychosocial, but since the interaction with the social environment is the cause of morbid conditioning and cathexis, we shall call these disorders *sociogenic* or *sociopsychogenic*.

TABLE 2
ETIOLOGIC CLASSIFICATION

	Organic	Nonorganic
Inherited	Genosomatogenic	———
Acquired	Ecosomatogenic	Sociogenic

All mental disorders are disorders of human behavior, the term behavior including all overt actions as well as covert and unconscious feelings and desires. Whether caused by genes (genosomatogenic), or by prenatal, natal or postnatal physicochemical offenses to the nervous or glandular system (ecosomatogenic), disorders are mental or psychological as long as they affect behavior. Besides the genosomatogenic and ecosomatogenic disorders, there are mental disorders caused by postnatal interaction between the organism and its social environment. Thus all mental disorders belong to one of the three categories or some combination of them.

The so-called organic mental disorders are actually either genosomatogenic or sociogenic. For, whatever is inherited, whether it results in physical or behavioral symptoms, is genosomatogenic. Some types of mental deficiency, not necessarily accompanied by physical symptoms, are inherited, and therefore ecosomatogenic. Genes and chromosomes are biochemical entities, part and parcel of living matter. The absence of physical deformity or malfunction does not make a mental disorder psychogenic. The proposed classification of mental disorders is not based on external appearances called symptoms, but rather on causes. If low intelligence is inherited, that is, transmitted by genes, it is genosomatogenic. Inherited disorders do not necessarily appear right after birth; some develop later in life. But, as long as they originate in genes, they are to be regarded as genosomatogenic.

Mental disorders acquired in interaction with the environment are sociogenic. If there is nothing abnormal in an infant's inherited endowment, the infant must be considered normal; whatever becomes abnormal is a result of interaction with the environment. Social interaction is the cause, and psychological abnormalities are the result. Thus, the proper name for this type of disorder should be sociogenic or sociopsychogenic.

Adverse Experiences and Mental Disorder

Adverse sociopsychological factors, that is, the interindividual relations reflected in disbalance of libido and destrudo, affect the intraindividual balance of cathexes. Rejection, hurt feelings, and hatred coming from without cause self-depreciation, self-hatred, or hatred toward others. Thus, economic hardship, frustrations and traumatic experiences might be regarded as among the main causes of mental disorders.

However, the earliest records of mental disorder tell of wealthy men and kings and not of poor shepherds. King Saul suffered severe depression; Democritus and Socrates were believed to be schizoid if not schizophrenic, and Tiberius and Caius Caligula were certainly far from normal. Moreover, Hippocrates, Asclepiades, and in modern times Freud and Jung treated wealthy patients. Most patients in analysis today are, by definition, affluent enough to afford it.

Moreover, were material success and socioeconomic status a factor in mental health, poor countries should have the highest rate of mental disorders. There is, however, not the slightest indication that such is the case. If one could trust statistics in this area, where results depend so much upon arbitrarily set definitions and inadequate diagnostic procedures, the United States with its high income per capita should have the lowest rate of mental disorders. Even the poorest Americans receive some public support; by and large, people in this country are not as destitute as those in developing countries where misery and suffering does not seem to cause mental disorder.

The Impact of a Trauma

There is a widespread belief that stress and traumatic experience are the main cause of social or sociopsychogenic behavior disorders, and that the nature of the trauma determines the nature of the symptoms. War experiences may shed light on this problem and a study of the so-called traumatic war neuroses viewed in an overall context of personality development, may elucidate the issue of symptom formation. Let us illustrate with the case of a marine who was unable to protect his best friend from being killed by the enemy and consequently felt guilty. Although he recalled the tragic event, with tears and anguish, the sad memories did not affect his mental health. Another marine, with a less healthy personality structure, developed amnesia and forgot entirely not only what happened on the battlefield, but his own name and whereabouts as well. The first marine, who was in good mental health prior to the event, retained full memory of the past, while the second marine's weak ego, unable to cope with the feeling of guilt, mobilized powerful repressive mechanisms which resulted in an amnesia and other neurotic symptoms. Apparently the traumatic war experience did not *cause* the amnesia and other neurotic symptoms of the second marine. The war trauma merely *precipitated* the symptom formation. The underlying causes for the neurotic symptoms were probably rooted in the past, in early childhood experiences. It seems that the radical change of environment and the transition from civilian to military life may revive childhood separation fears. The serviceman must become a member of a social grouping that is almost diametrically opposed to his past experience at home and in school. Familial groupings offer definite social satisfaction while securing distinct social roles of parents and children;

the family expects loyalty and cooperation without much coercion. The Armed Forces are built as a hierarchic and authoritarian social system, comprised of men only. The inducted man *must* carry out his duties and learn subordination to people he has never met and whom he does not necessarily like or respect. Cooperation is imposed by orders.

Service in the Armed Forces requires new adaptations and creates new conflicts, problems and stresses. The soldier, pilot, marine or sailor has to live in an atmosphere of continuous fatigue, boredom, subordination, loss of personal freedom and threat to life. He is deprived of sex and freely chosen companionship, and rarely has he an opportunity to relax. He is constantly watched and being judged in training and in his performance of duties. In that his shortcomings as a member of his team are always being pointed out, there may be severe damage to his self-esteem.

Family life is a continuous social experience. In most cases people perpetuate their family ties and turn to their close relatives in times of stress. The Army situation is viewed by most people as a transient hardship.

A frightening war experience may reactivate past worries and anxieties, thereby precipitating a neurotic or even psychotic regression. The type of symptoms may be related, in part, to a particular trauma; forgetting, for instance, removes the feeling of guilt and responsibility, while severe vomiting and diarrhea may prove to be effective in preventing future active combat.

One must conclude that the so-called traumatic or war neuroses do not comprise a separate clinical entity but are transient or lasting acute states of an already existing mental condition. The nature of the traumatic disorder is probably related to the personality type and clinical condition of a given individual. A hysterical individual exposed to shell shock may develop psychological blindness. "A patient with total hysterical blindness is generally able to get around better than a patient with an organic lesion. He says he sees nothing, yet he is able to avoid large obstacles in walking, handle eating utensils, etc. The patient reports being blind because he is consciously unaware of seeing" (Brady and Lind, 1961).

Combat Fatigue

One of the most common neurotic symptoms in war is *combat fatigue* (Kardiner, 1959), manifested by loss of appetite, insomnia, exhaustion, carelessness, jumpiness, unnecessary self-exposure to danger, freezing to the ground, fear of the noise of friendly artillery, and a total inability to relax, all of which may signal an approaching breakdown.

According to Kardiner (1959) the traumatic syndrome is comprised of the following patterns: (1) A deflated self-image; (2) Catastrophic dreams and nightmares; (3) General irritability and an accoustic startle pattern; (4) Impulsiveness and the tendency to act out aggressiveness; (5) Overall regression to childish behavior.

Rado (1956–1962) believes that the symptoms of traumatic neurosis have a "high demonstrative value to elicit pity" and to give support to the patient's diminished resources. Furthermore, Rado feels that the patient sets up a highly protective shield in a fierce attempt to protect himself against the possibility of a repetition of the trauma. The "traumatophobia" is a state of perpetual fear of an impending catastrophe. What the soldier fears most is his own fear. This fear of fear creates an unbearable tension and a desire to escape from the danger situation. Insofar as there is no real escape in war but to fight to the end the soldier feels trapped. Thus, the road of escape leads to a morbid denial of reality.

Several defense mechanisms can be applied, depending on the individual's past experiences and personality type. All these mechanisms are of a regressive nature in that they represent a search for refuge in an imaginary early childhood sanctuary. Some servicemen become incontinent; some regress to baby talk, regurgitate food, and even crawl on all fours.

Reverse Reactions

It has been observed that sometimes a stress situation brings not an increase but a decrease in mental symptoms. Hastings (1944) reported a decrease in psychiatric cases in the Air Force during World War II. Hopkins (1943) noticed a distinct decrease in the rate of admission to mental hospitals in Liverpool during the same period. In Sweden there was a decline in mental cases during the war (Ódegaard, 1954); in Israel, during the War of Independence, the mental health of the population improved (Wolman, 1953).

We know that external danger mobilizes the body's inner resources; e.g., glands of inner secretion and the autonomic nervous system respond to emergency situations with a mobilization of all inner resources. In circumstance of extreme danger, people who under ordinary circumstances are nonambulatory, have been known to flee for their lives.

Something similar happens in the psychological sense. A weak ego, usually unable to control unconscious impulses, may suddenly gain control over behavior in an emergency situation. A national emergency, for instance, forces the moralistic superego to support the ego; thus at least one conflict is removed. People in London under the Blitz and in Israel during the War of Independence showed unusual heroism. Public enthusiasm and generally high morale largely contributed to the improvement of mental health.

When only 650,000 people are available to wage war against 50,000,000, a country can hardly afford to disqualify anyone from service except the severely psychotic or badly mentally retarded. One young man who had been rejected by the Medical Board because of eye trouble, and by Psychological Services because of apparent neurotic tics and compulsions, nonetheless managed to gain acceptance into the Army and, despite pessimistic prognoses, excelled in five fierce battles with the Arabs.

Although extremely neurotic outside the Army, within the context of the military structure his neuroses were temporarily abandoned. When he told his unit how he had "fooled" both the medical examiner and the psychologist and, despite their opposition, joined a combat unit, he became a popular figure. Although scared to death in active combat, the feeling of being accepted by his buddies and the responsibility for the survival of his nation kept his neuroses in check.

The Hammer and the Anvil

A physical or mental trauma can seriously affect one's mental health, but it is rarely if ever an exclusive causal relationship. Consider a rock thrown at a window; the glass shatters not only because the rock is hard, but also because the glass is breakable. The same rock thrown against a wall or a shatter-proof window pane, or thrown with less force or from a different angle, is likely to cause significantly less damage.

Because the human psyche is remarkably durable, it is highly unlikely that a single trauma will precipitate mental breakdown. We will all experience adversity or even tragedy at some point in a lifetime, but only some people react with visible and lasting distress. In World War II most members of the Armed Forces who took part in active combat went through shocking experiences, but only a relatively small number of them were adversely affected to the point of developing mental symptoms. Some men became disturbed at the induction centers, unable to accept separation from their families. Others developed symptoms at a later stage of military training; still others adjusted to the separation from their families and coped satisfactorily with the hardship of training, but became disturbed when shipped overseas. Some servicemen became mentally disturbed in active combat when exposed to shelling and bombardment. However, most returned home sane after all the frightening experiences of modern warfare.

Obviously, there are significant differences in the way various individuals handle stress. Hardships can break maladjusted, immature, neurotic people, but it is rather unlikely that a well-balanced individual will collapse under stress. Although every human being has a breaking point, it is quite obvious that those who suffer mental breakdown under stress are predisposed to this kind of disorder prior to the traumatic event. A traumatic experience is usually a *precipitating factor*, a sort of straw that breaks the camel's back. But the camel's back must have been very weak or cracked before the final straw.

The Social Climate

The exasperating variety of clinical behavior disorders militates against the possibility of a single factor theory of mental disorder. There are however certain persistent patterns in mental disorders, which are easily discernible only in the most severe cases when the irrational behavior becomes extreme. Following the traditional classification, one can distinguish schizophrenia, depressive disorders (manic-depressive psychosis), and psychopathic behavior. A system of division into three "normal" behavioral patterns was suggested in the previous chapters, namely, vectorial (corresponding to Freud's obsessive type), mutual (corresponding to Freud's erotic type), and instrumental (corresponding to Freud's narcissistic type).

The question is, what are the factors that can transform a reasonably well-adjusted individual whose behavior tends to be vectorial, mutual or narcissistic into a schizophrenic, depressive or psychopath with an apparent powerful degree of hostility, and what are the gradual steps, if any, in this process of mental deterioration.

There is ample evidence to suggest that the attitudes of
one's peer group and public opinion can enhance or reduce
the ability of individuals to handle stress. Experimental studies on group cohesiveness have indicated that groups devoted
to an idealistic goal (vectorial) resist stress and failure better
than the mutual, and much better than the instrumental
groups (Wolman, 1960b). Studies in social psychology bear
witness to the reinforcement of socially approved behavioral
patterns, and emphasize the impact of cultural norms on
behavior of individuals (Deutsch, 1949; 1965; Inkeles and
Levinson, 1969; Klineberg, 1965; Lewin, K., 1951; Proshansky and Seidenberg, 1965). Kardiner (1935, 1945) stressed the
importance of child-rearing practices, but these practices
themselves are influenced by geographic, climatic, and economic factors (Proshansky, 1970).

Transient social norms and the way the individual views
himself in regard to his group exercise significant influence
on his behavior. Studies reported by Asch (1952), Bronfenbrenner (1967), Lewin (1951), Sherif and Cantril (1947),
Deutsch (1969), Sherif and Sherif (1964) and many others
have proven beyond doubt that group pressures can modify
the attitudes, decision-making processes, and overt behavior
of individuals. These group influences can be reinforced by
social learning (Bandura and Walters, 1962) and can affect
the balance of libido and destrudo cathexes. For instance, if
someone is exposed to prejudice and discrimination, his attitude toward those who discriminate against him will
justifiably be unfriendly, and at certain times his ideas concerning the outer world may appear to be paranoid. Yet, as
long as he has valid reasons to support his contention that he
is a victim of discrimination, he cannot be regarded as a
paranoiac. However, if he has been exposed to a prolonged
period of discrimination, he may carry over his suspicions
into a new environment which does not practice discrimination, and thereby call attention to himself as irrational and

disturbed. If unfortunate social experiences have a lasting impact, they are to be seen as having some etiologic role in behavior disorder. However, if the impact is transient, and the ensuing irrational behavior is temporary, the chain of events can hardly be described in terms of psychopathology, though there is no clear line of division between someone who loses his temper rarely and one who loses it frequently.

It is precisely to this issue that the current volume addresses itself. There is the undeniable fact that some individuals act in irrational and maladjustive ways, displaying serious shortcomings in four important areas of mental functioning, namely, the cognitive, affectual, volitional and social. Abnormal behavior thus defined reduces substantially the chances for survival; this definition is for the most part self-explanatory in severe psychotic cases. Extreme abnormality is eminently discernible.

Normal behavior is much more difficult to define. The term "normal" means more or less normal. No one's behavior meets all four criteria of mental health all the time, and normality merely indicates the degree of approximation to the four criteria, or the degree of distance from pathology.

Insofar as mental health is a matter of degree, the understanding of human relations and other events conducive to irrationality and mental disturbance can serve as an introduction to the study of etiology of behavior disorders.

The Narcissistic-Instrumental Pattern

Social upheaval, war and revolutions uproot thousands of people, deprive them of their possessions, jobs and homes, and force them to cope with life as a "sink or swim" alternative. Although some people drown, many manage to swim and survive. We cannot conclude that those who survive the murky tides of social catastrophe necessarily belong to a distinct personality type. However, certain social events seem to encourage and foster certain behavioral patterns.

Excessive stress, hunger, deprivation and danger foster a
redirection of interindividual libido and destrudo cathexes. A
severe threat to life usually activates self-directed libido and
object-directed destrudo which, in a regressive manner,
evokes narcissistic, oral-aggressive and instrumental-hostile
behavior patterns.

In Russia, after the November Revolution, hordes of
youngsters turned to robbery and murder. These "bezprizorn-
ye," children of hunger and despair, described by Makarenko (1955), fought for survival in a most primitive way.
Aichhorn (1935) analyzed a similar phenomenon of wayward
youth in Central Europe after the First World War; similar
developments took place in Poland and in Italy after the
Second World War. In times of disaster and famine people
tend to become more atavistic because they are unsure of
their own survival. In extreme cases of famine, civilized people have been known to regress to cannibalism.

However, not all people react in a hostile-instrumental
manner to adverse conditions. The hypothesis that links frustration to aggression seems to be overstated and overgeneral-
ized, for aggression can be produced also by other factors,
and frustration may lead to a variety of reactions.

It appears that some social climates foster a *bellum omnium contra omnes* (war of all against all). In instrumental
groups and societies where everyone pursues his own needs,
social upheaval strengthens these tendencies and produces
truly psychopathic mass behavior. The economic crisis toward the end of the third decade of this century produced
hardship in many countries, but only in Germany did a
well-organized clique of psychopaths seize power. The famous German phrase "Ich muss es haben" (I must have it),
and the notorious German inferiority feeling that manifested
itself in the song, "Deutschland über alles" (Germany above
all) were highly conducive to regressive narcissism and hostile instrumentalism, directed against whoever refused to subject themselves to the insecure, aggressive beasts.

The Schizoid-Hypervectorial Pattern

A threat of loss of support may precipitate severe anxiety. Consider catastrophic social situations where the bulwarks of society display their weakness, cowardliness and lack of moral standards. The decline of moral authority of public leaders has always led to a schizoid social climate. In times characterized by a loosening of cultural norms and social bonds, when people lose faith in the social order and value system, there is a growing tendency for escape into drugs, astrology, mysticism and supranatural beliefs and practices. A permissive, fatherless, spineless social climate ultimately leads to withdrawal from reality. In a society where no one can be relied upon, where authority figures and public leaders have abdicated their leadership functions, people lose the sense of belonging and security. Many individuals assume that no one cares and no one will; thus everyone feels he has the right to reform society and create a new world. The pseudovectorial attitude embodied in the hippie culture, combined with a false feeling of power, and rebellion against the pampering, infantilizing parents referred to as the "establishment," has certain correspondences with the schizophrenics' world-destruction hallucinations. In such an atmosphere of decline of authority and order, the perception of reality may become grossly distorted. It has been suggested that the sexual license of our times, mixed with crude mystical practices, increasing homosexuality, violence and boredom can be compared to conditions at the time of the decline of the Roman Empire. Infantile, nonsensical babbling is passed off as "poetry," and simplistic, awkward smearing of canvasses calls itself art. This regressive movement, born in Europe out of the despair of the First World War, put an end to the Victorian era and to the European balance of power. Such an antiintellectual and antirational movement, which I have described as "willful regression" (Wolman, 1971b), continues today in many areas under a variety of names, bearing witness to a feeling of despair typically transformed into an unrealistic assumption of greatness. Further regression in this direction results in mystical-obsessional rituals, and, in extreme cases, full-blown schizophrenic delusions of grandeur.

A schizoid type (see Chapter 8) perceives authority figures as helpless and unreliable creatures, and assumes that he has the power to destroy them together with the entire evil world of adults. Hence the megalomaniac, destructive, pseudorevolutionaries who act out their repressed infantile temper tantrums in catatonic frenzy. Other groups practice mysticism, astrology, spiritualism, and hold psychedelic orgies, deluded by a belief that they are fulfilling some lofty ideal.

It is highly unlikely that one becomes a severely regressed schizophrenic as a result of decadent cultural conditions. The search for particular etiologic factors must start with conception, but it seems that the distinguishing characteristics between classical schizophrenia and the pseudovectorial schizoid personality are none too clear.

The Depressive-Mutual Pattern

Rejected and persecuted people tend to be depressed. Such an exogenous depression is a normal emotional reaction to misfortune, for a positive change in fortune is usually accompanied by an appropriate mood shift.

Serious and repetitive adverse experiences are not conducive to cheerful moods. A continuous chain of failures and mishaps is likely to create an atmosphere of doom. The feeling of defeat and despair may create a desire to escape from further hardships by regressing to a stage of infantile helplessness where misery once evoked maternal sympathy and help.

Periods of despair, accompanied by a hope for sympathy and love, repeat themselves in the history of humanity. Every so often prophets and messiahs would appear and promise redemption and compensation for sufferings. Thus, self-depreciation, severe guilt feelings and feelings of worthlessness were interrupted by periods of ecstatic elation.

Messianic hopes are prevalent in Judaism and are even more pronounced in the Christian religion, which promises the regaining of the "Lost Paradise" and reward in Heaven for suffering on earth. The origins of Christianity are profoundly linked to the desperate situations of subjugated nations and enslaved people who dreamed about Redemption, and therefore believed in salvation through suffering. Whereas opulent Christian kings and lords paid lip service to the glory of the hereafter, preferring mundane joys of the here and now, the persecuted Jews clung to the Messianic idea.

The Jews and several other minority groups and members of subjugated nations (e.g., the Poles under Russian rule) have repeatedly maintained that the good Lord tests them, and ultimately that He will reward them for the years of misery. Messianic hopes and the feeling of being hated and admired at the same time flourish amongst persecuted groups.

Although it cannot be said that persecution and hope for redemption cause depressive disorder, with its unquenchable thirst for love, there is evidence to indicate that if the atmosphere of doom starts early in life, the unloved child develops a hatred for those who withold their love. This hatred is typically accompanied by a paranoid projection and a desire to regress to an infantile stage when sufferings did elicit maternal sympathy.

Early Childhood Experiences

It is obvious that the weaker the personality structure, the more damage can be caused to it. Adult men and women can take a good deal of stress without being permanently affected, but an infant's personality is easily damaged by unfavorable social relations, especially when these interactional patterns are persistent, and exclusive of other potentially compensating influences.

There is a growing body of evidence concerning the import of early childhood relations on personality development

(Escalona, 1968; Hartmann, 1950; Kris, 1950, Nagera, 1966; Ritvo and Solnit, 1958; Spitz, 1965; and many others). An adverse home environment systematically undermines or prevents normal development; early traumatic events foster fixations and prevent the formation of an adequate ego. The weak ego, when faced with severe frustrations and frightening experiences, must resort to defense mechanisms and symptom formation. Should these neurotic, ego-protecting symptoms fail, more severe or psychotic ego-deficiency symptoms come into play. In other words, a failed neurosis may turn into a psychosis. In neurosis the ego is still in control of the entire mental apparatus; in psychosis the ego collapses, and irrational behavior prevails.

Anxiety

My main assumption is that fight for survival is the most basic drive in all organic nature, and that hostility is the result of fear of death, starvation or destruction. All other forms of fear are derivatives of this fundamental fear of death. For instance, fear of darkness has its origins in primitive man's inability to see the approaching enemy and the initially apprehensive attitude to strange places and strange people is related to the fear of unpredictable situations and the inability to protect oneself against them.

Similarly, the fear of separation, abandonment and loneliness is directly related to the fear of annihilation. In terms of the power-and-acceptance theory explained in previous chapters, power is the ability to satisfy needs—and the supreme need is survival. Thus, the stronger one is, the less one need fear loneliness. Ibsen's hero rightly exclaims that he who stands alone is strongest. Those who are weak depend on being accepted and protected by others. Horney and Sullivan rightly regarded the need for acceptance ("safety") as of paramount importance. Unfortunately their conception of neurosis was reduced to this highly relevant but surely not the sole aspect of pathogenesis. The need to be accepted and protected is only a *means* to the goal of survival, applicable to particular situations when one cannot defend oneself and needs such support. Thus loneliness and rejection as such cannot be regarded as a cause of neurosis. Separation, rejection and loneliness will traumatize only those who are emotionally damaged to begin with.

The infant's survival is dependent upon the protection offered by parents or parent surrogates. When such protection is not forthcoming or when children believe that protection is being withheld from them—in short, when children feel *insecure,* the fear of death or its derivative fear of being forsaken may become *internalized* in the form of *anxiety.*

Fear can be a normal reaction to danger, thereby leading to adjustive reactions appropriate to the situation. In early childhood the appropriate reaction is to seek help from parents or parental substitutes. Gradually, as the child grows, he learns to cope with minor threats and to seek cooperation with other people. The estimate of his own power grows in a realistic appraisal of the external dangers.

I am in agreement with Freud that anxiety is a reaction of the ego to onslaughts coming from within, from the id or the superego, or both. The feeling of anxiety is however experienced as worry, apprehension, and doubts of one's ability to cope with dangers, for the ego's fear of the id and superego is actually an internalized feeling of fear of external dangers. "Anxiety," Freud wrote in 1933, "is the reproduction of an old danger—threatening event; anxiety serves the purposes of self-preservation as being a signal of the presence of a new danger" (p. 84).

We are not able to determine in any empirical fashion that the id of some individuals is more threatening than that of other individuals. We know very little about the state of the id in prenatal and early postnatal life. Certainly one can follow the line of reasoning of Melanie Klein (1932) and Segal

(1967, 1972) who assume that the formation of personality structure takes place in early months of life, but it might be methodologically more sound to keep our speculative hypotheses at a necessary minimum (Wolff, 1966). The inability of the ego to cope with id onslaughts could be related either to an overactive and omnipotent id or to an inadequately developed ego.

The hypothetical strength of inherited id impulses is apparently related to unknown genetic factors. "We can come nearer to the id with images," Freud (1933) wrote in the *Introductory Lectures,* "and call it chaos, a cauldron of seething excitement. We suppose that it is somewhere in direct contact with somatic processes, and takes over from them mental expression . . . Instinctual cathexes seeking discharge—that is, in our view, all that the id contains" (pp. 104–106). The id does not change; an instinctual force may be "innately too strong or too weak," and "the determining causes of all varying forms of human mental life are to be found in the interplay between inherited and accidental experiences" (Freud, 1938, p. 84).

Given a certain hereditary predisposition, the interaction with the physical and social environment will ultimately determine how much and to what extent the inherited potentialities will find expression and realization. The mental apparatus of the newborn, the id, might be likened to a body floating in water. Environmental forces, acting upon the id, cause changes in the surface of the floating body. This surface gradually separates from the id and develops into a separate mental agency, the ego.

The strength of the ego depends largely on life experience and especially on interaction with parental figures. According to Hartmann (1937), the child's personality develops through interaction between the nonconflictual (primary autonomous) space of the ego—including mobility, perception and thought processes—and the conflictual space, which is wholly related to interaction with the environment. A wholesome and stable parental attitude contributes to the growth of a strong ego capable of resisting regressive tendencies (secondary autonomy).

Parental Attitudes

There is an ample body of evidence to suggest that the amount of damage caused by stress and traumatic events in early childhood depends on parental attitudes. The studies of Brody (1956), Freud and Burlingham (1944), Glover (1955), Sander (1962) and others clearly proved the adverse impact of parental anxiety on children's behavior. In addition to similar clinical observations in my early practice in children's institutions in Poland and Israel, I had the chance during World War II and the Israeli War of Independence to observe children under stressful circumstances. I noticed that children living in areas exposed to heavy air raids and artillery fire suffered little emotional damage as long as their mothers behaved in a calm, self-assured manner and impressed the children with their competence. Apparently the calm attitude conveyed to the children by their mothers promoted a feeling of security which enabled them to continue their play in shelters and basements.

Mothers who reacted to danger in an exaggerated, frightened manner, brought out severe neurotic symptoms in their children. The neurotic reaction of the children hardly corresponded to the real danger, but it was highly correlated to the danger as communicated by the mothers. Because the present-day nuclear family structure reduces the child's close contacts to his parents or one or two siblings, he has become more dependent on parental moods and more exposed to interparental strife than ever before in the history of man (Ackerman, 1958; Parsons and Bales, 1955; Bronfenbrenner,

1967; Wolman, 1970). A detailed description of pathogenic family patterns is given in the three following chapters.

As previously mentioned, the normal development of personality depends to a large extent on the amount of love one has received in his childhood. Abundant parental love enables the child to grow in an atmosphere of security and acceptance. As the child develops, he learns to give to and share with his peers. Gradually he becomes capable of mutual, nonsexual relationships in friendships and mutual, sexual relationships in courtship, until he is mature enough to assume parental and vectorial responsibilities. Reich (1945) in his first edition of *Character Analysis* pointed to disbalance in libidinal cathexes as the fundamental, quantitative, "economic" factor in personality organization (p. 12 ff). The division into the three behavior patterns, namely, instrumental, mutual and vectorial, is isomorphic to economy of cathexes.

The physical and mental growth of infants who have not received adequate love may be seriously impaired, even when their physical needs have been satisfied.

Apparently, milk is not enough. When the feeding situation is accompanied by unfriendly irritable or angry gestures, the infant may refuse to accept the food or hold it inordinately after intake. Most feeding problems in infants are caused by impatient, frustrated, unhappy and unloving mothers whose unwillingness to give love is somehow perceived by the infant. In the extreme cases described by Spitz, unloved infants succumbed to marasmus (Spitz, 1945, 1965).

There is an abundance of scientific literature describing patterns of irrational treatment of children (Bateson et al., 1956; Cheek, 1964; Framo, 1962; Davidson, 1961; Fleck, 1971; Klebanoff, 1959; and many others). In these manifold patterns one can distinguish three noxious types of parent-child interaction—outright rejection, shifting from love to hate, and overdemanding attitudes.

The Rejecting Parents

Some parents do not demand love from their children nor do they offer any love to them. The child growing up in this kind of environment feels lonely and rejected, and perceives the world as a place where one either exploits others or is exploited by them. Rejected children soon learn to take advantage of other people's weaknesses, assuming that everyone else does the same. Viewing the world as a jungle serves as a justification for their own extreme selfishness. They regard their exploitative and hostile behavior as the self-preservatory response of an innocent creature facing a hostile world.

Clinical observations indicate three prototypical settings which are conducive to fostering such selfish, hyperinstrumental, hypernarcissistic personality types, namely, institutions, underprivileged homes and wealthy families. The institutional environment, where anonymous counselors deal with anonymous "cases" in a cold, uninvolved, matter of fact way, distri¹ 'ing so many cups of milk, and so many penalties for violation of the institutional discipline, is most likely to produce secondary narcissism (A. Freud, 1967).

Many hyperinstrumentals are underprivileged children who have been reared in an atmosphere of constant bickering, and were rejected by parents who resented the burden of taking care of their offspring. Members of underprivileged families often create an atmosphere where the jungle ethic prevails and the entire world seems to be populated by enemies.

In the third category are children of well-to-do families where the parents have characteristically substituted money for affection and nurturance. The child of such a background has no one to emulate, or to identify with, and is forced to live a hollow, selfish existence of unfulfilled wishes.

These *narcissistic, hyperinstrumental* children, when they deteriorate, typically become psychopaths. Milder cases of hyperinstrumentals are selfish and hostile people who feel that others are hostile. They are sensitive to their own suffering and deprivations, but have no empathy or sympathy for anyone else. In more severe cases, there is a total lack of moral restraint, consideration, and compassion for one's fellow man, and often a tendency to defy the law while proclaiming and believing in one's own innocence. The hyperinstrumentals who are exploitative and generally oral-cannibalistic, operate on the principle that weak enemies and neutrals have to be destroyed and friends are to be used. The destrudo of hyperinstrumentals is highly mobilized and ready to strike against the outer world (object-directed). A hyperinstrumental, perceiving himself as an innocent, poor, hungry animal, sees people as enemies: either he will devour them or they will devour him. Highly aggressive, the narcissistic hyperinstrumental type is actually a coward, brutal and cruel to those who fear him but obedient and subservient to those he fears. In the milder, neurotic cases, he appears as a selfish, frightened individual. In more severe cases he is cruel when deteriorated. The most severe cases are described in terms of psychotic psychopathy, called by J. C. Prichard (1835) "moral insanity."

The narcissistic, hyperinstrumental type has weak moral principles, distorted human standards, and no sense of social obligation. He is concerned about no one but himself, and often develops hypochondriacal worries. If he happens to be religious, his gods are either masters whom one bribes, or warriors who are to help him conquer the world. His gods are always on the side of the big batallions.

Not all human fears are internalized and turned into neurotic anxiety. Well-adjusted people cope with fears in a constructive manner. For example, they cope with the fear of hunger by seeking gainful employment and providing an adequate income. They put locks on their doors to defend themselves against burglars, and they pay taxes to the government, expecting adequate police and fire protection. Extremely threatening situations call for fight or flight, depending on an estimate of one's own power and acceptance and the power and acceptance of the adversaries. (Power is defined as the *ability* to satisfy needs or prevent their satisfaction, and acceptance is the *willingness* to satisfy needs or prevent their satisfaction.)

Distortions in the estimation of power and acceptance are a distinct sign of neurosis. Narcissistic, hyperinstrumental neurotics perceive themselves as weak and friendly, while viewing the outer world as strong and hostile. People with strong narcissistic, hyperinstrumental tendencies are prone to have a distorted image of themselves as being small, weak, innocent, friendly creatures exposed to an inimical world. The apparent disbalance in libido and destrudo cathexes, with the libido directed toward oneself and the destrudo toward the outer world, calls for a corresponding perceptual distortion.

The feeling of one's own weakness in the face of a threat gives rise to hostile feelings. Most often it is a combination of defensive and aggressive hostility, defensive against stronger creatures and aggressive against the weaker ones. The narcissistic, hyperinstrumental type is a notorious coward who fights only against easy prey and is subservient to the mighty ones. One meets in daily life scores of individuals of this kind, who are eager to attack, to loot and exploit minority groups, women, children, the lonely and the helpless. However, there are degrees in the narcissistic regression. The less mature the hyperinstrumental type, the more is he prone to act in a hostile, aggressive-defensive manner. There is a gradual transition from the more or less "normal" selfish, narcissistic-instrumental individual toward a clear-cut psychopath or sociopath, referred to in chapter 7 as the "innocent criminal." One may hypothesize that the economic crisis of the late twenties, the defeat in the first World War, combined with the notorious German inferiority feeling, was conducive to a mass-psychopathic Nazi behavior. The main causes however must be traced elsewhere, for psychopathic-narcissistic behavior is found everywhere else (see Chapter 7).

The Overdemanding Parents

It is becoming increasingly apparent, in the light of clinical evidence, that the vast majority of mental disorders are caused by mistreatment of people (children) by people (parents). There are innumerable patterns of faulty interindividual relations within the framework of family life, but apparently some of them are more harmful than others.

Certain intrafamilial relationships seem to be particularly detrimental to the child's personality. One of these is the *reversal of social roles*. Some parents act as if they were the children who need to be loved, and demand the kind of love and affection from the child that would more properly be expected to come from their own parents. In such families, the parents' attitude toward the child is instrumental, and the child is forced too early into a costly, loving, vectorial attitude toward his parents. The child, in effect, is robbed of his childhood and must prematurely become an adult. His parents, disappointed in one another, expect him to compensate for all the love and affection they failed to obtain from each other. Moreover, the child is not allowed to express his dissatisfaction, discomfort, and dissent, nor is he permitted to act out childhood tantrums. In short, a child exposed to immature, overdemanding and instrumental parents is expected to become a model child who renounces his own desires to please his parents. The child is forced into an extreme and too early *hypervectorial* attitude.

Parsons and Bales (1955) described the child's dependency on the mother as follows:

> The neonate . . . as an object of possession is valued, and *taken care of*. He is an object of pride, and must be "kept in good condi-

tion." This means of course that his organic needs must be adequately met, but also as an object of pride he is attractively dressed, encouraged, when he can, to smile in order to please people, etc. He is "shown off."

At the same time, of course, parents even of the newborn, do not see the child exclusively in terms of his present state but also of his potentialities for the future. From their point of view his status as a possession is inherently temporary. They also tend, in orienting themselves to him, to recapitulate their own developmental histories.

When this process goes on for a while, two important things tend to happen. First, the child develops a set of *expectations*, not only about being cared for as such but with respect to specific agency. He establishes, that is, a dependency on the specific agent of care. He receives, not merely segmental gratifications, but "care." The specific acts of care then acquire a new and more extended meaning for him, they not only in fact gratify the particular need, but they come to *symbolize* the mother's attitude of wanting to take good care of him and his own right to be taken care of. Furthermore, the qualitatively different acts of care come to be associated with the same object, the same agent, so that he acquires a diffuse attachment, to *her*, a *dependency on her*. There is generalization across the lines of differentiation between segmental needs, so that being taken care of becomes a single *system* of expectations which can function as a system [p. 63].

Insecure, frustrated parents often present themselves to the children as pitiful, helpless creatures incapable of offering protection and very much in need of it themselves. In terms of the power and acceptance theory, they are perceived by the child as being weak and friendly, that is, unable to help but willing to do so.

The fear of the parents' downfall and death forces the child to support them. The child's libido becomes object-hypercathected on parents or their substitutes, with very little libido left for self-cathexis. On the other hand, the destrudo becomes self-cathected; the child fears to hurt his allegedly dying parents and blames himself for whatever misfortunes befall them. This object-libido hypercathected attitude combined with the fear of one's own hostility creates the hypercathected personality type that corresponds to Freud's obsessional type.

Chapter 7 entitled "Fallen Angels," describes the schizohypervectorial disorders.

Human beings are not angels. The model child may try, at the devastating cost of impoverishment of his own emotional resources, to overcontrol his impulses. However, as soon as the emotional resources of love (the libido) have been overspent, the emotional energy of hate (the destrudo) takes over. Overspent love turns to hatred for oneself and others. The fallen angel soon becomes a hateful devil who is no longer able to control his hostile impulses. He hates himself for hating others, and is afraid of love that becomes overdemanding and threatening. The extreme result is schizophrenia. Typically, schizophrenics are individuals who as small children were forced to worry about their parents. Throughout their lives they feel compelled to strive for perfection and are unreasonably harsh on themselves. They appear to treat life as an obligation to be honored, as a ritual to be followed or as a mission to be fulfilled, showing unlimited sympathy for those who suffer. Their love tends to be excessively loyal, often to the point of a domineering and despotic overprotectiveness. The loss of controls results in a full-blown schizophrenic episode, driven by uncontrollable hatred (Bellak and Loeb, 1969; Hill, 1955; Jackson, 1960; Wolman, 1961; 1970).

Victims of Inconsistency

A particularly malevolent kind of parenting is that which swings from one polar extreme to the other, typically from overprotection to outright rejection. Most clinical studies stress the role of the mother, insofar as mothers spend more time with the children, especially when the children are very young, but fathers play a significant role in this rejecting-accepting familial pattern as well (see Wolman, 1961).

Some of these mothers never wanted to be mothers in the first place; some resent their husbands and feel that the child stands in the way of their escape route from marriage; many see the child as an overwhelming burden; some show unmistakable preference for another sibling; others are incapable of loving anyone but themselves.

These mothers are never entirely consistent in their rejection. Typically, when the child is severely ill or badly hurt, the rejecting mother, torn by guilt feelings, showers the child with affection. However, her love is of short duration and as soon as the child recovers, he feels rejected again.

The rejected-accepted child can't help blaming himself for not being loved. Eventually he becomes a "love-addict" (Fenichel, 1945), idolizing the mother and at the same time hating her for rejecting him. His prevailing mood is one of depression, that is, self-directed hatred combined with self-love and self-pity. His experiences teach him that he can win maternal love only by the evocation of compassion; thus self-defeat appears to be the only road to love and happiness. A child who has been patterned in this manner will become a depressive, with intermittent periods of elation associated with his misfortunes.

The dysmutual, depressive type corresponds to Freud's erotic type. He overextends himself in love for others as the hypervectorial schizophrenics do, and when rejected, he feels hostile, as do the hyperinstrumental psychopaths. The depressive dysmutuals expect their love to be returned with a high rate of interest; when in love they are hyperaffectionate, but, if not repaid in full, their love turns to hatred with remarkable facility. By the same token, the self-directed love which is considerable, turns easily into hate upon narcissistic injury, and frequently leads to suicide attempts. These cyclic mood shifts, reflecting the disbalance in libido and destrudo, present a clinical picture of manic-depressive illness. When these patients feel loved, they believe themselves to be strong and friendly and their mood is elated. When they feel reject- ed, they experience themselves as weak, small, destitute and hostile and their mood is depressed. In a loving mood they resemble Dr. Jekyll; in a hating mood they are Mr. Hyde. Since none of these moods is lasting, the dysmutual creates the impression of being insincere. Actually he swings from extreme honesty to dishonesty, from love to hate, from he- roism to cowardice (Beck, 1967; B. D. Lewin, 1950; Wolman, 1966b).

Sociodiagnostic Categories

It may be useful to compare the three types of disorder on certain significant and observable issues.

The first observation category is (1) *activity and vitality.* Hypervectorials (schizophrenic type) display as a rule less vitality as compared to average normal subjects. They are more precise, pay more attention to detail, but usually ap- pear to be more enervated than other people. The hyperin- strumentals (narcissistic type) are active only when such efforts serve the satisfaction of their needs. The dysmutuals (the depressive type) fluctuate between the extremes of hy- peractivity, and passivity.

(2) Hypervectorial schizophrenics show certain *intellectual peculiarities.* They may be keen, attentive, and alert in one area and show complete lack of interest and apathy in many others. Unless badly deteriorated, when involved in some- thing, they are perceptive, and show a sharp, logical and crit- ical judgment. Hyperinstrumental narcissists are seldom seri- ously involved in anything outside their own immediate needs. Dysmutual depressives can be remarkably alert or ob- livious, depending on their mood.

(3) There does not appear to be any relationship between intelligence and mental disorder. However, certain peculiarities in thought processes are distinguishable by psychological tests, and in extreme cases, even by a simple observation. The hypervectorials overlook gross detail; they are logical (unless deteriorated) but not empirically minded. They are inclined toward abstract thinking and an overemphasis on minute detail with little regard to reality.

Hyperinstrumentals with a high I.Q. are shrewd rather than wise and cunning rather than planning. Dysmutuals are rarely as shrewd as hyperinstrumentals or as precise as hypervectorials; they are, as a rule, more practical than the hypervectorials and more philosophical than the hyperinstrumentals.

(4) Food is overdetermined for hyperinstrumentals; they tend to be exceedingly finicky eaters, often ritualizing the eating process. Either they refuse to eat, overeat or mess with food. Dysmutuals eat quickly and excessively.

(5) Hypervectorials are given to sleep disturbances and often cannot *sleep* the night through. The hyperinstrumentals sleep deeply and for long stretches at a time. Dysmutuals either fall asleep whenever they feel depressed or are unable to sleep when excited. Depressive psychotics wake up very early in the morning hating themselves and the world; in the early morning hours the danger of suicide is high.

(6) Hypervectorials do not care for themselves but worry inordinately about what other people will think about them. In milder cases there is a meticulous attention to neatness. Neglect in personal cleanliness and appearance is usually a sign of serious deterioration, often the onset of manifest schizophrenia. Hyperinstrumentals do not care much about personal cleanliness, though they are concerned with their external appearance. Dysmutuals swing from one extreme to another, from hyperconcern about personal care to a complete self-neglect.

(7) In regard to material possessions, hyperinstrumentals are acquisitive, hypervectorials retentive, dysmutuals inconsistent. Hyperinstrumentals take whatever they can and are unwilling to share; hypervectorials cannot part with their possessions but will occasionally spend money on others rather than on themselves; dysmutuals are acquisitive and spendthrifts at the same time.

(8) Hyperinstrumentals work hard only when driven by fear or reward and will cheat whenever they can. Hypervectorials are conscientious workers. Dysmutuals' efficiency depends on their fluctuating moods.

(9) Hypervectorials worry whenever successful and blame themselves whenever they *fail.* Hyperinstrumentals are boisterous in success and cowardly and subservient in defeat. Dysmutuals exaggerate with joyful self-praise in success and with brooding and self-accusations in defeat.

(10) Hypervectorials frequently neglect their own health notwithstanding pain. Hyperinstrumentals are highly sensitive to pain and overconcerned with their health. Dysmutuals vacillate from one extreme to the other.

(11) Schizophrenics and all other hypervectorials fear their own hostile impulses. Hyperinstrumentals distrust and fear people. Dysmutuals in elation have no fear; in depression they fear everything.

(12) Feelings of inadequacy and dissatisfaction with oneself accompany practically all mental disorders. The hypervectorials feel most dissatisfied with themselves because they are convinced of their hostility and worry that others will blame them for it. Hyperinstrumentals are not concerned with what others think about their moral standards unless there is a danger of being punished. As one psychopath put it, "I feel either as a tiger that can tear the world apart or as a vegetable anyone can step on." The dysmutuals feel strong and friendly when accepted; when rejected, they feel weak and hostile to themselves and to the outer world. The self-esteem

of hypervectorials depends largely on whether their love has been accepted, i.e., whether the parental figures or love-objects have accepted their love. The dysmutuals need to receive love from everywhere and are never satiated.

Social Behavior

(1) Hypervectorials sense or empathize with the feelings of others; hyperinstrumentals are concerned only with themselves; dysmutuals are less empathic than hypervectorials and more so than hyperinstrumentals.

(2) Hypervectorials excel in sympathy; hyperinstrumentals have no sympathy for others. Dysmutuals are either hyper-sympathetic and self-sacrificing or they swing back to an almost psychopathic selfishness.

(3) Schizoid hypervectorials are tactful and considerate, but become cruel when they develop character neurosis or manifest schizophrenia. Narcissistic hyperinstrumentals are tactful toward those they perceive as strong, and brutal toward those they perceive as weak. Manic-depressive dysmutuals are oversentimental toward those whose love they seek and tactless and even brutal toward those they don't care for.

(4) Moral rigidity characterizes hypervectorials; lack of morality is typical of hyperinstrumentals; moral inconsistency is the sign of dysmutualism. Hyperinstrumentals have no moral principles whatsoever; they are opportunists. Dysmutuals can be hypermoral in one situation and totally immoral in another.

(5) Hypervectorials blame themselves; hyperinstrumentals blame others; dysmutuals blame themselves and others.

(6) Hyperinstrumentals lie whenever it is profitable. Hypervectorials lie rarely—only when they are afraid people may think they are bad or stupid. Dysmutuals lie frequently, usually for self-aggrandizement, telling exaggerated stories about their victories and defeats.

(7) Hypervectorials perceive others as better, stronger,

smarter than themselves. Their sense of inferiority often generalizes to those for whom they feel responsible, especially their own children. Hyperinstrumentals divide the world into those whom they fear and those whom they exploit. Dysmutuals divide the world into those who love and those who reject.

(8) Hypervectorials are selective in the choice of their friends, but become deeply involved and are unable to break off friendships. A friend to a hyperinstrumental is someone to take advantage of. Dysmutuals easily develop strong attachments, but their feelings are rarely lasting or persistent.

(9) Hypervectorials are persistent and become deeply involved in sexual love. When their love is not accepted it turns into hate. Dysmutuals easily "fall in love" and hate those who refuse to give them love; they are constantly in search of new love-objects, and their feelings are an ambivalent combination of love and resentment.

(10) Sexual deviations are found in many mental disorders. Psychopaths are frequently polymorphous perverse, i.e., capable of and willing to participate in any type of sexual activity. Schizophrenics have difficulty in sex-identification roles and fear homosexuality. Manic-depressives have a tendency toward impotence, frigidity, homosexuality and other sexual disturbances.

(11) Hypervectorials display hostility when rejected and are unable to deal with inner hostility. Narcissistic hyperinstrumentals are hostile when their needs are frustrated. Dysmutuals display ambivalent hostility, hating friends who do not meet their demands for love. A hypervectorial schizophrenic becomes aggressive when he cannot control his hostile impulses; a hyperinstrumental narcissistic type attacks to rob or to win; a manic-depressive vents his hostility when he feels rejected. The hypervectorial schizophrenics are often themselves hostile but cannot tolerate hostility, blame or

criticism. Hyperinstrumentals accept criticism from whomever they fear. Dysmutuals become aggressive-depressive (that is, hostile toward others and themselves), whenever they are criticized by those from whom they expected love.

When deeply regressed to a level of dementia the hyperinstrumental, narcissistic psychopaths become atavistic; they may regress to bestiality, murder, cannibalism. The dysmutual manic-depressives tend to regress into a sleepy, intrauterine, parasitic existence. The severely regressed hypervectorial schizophrenics withdraw libido from life and, if not taken care of, may die or will themselves to death.

Five Levels of Mental Disorders

The above outlined divisions represent the three main types of disturbed behavior corresponding to what has been traditionally called the schizophrenic and schizothymic type, the manic-depressive or cyclothymic type, and the psychopathic type. These categories also relate to the distribution of libido. In the hyperinstrumental psychopath, the libido is hypercathected in the self. In the hypervectorial schizophrenic, the libido is hypercathected in others. The dysmutual type swings from one extreme to the other.

While social adjustment is a significant criterion in diagnosing the three major types of mental disorder, personality structure together with the degree of cognitive rationality and emotional balance determine the level of clinical pathology.

Distribution of libido and destrudo serves as a guidepost in the distinction of the three types. The distinction of levels or degrees of severity of disorder within each type is based on other aspects of personality structure. The level (neurosis, psychosis, etc.) of a mental disorder, whether it is hyperinstrumental, hypervectorial, or dysmutual depends on the topographic aspects of personality, that is the unconscious, preconscious, and conscious together with the relative position of the mental apparatus, that is, the id, ego and super-ego.

Such a system will follow along horizontal lines, classifying all mental disorder in accordance with the two above-mentioned criteria, topography and apparatus. Five levels of pathology can be distinguished, starting from *neurosis,* through *character neurosis, latent psychosis, manifest psychosis,* toward the complete *dementia* or collapse of the mental structure.

Neuroses are characterized by repression of unconscious material and the struggle of the ego against the pressures stemming from the id and superego. A profound feeling of anxiety accompanies the mounting tensions. In neurosis the ego still clings to reality in warding off the inner pressures.

In character neurosis, as it were, the neurotic symptoms "take over." The ego does not fight any more insofar as it has come to terms with the symptoms. Primary and secondary gains dominate the dismal picture which is further characterized by a "character armor" that serves as a protective shell. Character neurotics develop a set of permanent, rigid attitudes.

In psychosis the ego fails in its tasks of reality testing and of control of emotions and motility. In neurosis and character neurosis most symptoms are "ego protective." The ego-protective symptoms represent the efforts of the ego to preserve its role as the controlling apparatus. Ego-deficiency symptoms develop in psychoses, bearing witness to the loss of contact with reality and failure of the ego in its control of the id. In the latent phase of psychosis the ego is still engaged in a losing battle, but when the protective symptoms can no longer protect the ego, a full-blown psychosis develops. In neurosis the individual is torn by inner conflicts and anxieties; character neurosis can be compared to a state of a bottled-up fright; psychosis is a state of panic.

In character neurosis the ego accepts the neurotic symptoms as if they were the best protective shell against further deterioration and eventual breakdown. Sometimes character neurosis prevents further erosion and overt psychosis. However, it does not prevent it all the time and in all cases.

Differential diagnosis should take into consideration both the vertical and horizontal lines of division. The vertical lines discern three types of mental disorder namely, the hyperinstrumental, the dysmutual, and the hypervectorial. These three types correspond respectively to a self-hypercathexis of the libido, cyclic cathexis, and object-hypercathected types. When the five levels are added, 15 clinical pictures emerge, representing the five levels of each type.

The five levels represent degrees of damage caused to the ego. In neurosis the ego is still fighting against the inner pressures, as born witness to by ego-protective symptoms. In character neurosis the ego has already been partly defeated and reconciled with the morbid symptoms which form the core of personality. In latent psychosis, although the battle is practically lost, the ego somehow manages to preserve some vestiges of its control over the mental apparatus. In manifest psychosis the defeated ego exercises no control over the mental apparatus; the unconscious floods the conscious, and the individual is at the mercy of his irrational impulses. On the dementive level the total personality structure is in a state of shambles.

According to the five-level plan, the hyperinstrumental psychopathic disorders can be divided into (a) *narcissistic hyperinstrumental neurosis* in which the neurotic personality structure (topography and mental apparatus) is geared to the struggle of the ego against powerful instinctual forces that violate the reality principle. Fear of external danger leads to symptom-formation and escape into illness; many cases of so-called anxiety neurosis and traumatic neurosis fall into this category. The second level of hyperinstrumentalism is represented by the (b) *narcissistic hyperinstrumental character neurotics,* who give an impression of being pleased with their extreme selfishness and neurotic symptoms, from which they derive primary and secondary gains, and about which they rationalize. On the third level the "armor" can no longer help and the (c) *latent psychopathic (narcissistic) psychotics* are forced to act out their primitive impulses. The ego is shattered and the instinctual drives excercise decisive influence. It is the uncontrollable *haltlos* type of behavior, with little if any inhibitions, leading to manifest antisocial behavior. The fourth level is the (d) *hyperinstrumental psychosis* or *moral insanity.* This represents a total victory of secondary narcissism and object-directed destrudo. Many cases described in the literature as criminally insane belong to this category. The fifth and last level is the (e) complete *dementia* encountered in jails or in mental institutions. In times of social upheaval such as war, famine, etc., such individuals have been known to regress to animal-like behavior.

The dysmutual manic-depressive type can be presented on a similar five-level scheme. The first is the neurotic level; it is the (a) dysmutual neurosis, inclusive of hysteria with its inconsistencies, changing moods, and dramatic personality dissociations in the style of the Dr. Jekyll and Mr. Hyde model. Following are the (b) cycloid (or hysteroid) dysmutual character neurosis; the (c) latent dysmutual or manic-depressive psychosis and finally (e) the dementive stages of a deep regression to a prenatal type of behavior.

The hypervectorial schizophrenic type can also be divided into five levels, starting with (a) hypervectorial neurosis, inclusive of the obsessive-compulsive neurosis, characterized by severe superego and guilt feeling; then (b) hypervectorial or schizoid character neurosis that uses compulsions as protective shell; (c) latent schizophrenia when the ego exercises tenuous control; and (d) manifest schizophrenia when the ego loses the battle and regresses; and finally the (e) dementive stage. On the level of dementia the differences between the three types are less pronounced. When a house is completely destroyed, it doesn't make much difference whether it was by fire, bombs, or artillery shells.

These five levels are not static entities. If mental disorders are, as it is hypothesized in this volume, a product of disbalanced libido and destrudo cathexes, and this disbalance has been brought about in the process of social interaction, further interaction between the disturbed individual and his environment may be either detrimental or beneficial. In the final analysis, psychotherapy is an interaction process aimed at the restoration of a normal personality structure (see last chapter.)

Deterioration Processes

The course of any mental disorder depends upon at least seven groups of determinants: (1) the predisposing factors, i.e., the constitutional endowment of the individual in terms of heredity, social and cultural factors, etc.; (2) the specifically noxious pathogenic factors in one's life history. (3) the time when these factors, conflicts, frustrations, etc. began to act upon the individual and the developmental stage when the main damage was done—a factor unduly emphasized by Abraham; (4) the personality structure of the individual and his frustration tolerance threshold; (5) What happened later on in terms of compensation, aggravation, generalization, etc. of the initial damage; (6) the nature of the damage, in terms of degree and magnitude; (7) cultural influences that may facilitate certain types or levels of mental disorder.

In brief, only a careful study of all seven factors can determine the continuity or discontinuity of the deterioration processes in each individual case. In some cases of hypervectorialism there has been a gradual transition from the level of neurosis, through all four levels leading to total dementia. This group is apparently the most vulnerable, for an abundant object cathexis leads to a dangerous impoverishment of the mental system. In some instances, the hypervectorial process starts early in childhood and the individual has no chance to develop neurotic defenses. This is true of early childhood schizophrenia.

Hyperinstrumentalism probably offers less opportunity for severe deterioration from level to level in that the strong self-cathexis provides a protective shell. I can recall a group therapy session where a latent schizophrenic said to a psychopath: "You will last forever; your only worry is yourself, your comfort, your pleasure." Undoubtedly, there is some seed of truth in this observation. However, even psychopaths, when exposed to repeated disappointing encounters and excessively unfavorable life circumstances, begin to deteriorate.

The dysmutual manic-depressive type falls between these two categories. There is less danger of early psychotic development than in the hypervectorial type, but a greater risk of its occurrence than is true of the hyperinstrumental.

One must therefore arrive at a qualified acceptance of the continuum hypothesis. It is to be borne in mind that this hypothesis does not constitute a hard-and-fast rule. Under certain circumstances conducive to breakdown, an individual will move step by step toward disaster, unless there is successful intervention. However, in other cases, there may be sudden collapse of the mental apparatus or conversely, permanent arrest before the deteriorative process has made any significant advances.

The three types and five levels require a more detailed description. But first, some remarks on symptom formation.

Life Histories

The story of each individual life assumes its shape according to the peculiarities of his social environment. Fixation and regression, two key factors in Freud's theory of neurosis, are produced by gratifications and frustrations of libido at each respective stage. These gratifications and frustrations are a product of social interaction, chiefly between the child and his parents. The sociologically oriented Adler, Horney and Sullivan went even further than Freud in emphasizing the importance of parent-child relationships.

These early social relationships definitely affect the child's personality. Actually we do not know exactly how these changes take place. We may only hypothesize that there is a combination of several factors, to wit: (1) genetically determined developmental tendencies common to the species; (2) developmental potentialities of each individual determined by his particular set of genes received from his parents. Mental abilities, special talents and dispositions and the total constitution of the individual belong to that category; (3) the interaction between the organism and his environment.

The last factor is of special significance in that the general and individual genetically determined potentialities are ultimately affected by this interaction which determines phenotypical development. Even the best seed will not take root in barren soil. The human neonate is poorly prepared to struggle for survival and desperately needs help and care, milk and love. When the newborn does not receive the necessary emotional supplies, he may try to adjust to the barren and unfriendly environment. Mental disorder is related to the efforts to adjust to malevolent conditions; by and large, it is an effort that has failed.

Conditioning and Cathexis

The interaction between the organism and its social environment can be presented as a stimulus-response continuum in accordance with Pavlov's theory of conditioning. Accordingly, morbid patterns of overt and covert behavior are conditioned by noxious stimuli associated with the parents and other significant adults. Yet the conditioning theory, whether Pavlov's, Tolman's, Hull's or Skinner's, cannot fully explain the formation of abnormal patterns of behavior. Many people enjoy alcoholic drinks but only some of them become alcoholics; obviously there is more to alcoholism than simple reinforcement.

Although an existing symptom can be reinforced, the choice of symptoms lies largely outside the realm of conditioning. However, the persistence of symptoms which appear to go unreinforced raises additional questions. Perhaps if we regard symptom formation as having a survival function we can better understand its proliferation, although it could be argued that survivalistic behaviors are basically reinforcing.

Pavlov never denied the idea of innate instinctual forces. The main reflex or instinct, wrote Pavlov (1928) was the instinct of life. This general instinct for life can be divided into *positive movement* reflexes toward conditions favorable for survival and *negative movement* reflexes guarding the organism against injury. I have stated it another way. There is one instinctual force, "Lust for Life," which is divided into a life-promoting force, Eros, and a destructive force, Ares. Both instinctual forces, Eros and Ares, serve life through the investment of their respective energies, libido and destrudo, into objects (i.e., cathexis). Normally, cathexes are more or less balanced. When the child is exposed to adverse conditions, his cathexes become disbalanced. Such a cathexis of libido or destrudo follows the main instinctual objective, survival, but fails to serve its purpose in that it is morbid.

Symptom formation serves a kind of morbid adjustment, as if without the symptoms, the organism would be worse off. Mental disorder may offer certain gains and serve as an escape from real trouble into imaginary dangers. *Primary gain* is manifested in the alleviation of inner tension; *secondary gain* is expressed in the winning of social approval. When an

TABLE 3

CLASSIFICATION OF
PSYCHOSOCIOGENIC MENTAL DISORDERS

	NARCISSISTIC-HYPERINSTRUMENTAL TYPE (I)	DEPRESSIVE-DYSMUTUAL TYPE (M)	SCHIZO-HYPERVECTORIAL TYPE (V)
Neurotic Level	Hyperinstrumental Neurosis (Narcissistic neuroses)	Dysmutual Neurosis (Dissociations, hysterias, and depressions)	Hypervectorial Neurosis (Obsessional, phobic, and neurasthenic neuroses)
Character Neurotic Level	Hyperinstrumental Character Neurosis (Narcissistic character)	Dysmutual Character Neurosis (Depressive and hysteric character)	Hypervectorial Character Neurosis (Schizoid and obsessional character)
Latent Psychotic Level	Latent Hyperinstrumental Psychosis (Psychopathic narcissism bordering on psychosis)	Latent Dysmutual Psychosis (Borderline depressive psychosis)	Latent Vectoriasis Praecox (Borderline and latent schizophrenia)
Manifest Psychotic Level	Hyperinstrumental Psychosis (Psychotic psychopathy and moral insanity)	Dysmutual Psychosis (Manifest depressive psychosis)	Vectoriasis Praecox (Manifest schizophrenia)
Dementive Level	Collapse of Personality Structure		

individual develops compulsions to ward off unbearable obsessive thought, it is primary gain. When an individual's mind goes blank to avoid responsibility and reproach, it is secondary gain.

As long as the precarious balance of libido and destrudo cathexes is preserved, as long as hatred is kept under reasonable control and love for oneself is balanced with love for others, one is more or less mentally healthy. Again, it is to be emphasized that no one is perfectly balanced or balanced all the time. If there is progressive regression and deterioration, object-directed and/or self-directed destrudo will dominate the personality.

The following chapter will describe in detail the three paths taken by the three libidinal types: the obsessional-hypervectorials' road to schizophrenia, the narcissistic-hyper-instrumentals' road to psychopathy, and the erotic-dysmutuals' road to depressive psychosis.

✖ 7 ✖

Fallen Angels

The Schizogenic Mother

During the last 20 years scores of books and papers have dealt with the mothers of schizophrenic patients. Although descriptions of these mothers have included a multitude of personality types, temperament, cultural backgrounds and socioeconomic status, a basic picture emerges. In all cases, the mothers were self-conscious individuals, ridden by inner anxieties and fear of others, typically perceiving themselves as being weak and threatened by the outside world. In an attempt to counteract their fears, they became manipulative and controlling, as if dictatorship could allay their fears and anxieties. Although the tendency to manipulate others is perhaps their outstanding trait, this tendency is not limited to any particular clinical type (Alanen, 1958, 1960; Arieti, 1955; Bowen, 1960; Cheek, 1964; Davis, 1961; Esman et al., 1959; Fleck, 1971; Framo, 1962; Farina, 1960; Goldfarb, 1961; Haley, 1962; Kanner and Eisenberg, 1957; Lidz et al., 1955; Nuffield, 1954; Wolman, 1961; 1965b; 1966a; 1970).

Before the first child was born, these women tried to control, overprotect, and manipulate their husbands, ultimately forcing them into the role of a child. They were demanding and authoritarian, easily reversing their overprotective attitude to resentment whenever it became apparent that their smothering attentions were not properly appreciated. I should like to stress that none of the mothers of schizo-

167

phrenic patients I have interviewed was a "rejecting" mother. None were guilty of abandonment, neglect or indifference to the needs of the child.

Three decades of private and hospital practice, in addition to research, have brought me into contact with a great number of patients and members of their families. The present book, especially chapters 7 through 9, is based on my own clinical observations. As stated above, the in-depth interviews conducted with parents of mental patients reveal a variety of personality types, but the mothers of schizophrenics represent an almost homogeneous group. In reply to all my questions, the mothers had one all-pervasive answer. They uniformly described their great love for the schizophrenic child. They never missed an opportunity to tell the child how good and self-sacrificing they were but in return demanded unlimited gratitude and unconditional obedience. They spread their wings, like colonial powers, to protect and to exploit, to give and to prevent growth, to nurture and to bind, to feed and to swallow (cf. Bettelheim, 1967). They were *martyr-tyrants* who imposed their tyranny and extorted blind obedience through true or pretended suffering and by binding their victims with permanent indebtedness. Any effort at rebellion was squelched by vehement parental accusations which never failed to create in the child a profound feeling of guilt (Hill, 1955).

Mothers of schizophrenics go to great lengths to demonstrate the extent of their suffering and make much of their illnesses, either real or imagined. Most of these mothers hated their husbands and maintained that they would have "run away," but "for the sake of the children." Some women, hating the social and economic success of their husbands, claimed that they had married basically inferior men. They typically portrayed themselves as suffering, poor, rejected, betrayed human beings. Never would an opportunity be missed to communicate their misery to the preschizophrenic child, who was forced to become his mother's confessor and sometimes protector (Waring and Ricks, 1965; Weakland, 1960).

People who genuinely suffer will generally make some attempts to avoid or at least reduce the intensity of their pain. On the contrary, the mothers of schizophrenics appear to heighten the effects of their suffering in order to prove their martyrdom. Some of them neglected their own physical health in what could only be described as an ostentatious manner, pretending that they had no time to visit a doctor, or claiming that "it would not help." They expressed the hope that their children would realize how "unfair" they have been to their self-sacrificing mother.

It is irrelevant to a child whether the mother is actually ill or only pretending. The child who becomes schizophrenic trusts his mother and accepts her statements on face value.

Little, if any freedom, and no independent action was permitted children who became schizophrenic. Most were strictly supervised and forced to become "model children." Privacy, in terms of living space or property, was an unknown concept to these children. One patient, even at the age of 24 had to obey all her mother's demands; another 20-year-old was not permitted to make her choice of dresses. A man of 25 could not leave home without giving his mother a detailed report of his every movement—the where, when, and what of his plans. In short, the mothers of schizophrenic patients were self-styled dictators, totally convinced of their own righteousness, and deluded by the belief that they wanted only what was best for their children. Demanding absolute obedience and conformity, they frequently punished the child for disobedience, but even punishment could not erase the child's guilt. One such mother, given to hitting her child, complained that "he made [her] sick and [she] would die soon because of him." Another mother used to beat her daughter for minor transgressions and cry for months that she

had a monstrous daughter who "killed her own mother."
When the preschizophrenic child behaved as any other normal child would, he was accused of being unfair, ungrateful,
unjust, and cruel to his poor, sick, self-sacrificing mother
(Waring and Ricks, 1965; Wolman, 1957).

Mothers of schizophrenics were masters at implainting
guilt feelings in their children regardless of the child's supposed offense. Whenever the child had a quarrel with another child, he would be blamed by his mother for starting
the fight. Even when the preschizophrenic child proved that
he was attacked, his mother replied that had he been wiser
and more understanding he could have avoided the fight. If
the child received good marks in school, they were taken for
granted as something to be expected but not to be praised.
When the child failed, he was harshly criticized for not exercising enough insight, tenacity, self-control and effort.

Perhaps the most important trait common to all of these
schizogenic mothers was their subtle hostility to the child.
Although these children were constantly being punished for
one thing or another, even the most brutal punishments were
mild in comparison to the ubiquitous threat of death of the
mother. It is this imminent sense of doom which leads to the
unbearable feelings of guilt in the child.

The Schizogenic Father

The fathers of schizophrenic patients were not necessarily
hostile to their wives or children, but most of them felt neglected at home and competed with their children for the
wife's love and attention. Some of them were quite successful
in their professional lives but at home they failed to exercise
any leadership whatsoever and acted as if they were themselves children, rather than husbands and fathers. Thus, one
young preschizophrenic girl brought home good marks from
school; her father interrupted the conversation to relate his

own successes in childhood. Another father could not stand his son's "boastful talk." Many of these fathers resented their children's college studies. None offered their children protection and guidance; none made the child feel secure at home. Many complained about unhappy marriages but seldom had the courage to end them.

We can distinguish four types of morbid paternal behavior. Some fathers of schizophrenics tried to win their wives' love and attention through the role of "helpless, sick child." Some tried to accomplish the same by playing the prodigy, the "favorite child." Other fathers fought bitterly for their social position at home by playing the "rebellious child" role. The last group gave up the fight but did not give up hope; they were the "runaway" children who did not run too far. The methods used by the fathers were diverse, but the objective was always the same: to be the beloved, admired, only child of his wife, to the exclusion of his own children.

Many fathers resented being fathers and competed overtly with their preschizophrenic children for the favors of their wives. One father competed and fought with his daughter at the dinner table for an additional serving of dessert. Another would grab his little son's toys. In each case, the father tried to prove to his wife that he was nicer, better, smarter, or sicker than his children, and that he deserved all the attention the child was receiving.

One father used to display his drugs and medicines whenever his child was sick as if to say, "I am sicker than you." Another father did not approach the bed of his sick child out of fear of contagion. When a preschizophrenic child boasted his success in foreign language studies, his father started to study Latin to show his wife that he could master a more difficult language.

The schizogenic father is basically narcissistic, continuously concerned with his own problems, hardships, and achievements. He typically ignores the child although some

are manifestly hostile. Frustrated instrumentalism leads easily
to overt hostility. When a preschizophrenic girl broke her leg
and was brought home by neighbors, the irate father slapped
her face for "what she was doing to [him]" (i.e., forcing him
to take care of her). Some of the fathers appeared eager to
beat the "bad child," either to please mother, or as an act of
revenge against the child's loyalty to her, or without any
apparent reason.

Some fathers were overtly seductive toward their own
daughters. Having failed to win their wives' affections or
motherly ministrations, they turned to their daughters for
these purposes. Finding it easier to play the role of the "hurt
hero" with the child, the father would become physically
abusive to the wife because she "was mean to his nice little
girl." Such fathers would engage in overtly sexual activities
with their daughters, and might even engage in actual intercourse, although this practice was more frequent in the lower
socioeconomic classes.

Despite the various destructive attitudes these fathers
demonstrated toward their children (jealousy, rivalry, neglect, hostility, seduction, exploitation, etc.), the children har-
bored remarkably little hatred or resentment in kind. Rather
the schizophrenic perceived the father as a weak and friendly
or weak and unfriendly individual, rejected or terrorized by
mother. Thus, a prominent pattern emerges of considerable
sympathy toward the "poor daddy," regardless of his brutality. Fearing mother, with her merciless demands and scolding
criticism, they tried to team up with the father in the hopes
that there would be greater strength with an ally at their
side.

Pathology of Marriage

In my research work on schizophrenia (Wolman, 1966a), I
interviewed a large number of parents of schizophrenic pa-

tients. A feature common to all these parents was extensive complaints about the lack of understanding, consideration, and tender care they had expected, and often demanded, from their marital partners. The tone, the character of the complaints, and the nature of the disappointment were all indicative of a childlike demand. It would appear that these men and women required of their marital partners that which was beyond the scope of reasonable expectations. They wanted to receive love, affection, admiration, and protection, but were prepared to give little in return. In short, they wanted to be respectively mothered and fathered by their wives and husbands and, when frustrated, drew their children into the conflict.

None of these mothers accepted marriage as an equal partnership and all of them expected more than marriage could offer. Initially they had hoped that their husbands would prove to be omnipotent "dream-fathers," who would be able to satisfy their childish fantasies. When disappointed, these women assumed the dominant role in the family, but with a vengeance. They became tyrannical and manipulating, and held nothing but contempt for the husband who failed to become the ideal father.

With the birth of the first child, the situation became markedly exacerbated. The mothers placed excessive demands on their husbands, requesting extensive help in the household, unlimited attention and consideration, and an exaggerated amount of moral support. It is quite possible that were their husbands more considerate, more supportive, less narcissistic and more rational, these women could have become adequate mothers. But since their husbands failed lamentably, both as husbands as well as fathers, the women became even more domineering, more dictatorial, more demanding, venting their frustrations on the child with the tyrant-martyr attitude described above. They expected to receive from the child what they failed to receive from their husbands, and entangled the child in a web of frustrated sexual needs and hurt emotions. In most instances the mothers of schizophrenics evaded sexual relations with their husbands. A typical pattern was the use of sex as reward and its denial as punishment.

Thus a vicious cycle evolved in which the husbands, feeling neglected and rejected by their wives, maintained that the wives gave all their love to the child. The wives, disappointed by their unfriendly and uncooperative husbands, turned marital relations into a cold, detached coexistence with the husband, an overt tug-of-war, or total denial. In such an atmosphere it became patently obvious to the child that his parents were enemies. The most severely disturbed children were those whose parents' hatred manifested itself in verbal and physical abuse.

As described above, these fathers and mothers developed peculiar, nonparental attitudes toward their children. The fathers became either competitive or seductive, most often competitive with their sons and seductive with their daughters, as will be discussed later. Since overt hate causes more damage than inadequate love, the number of early childhood schizophrenic cases of boys is higher than that of girls.

The mothers developed either a parasitic-symbiotic or a hostile-protective attitude toward the child. The symbiotic mother did not offer her child a chance to develop his or her own personality. Even worse was the situation where mother involved herself in a tug-of-war with father whereby she "protected" the child from the father while at the same time expressing overt hatred for "his" child. None of these mothers was cold or detached; on the contrary, all were rather overinvolved and tried to "conquer" the child, either by a symbiotic web that destroyed the child's desire for independence, or by tearing him down in protective hostility.

There is no evidence that schizogenic fathers and mothers belong to any specific pathologic category. However, it is their interrelations which are pathologic. Whatever their individual personality deviations had been, the outstanding feature of mother's attitude to father was hostility. No mother in this group ever tried to hide her profound disappointment in her husband. They referred to their husbands as stupid, lazy, selfish, and invariably blamed them for the patient's troubles. From the patients there were reports of obscene language, violence and physical assaults at home. In the lower socioeconomic groups studied at the hospital, the language was even more profane and physical violence more frequent.

Children Without Childhood

Not all children of schizogenic parents became schizophrenic. Sometimes it was only the first-born child whom the parents chose as the target of their devastating "love"; sometimes other siblings were involved as well. The child from whom the parents expect love or who is forced to give love, invests his emotional energy too early and too lavishly; thus very little energy is left over to be invested in the ego.

An inadequate self-cathexis of libido affects pain-pleasure tolerance. That the schizophrenic has high tolerance for pain suggests that he is less self-preservatory. Pleasure is associated with discharge of abundant energy. The self-invested libidinal energy of schizophrenics is scare; hence, the exhaustion, disillusionment, and flatness.

The *pleasure principle* refers to immediate discharge of energy and immediate gratification of needs. As we develop we learn to act in accordance with the *reality principle* and give up the immediate gratification of needs for a future, more rewarding and less threatening gratification. The preschizophrenic child is coerced into renouncing his pleasure principle without any compensation. He is forced to please his parents, to control his impulses, and to become a model child. An early bowel control and striving for perfection are the usual patterns of preschizophrenics, especially on the neurotic level.

Such lavish object cathexis of libido cannot be indefinitely sustained. Gradually or suddenly the preschizophrenic begins to feel tired, disgruntled and discouraged. As the deterioration process sets in, they begin to fail in their household and occupational duties, often neglecting their physical appearance.

A child who believes that his parents are weak but friendly, is less likely to become severely disorganized than one who sees his parents as evil. When one of the parents presents the other as contemptible, and if the child accepts the characterization (especially, if it is the mother), all his self-sacrifice appears to have been in vain, and a rapid deterioration may ensue (Arieti, 1955; Wolman, 1966a).

Sex

Schizogenic parents are seductive and incestuous. The mother expresses great love for her little son, advertising her willingness to sacrifice everything for him. Often she will form an alliance with the preschizophrenic child against the father. In such an atmosphere there is little if any chance for a resolution of the Oedipus complex, and the child may never outgrow his incestuous desires.

Latent and manifest schizophrenic males typically fear and avoid women—especially those who are feminine and attractive. Fantasies combining sex and violence are common insofar as the barrier between libido and destrudo is weak. When the defenses crumble, the destrudo becomes the dominant force. Hence the phenomenon of the withdrawn schizophrenic turned rapist or murderer, driven by powerful impulses beyond his control.

Whereas some female schizophrenics appear to avoid sexuality, others are overtly promiscuous. This self-contradictory pattern is reminiscent of many other contradictions in schizophrenia. One explanation is that because there is so much anxiety in connection with sexuality, a tremendous amount of energy is bound up in repression and rigid self-imposed controls. Thus, when the control apparatus fails, these heretofore pent-up impulses are unleashed indiscriminately.

Homosexuality

Homosexual tendencies have been observed in varying degrees in most ambulatory and hospitalized cases of schizophrenia. The severity of the homosexual conflict depends largely upon the extent of paternal seductiveness and interparental strife. A 32-year-old hospitalized, paranoid schizophrenic man complained that he was attracted to men and feared becoming homosexual. Background information revealed a seductive father who had tried to "win over" the son in fights with the mother.

Homosexuality in male schizophrenics represents a combination of wish and fear, produced by the schizophrenic confusion of sex and age roles. The identification with the mother and a concomitant attraction to the father creates a conflict between homosexual wish and fear that the wish may come true. It should be noted that not all homosexuals fear homosexuality; some of them, especially the psychopaths, yield easily to homosexual temptations.

The homosexual tendency is also frequent in female schizophrenics. One patient admitted that when she was very disturbed, she attempted sexual relations with another girl. At that time her fear of homosexuality was substantially reduced, and she was not motivated to control her desire to become intimate with a girl who resembled her mother.

The shaky sexual identity of schizophrenics is pointed up in their alternation between masculine and feminine roles which occurs with frequency in their dreams. This blurring of sexual identification appears to be a function of the confused parental roles which did not permit a clear-cut identification with the parent of the same sex.

Hostility

Schizophrenia is an irrational struggle for survival. The fear of losing the overdemanding mother forces the future schizophrenic to invest more and more emotional energy into the relationship in which he assumes the role of lover-protector. This hypervectorial cathexis of libido reduces the individual's own resources and prevents an adequate self-love. When the amount of libido left for self-cathexis drops very low, the energy of hate, the destrudo, takes over. This is, in essence, the core of schizophrenic hostility. Although the schizophrenic's fight for survival is irrational, as long as he engages in the battle, the prognosis is more favorable than is the case when there is withdrawal and resignation from life. In the hebephrenic syndrome of schizophrenic behavior the schizophrenic acts as if he were saying, "I tried to live a normal life, but I had to pay too high a price. Now I am trying to survive while giving up self-control, responsibilities, etc." In the simple deterioration syndrome, the schizophrenic ego has given up the fight for survival altogether.

But why do schizophrenics fight for life in an irrational way?

The preschizophrenic child is constantly restrained, overcontrolled, criticized, and blamed by his mother. As would be true of any other child, he resents his mother and requires ventilation of his hostility in words and deeds. However, whereas the average mother brushes off the occasional outbursts of the child's hostility and offers him soothing reassurance, mothers of schizophrenics exploit the child's tantrums and retaliate with malicious accusations. Thus a typical reaction to her angry child is: "You are killing your mother;

it is because of *your* bad behavior that your mother is sick and will die soon." As a result of this association, the child begins to believe that his hostility may jeopardize his mother's life, that he is the villain who kills his own mother.

The child's fear of his own hostility is constantly fed by his mother's complaints that she is sick and dying, by her accusations that the child "is going to be the death" of her and by the child's fear that he may really hurt his mother to protect himself against her exaggerated demands and merciless criticism.

Fear of one's own hostility in obsessive-compulsive neurosis has been described by Freud (1894, p. 58), Fenichel (1945, p. 284ff) and others. Fenichel emphasized that "not genital but anal-sadistic wishes have to be warded off" in the obsessive-compulsive neurosis.

Hypervectorials try to control hostility with the help of defense mechanisms, such as repression, denial, reaction-formation, and displacement. These defense mechanisms, easily recognized in the formation of obsessive-compulsive neurosis and schizophrenic psychosis, are unconscious barricades erected against one's own hostility. Compulsive behavior keeps in check the obsessive wishes of a hostile and sexual nature. The obsessive-compulsive neurosis and schizoid character neurosis are, respectively, the first and the second steps toward a full, manifest schizophrenia.

There are several behavioral patterns in the destructive behavior of schizophrenics. The first and mildest pattern is *pseudorational*, where the ego applies the defense mechanisms of rationalization and projection, and the destructive energy turns inwardly in self-accusation or outwardly in paranoid accusations of others. Paranoid schizophrenics believe that they fight in self-defense; thus a vestige of reality is preserved.

Another pattern of hostile behavior is the *depressive-aggressive* syndrome, culminating in outbursts of an uncontrollable violence that may become genosuicidal, and driven by the desire to destroy everything and everybody including oneself. The catatonic schizophrenic will set his own house on fire, making no provisions for escape. Some schizophrenics will start a senseless struggle against overwhelming forces, fighting blindly and hurting everyone including themselves.

Depression

Depressive moods are primarily brought about by self-directed aggression, frequently the result of traumatic relationships. Schizophrenics find it particularly difficult to renounce their overcathected love objects. A young, latent schizophrenic was rejected by her lover, who could no longer tolerate her overinvolved attitude. Consequently she developed an intense hatred for him but, at the same time, believed that she deserved to be rejected and thus developed marked feelings of self-hatred which culminated in a severe depression. The more she hated herself, the more she hated her former lover as the cause of her self-hatred. Her self-hatred grew as she became more convinced that it was she who made him hate her. From a psychodynamic point of view, her superego was destroying her ego and a distinct feeling of inadequacy, worthlessness and guilt ensued. These feelings, emanating from within, form the core of endogenous depression, to be distinguished from exogenous depression, which is generated by an aggression coming from an outside source.

Endogenous depression is more painful that exogenous, because one cannot escape an intrapsychic condition by fight or flight. Whereas psychopaths become exogenously depressed whenever they fail in self-protective endeavors, schizophrenic depression is usually endogenous. Its original source was, however, exogenous and, more specifically, sociogenic, for it stemmed from the onslaught of unfair accusations they had been exposed to in childhood. Internalized parental criticism is the constant source of a severe feeling of worthlessness and guilt.

In the dysmutual, manic-depressive disorders, depression is a self-terminating process. The childhood of the manic-depressive was characterized by severe parental rejection, but whenever the child was ill or injured, the rejecting mother became attentive and caring. Therefore the manic-depressive learns to derive secondary gain from his misfortunes.

The situation was entirely different in the childhood of the hyperinstrumental psychopath or the hypervectorial schizophrenic. The psychopath having come to the realization that his mother was totally unconcerned about him, developed a powerful secondary narcissism for self-protection. Hyperinstrumental psychopaths love only themselves and hate whoever stands in their way.

The hypervectorial learned a different lesson. Whenever he failed in a squabble with peers or in scholastic efforts, his mother took the side of his enemies and blamed him, unlike the manic-depressive who learned to win maternal love by self-defeat. The schizophrenic knew that mother loved him, but an unlimited gratitude and renouncement of his own identity was the price he had to pay.

Schizophrenics are less impulsive and less dramatic in their suicidal attempts than are manic-depressives. They rarely commit suicide on the pseudorational level. The danger is substantially increased when there are genosuicidal implications, and great when an "I don't care" mood develops, especially in the simple deterioration syndrome.

The Superego

The superego develops out of fear of parental punishment and need for protection and affection. The child "internalizes" parental prohibitions and identifies with the parental

figures. Conformity with parental demands lays the founda-
tions for social adjustment of the child and for his acceptance
of the cultural value system of his social environment.

In the hyperinstrumental psychopathic disorders, there is
very little if any identification with parents. In the dysmutual
manic-depressive disorders, the identification is tenuous and
the superego fluctuates from permissiveness to a punitive attitude. In the hypervectorial schizophrenic personality structure, the superego plays the role of an absolute, overdemanding, rigid ruler.

Schizophrenic illness may be likened to a fortress erected
against rebellious forces. The garrison of the fortress represents the ego; the rebels, the id. The garrison is controlled by
fanatic leaders who know of no compromise, no concessions,
no realistic evaluation of their own resources, and no consideration for anyone. The superego is represented by dictatorial fanatics.

Under normal conditions the ego accepts the moral guidance of the superego, exercises a rational control over the id,
while maintaining a reasonable equilibrium between the id,
the superego, and the demands of the outer world. In hypervectorial types the superego assumes absolute control over
the ego and insists on a severe restriction of the instinctual
demands of the id. The hypervectorial child is so involved
with his mother that he can relate only marginally to the
outside world. Thus, despite his abilities, his willingness to
learn and his friendliness, he may fail in school work and in
social relations.

There is no lasting joy, no true victory, no sense of
achievement for hypervectorials. Obsessive-compulsive symptoms pile up, fears and phobias multiply, anxieties and guilt
feelings perplex and overwhelm such individuals. They fear
defeat, but cannot enjoy victory because of the fear that success may bring new demands and new obligations. This fear
is based on the prototypical fear that they may not be able to
live up to the demands and expectations of their mothers.

Making decisions presents special difficulties for hypervectorials, for no matter what they decide, there will be criticism from the superego introjects.

In schizogenic families, parental prohibitions and admonitions are often at odds with common sense, offering little if any help in adjustment to real life. Parental restrictions are often whimsical, inconsistent, and irrational, destroying any chance for a sensible and realistic judgment. One mother warned her preschizophrenic child not to cross the street even on a green light until the child was 12; another mother forbade her son to go to school on rainy days but later on blamed him for missing so many classes. The child is caught in a web of forced impossible choices, where for example, obedience is criticized as lack of initiative, but disobedience is seen as an act of defiance. It is this same method which is adopted by the schizophrenic superego; small wonder that the schizophrenic feels doomed when he does and doomed when he doesn't.

Projection is an irrational defense of the ego against the attacks of the superego. When the superego says, "You are hateful," the ego protects itself by saying, "I am not, but I must defend myself against those who hate me."

When the despotic superego presses the ego too hard, the failing ego loses contact with reality and perceives the superego manipulations as if they were coming from without. Some schizophrenics feel that people steal their energies, control their thoughts, and compel them to do things they don't want to do. These *ideas of reference* indicate that the ego has lost most of its contact with reality and has externalized the superego pressures.

A victory of the superego over the ego will result in hallucinations and delusions that one is a super-parent, God-Father, creator-protector or judge-destroyer of the world. Schizophrenic hallucinations carry the voice of the morbid superego.

The Ego

The ego is the guardian of the organism, the link between it and the outer world. In order to accomplish this task the ego performs four functions: (1) control of the cognitive functions by reality testing; (2) control of emotionality by countercathexes; (3) control of voluntary motility, and (4) self-protection.

The severity of a mental disorder depends largely on the damage sustained by the ego. The earlier the damage incurred, the more dangerous it is likely to be. Early childhood schizophrenia or *vectoriasis praecocissima,* is the most severe disorder in the group of hypervectorial disorders. It is a failure of an as of yet undeveloped ego.

While the ego faces external dangers, it must also control the instinctual forces of Eros and Ares. Although both Eros and Ares serve survival, they operate on the principle of impulsive and immediate discharge of energy (the so-called "pleasure principle") and may therefore run into unexpected danger. The ego, which functions on the "reality principle," delays, modifies, or even renounces immediate gratification if there is the possibility of unfavorable consequences.

In the hypervectorial schizophrenic the ego faces two initial difficulties, caused by (1) depletion of emotional energy, resulting from the lavish giving away of love (hypercathexis) and (2) an unbearable pressure from the environment (parents) and from the id, which is the natural reservoir of all mental energies. When the ego cathects a considerable part of its emotional energy in external objects (parents or parental substitutes), the ego itself becomes less self-cathected. The less the ego is cathected, the less it is capable of performing its tasks. At all levels of hypervectorialism there is some deficiency in ego cathexis, but the "undernourished" ego is usually also an "overworked" ego. When the overgrown superego assumes a totalitarian position, the ego must be on constant duty as an ever-obedient servant.

On the prepsychotic levels of hypervectorialism, the picture is typically characterized by a ceaseless striving for perfection, an unrelenting tension, a compulsive need for cleanliness and order, and an ever-present fear of being wrong or losing. The obsessive-compulsives, the schizoid character neurotics and the latent schizophrenics are, as a rule, highly conscientious.

Interestingly, severe physical illness may effect a substantial improvement in schizophrenics. A serious threat to life signals the organism to mobilize its resources for survival. Thus a reasonable normal libidinal balance may be restored. This mobilization of resources in the face of danger may also explain the reaction to shock treatment, i.e., the organism responds to a severe shock with a reversal of cathexes onto the self in the service of self-preservation.

Control of Motility and of Emotionality

Most latent schizophrenics avoid intense human relations because they fear deep emotional involvement. Many refuse to accept human warmth because they fear a repetition of the parental relationship, where they were forced to be the givers. Thus latent schizophrenics will convey the impression of being aloof, cold, shallow and uninterested in other people. Their social encounters have hostile-protective overtones which appear to serve the purpose of discouraging intimate friendship. However, in the event that a hypervectorial does develop friendship or love relationships, he is inclined to take them seriously, usually to the point of overinvolvement.

Hypervectorials tend to overcontrol their motor apparatus; on the preschizophrenic levels their motor control approximates perfection. When there is deterioration, the overcontrolled behavior becomes rigid, and in manifest psychosis symptoms take the form of trembling, rigid postures, tics, clonic and tonic stupors, disturbances of speech and bizarre

mannerisms. These well-known symptoms of manifest schizophrenia point out the inner conflict in the control mechanisms of the motor apparatus.

Self-Esteem

One's self-esteem is a reflection of the relationship between
the superego and ego. When the superego tears the ego
down, the individual experiences feelings of inferiority and
inadequacy; when the superego approves of the ego, a feeling
of power and elation develops.

Tormenting feelings of worthlessness, guilt, and inadequacy are common to all hypervectorials. On a prepsychotic
level they doubt their appearance, intelligence, judgment,
and honesty, blaming themselves for whatever hardships they
or their friends have endured. The attacked ego may invite
external punishment to alleviate the guilt provoked by the
superego. Thus schizophrenics will often provoke fights,
wishing to be defeated and to thereby accept defeat as a deserved punishment.

Lack of self-esteem in hypervectorials differs from the self-
degradation of manic-depressives. The moods of manic-depressives are cyclic, swinging from total despair to total optimism.
In the depressed phase the manic-depressive is self-destructive
and suicidal. In hypervectorials the feeling of inadequacy is
always present, even when there is realistic awareness of their
good qualities. Schizophrenics, compulsives, and other hypervectorials are always highly self-critical, even when successful. The schizotype superego always reminds them that they
should have done more and better. Although the manic-
depressive's superego is hostile to the ego as is true of the
hypervectorial, at moments of utter misery and despair the
superego merges with the ego in a blissful mood, as if repeating the moments of maternal affection.

The mothers of schizophrenics are not overtly hostile; they

love and protect the child who will become schizophrenic, but their "love" is symbiotic and imperialistic. Ultimately, the superego of the schizophrenic resembles the demanding and hypercritical mother which exerts its tyranny on the ego. Although the schizophrenic superego does not aim at the destruction of the ego, it demands an unconditional subservience. Preschizophrenics and schizophrenics live under constant fear that they may have neglected their duties and blame themselves for not being able to be as strong as they feel they have to be in order to protect those whom they love.

Conscious and Unconscious

The balance of the mental state is a most significant diagnostic clue. A conscious-preconscious dominance is a sign of adjusted and controlled behavior. An unconscious-preconscious dominance leads to a neurotic, rigid, and stereotyped behavior.

Unconscious behavior is at odds with external reality and does not process in a logical manner the information it possesses. In the realm of the unconscious, wish and fact are confused, and inner stimuli are mixed with those that come from without. In an unconscious state, the individual does not react in an adjusted way to his physical and social environment, but is guided by irrational fears, wishes and images, and lives in a world of dreams.

Dreams reflect the primary irrational processes of the unconscious. It is in this state that the impossible becomes possible, the forbidden is permissible, and the nonexistent exists. In short, fact and wish are confused as is true of psychosis. In normal waking life conscious controls keep in check the unconscious forces; when the unconscious prevails, behavior becomes irrational and disturbed.

Although rationality is a major prerequisite of mental

health, there need not be complete shutting off of the unconscious. The creative artist is very much in tune with his primary processes as is the psychoanalyst. To use Freud's analogy, the ego resembles a rider who rides on the back of a wild horse, the id. A neurotic fights his horse, a psychotic is overthrown by the horse and trounced, while the well-adjusted individual harnesses the horse and uses it for transportation.

The psychoanalyst is continually exposed to the bizarre communications of his patient's unconscious. Access to the unconscious may become dangerous when one is unable to control the unconscious impulses. This is precisely what happens in the mental disorders of hypervectorials. The emotional climate of their childhood was not conducive to a quiet and balanced life. Parental demands stirred powerful emotional drives in the child, resulting in a series of desperate efforts to control the unconscious impulses of love and hate. It is the failure of these repressive efforts which may lead to the beginnings of a full-blown manifest schizophrenic psychosis.

The weakness of the hypervectorial ego intensifies and aggravates the conflict. The healthy ego grows and thrives on contacts with reality, on reality-testing, on playing an active part in interindividual relationships. Thus the overprotective and parasitic attitude of schizogenic parents further isolates the child limiting his outer contacts and impoverishing his ego.

Another reason for the increased intensity of repressive efforts of the ego is the content and intensity of the unconscious wishes. The peculiar family situation of the hypervectorial child is a powerful stimulant of incestuous and aggressive impulses. These impulses, latent in all of us may be stimulated and brought to a pitch of excitement by the morbid interindividual relationships in schizogenic families. In normal circumstances the incestuous oedipal impulses become aim-inhibited and desexualized during the latency period. Hostility toward the parent of the same sex has been mitigated by love and fear, with gradual "introjection" of the parental image and identification with the parent of the same sex.

This process is highly distorted in hypervectorials. The mother's pseudovectorial, actually parasitic-instrumental attitude, together with the father's overtly instrumental attitude, strongly militate against normal identifications. Hetero- and homosexual impulses are confused, there being no way to break away from the seductive parent of the opposite sex nor to identify entirely with the parent of the same sex. Hence he is unable to even approximate a solution of his oedipal wishes.

In neurosis and character neurosis, the ego strives to ward off unconscious impulses. In latent psychosis, the unconscious elements begin to seep through and the individual feels as if he is existing, so to speak, on the edge of a volcano. In manifest psychosis the unconscious elements flood the conscious and by eruption or erosion the unconscious breaks the dams established by the ego. In the dementive stage the total personality structure is destroyed.

The First Level: Hypervectorial Neurosis

The three types of disorder, each subdivided into five levels, together comprise 15 clinical patterns. These 15 patterns include *all* nonorganic (i.e., functional) mental disorders.

In the hypervectorial disorders the first neurotic level is associated with obsessive-compulsive symptoms. The basic similarity between obsessive-compulsive neurosis and a full schizophrenia has been observed by several investigators among them Bleuler (1911, p. 449ff.). The Rorschach responses of obsessive-compulsive neurotics and neurasthenics are practically the same as the responses of schizophrenics who are not yet too deteriorated. Rigidity, preoccupation with minute details, perseveration and compulsive accuracy have been noticed in both (Klopfer et al., 1956, vol. 2, p. 288).

Not all hypervectorials go through the neurotic stage before becoming psychotic, but the vast majority do develop certain obsessive-compulsive symptoms prior to the onset of psychosis. The obsessive-neurotic may be regarded as a potential schizophrenic, overinvolved with his parents and ravaged by guilt feelings. Depletion of narcissistic libido and an overly punitive superego, which loosens the ego's hold on reality as well as the unconscious impulses, all threaten the neurotic hypervectorial with hypervectorial psychosis (i.e., schizophrenia).

Hypervectorial neurosis is not necessarily limited to the obsessive-compulsive syndrome. At the onset of the hypervectorial process, the ego utilizes a great array of defense mechanisms, the most common of which are compulsions and phobias. With collapse of the ego, compulsions may turn into catatonic automatisms, and phobias into hallucinations; for instance, a fear of and simultaneous unconscious wish for incest may become a hallucination of incest. On the neurotic level "the ego rejects the unbearable idea together with its associated affect and behaves as if the idea never occurred to the person at all. But, as soon as this process has been carried through the person in question will have developed a psychosis and his state can only be described as one of 'hallucinatory confusion,' " (Freud, 1894, p. 58).

On the neurotic level of the hypervectorial disorder the ego tries to please the superego and to overcontrol the id. Compulsions and phobias are the choice ego-protective mechanisms.

Many hypervectorial neurotics experience a paralyzing fatigue due to impoverishment of their own life and the tension originating in the warded-off impulses. These neurasthenic symptoms comprise another syndrome on the neurotic level of hypervectorialism. In neurasthenia one finds the same basic family background, the same hypercathexis in parental figures, the same impoverishment of self-cathexis and the same struggle to please the superego and overcontrol unconscious impulses.

The typical hypervectorial personality structure, with its overdemanding superego and overmobilized ego, is characteristic of all the neurotic syndromes of hypervectorialism. Whether the syndrome is compulsive, phobic, neurasthenic, or some combination thereof, the ego struggles against the unconscious sexual and aggressive impulses, using displacement, reaction formation, undoing, isolation and repression. Guilt feelings, striving toward perfection, rigidity in moral norms and compulsions, all bear witness to the superego pressures.

To summarize, the essence of the hypervectorial neurosis is the struggle of the overmobilized, overworked ego to please the superego and ward off the unconscious id impulses. As long as the struggle goes on, it is neurosis. But not infrequently the ego succumbs and further deterioration takes place.

Character Neurosis

Freud distinguished between cathectic and anticathectic or reactive character formation. When the ego is strong enough, it finds proper outlets for the instinctual impulses and a wholesome, "cathected" character or personality pattern develops. When the ego is unable to cathect or sublimate the instinctual demands, it establishes rigid barriers (armoring) or character defenses. These neurotic defenses reduce anxiety but distort the total personality, thus leading to an impoverished, character neurotic way of life.

The character neurotic piles up one defense mechanism on top of the other, making it increasingly difficult to unravel the initial conflict. In the hypervectorial, or schizoid character neurosis, the initial primary gain of social withdrawal was avoidance of love which could end in disappointment. But this avoidance increases the attacks from the superego, thereby creating more inferiority feelings, and new rationalizations to cover up the earlier ones.

When these rationalizations fail to hold out against the inescapable feelings of failure, denial mechanisms are invoked. The schizoid or hypervectorial character neurotic makes himself believe that he has no feelings for anyone. Thus he appears cold and detached, as if he were devoid of humane feelings.

"Constricted personality" is perhaps the best description of this level of hypervectorial disorder. The hypervectorial (schizoid) character uses rationalized compulsions as an armor. Frugality, for instance, becomes a virtue; a paranoid hate toward minority groups becomes identified with patriotic feelings. Through such mechanisms, the schizoid character becomes proud of his alleged virtues and imaginary services for a true or imaginary cause.

In character neurosis the compulsions turn into a rigid system. Schizoid characters who have achieved leading positions in industry or education, as supervisors, teachers or administrators, are cold, dictatorial, overdemanding and self-righteous. Their behavior is an attempt to force others into the mold created by their rigid superegos.

The hostile attitude maintained by the superego toward the ego will appear, albeit in disguise, as a moralistic and usually fanatical concern. Thus some of the worst crimes against humanity are performed under the guise of high moral standards espoused by the rigid superego. This channelling of intrapsychic hostility into social hostility is one of the outstanding symptoms of character neurosis. Fearing their own hostility, in counterphobic fashion the fear is transformed into a compulsive pursuit of "justice." Of course, it is a highly subjective, self-righteous, dogmatic and dictatorial concept of justice. The entire life of a schizoid character becomes a dull routine, a duty to be fulfilled, ritualistic, self-sacrificing, ultimately empty.

When this "armor" spreads to moral, religious or political issues, the schizoid character becomes a public menace through his self-righteous, domineering and fanatical demands. Professed love has always been an effective disguise for hate, a teaching well-known to religious fanatics. It appears to be easier to hate people in the name of God or Love than it is to love them. Apparently Ares is a more primitive and more basic drive than Eros.

All hypervectorials suffer from a profound feeling of inadequacy, viewing themselves the way their mothers saw them, namely as weak and hostile individuals. When a schizoid character channelizes his hostility into a self-righteous behavior, he in effect becomes a self-appointed saint persecuting the infidels. In the name of whatever ideal or principle he advocates, he acts out his hostile impulses in a way approved by his own superego. Many "holy" wars, crusades, mass persecutions and outbursts of mob violence against the "unfaithful" were generated by schizoid character neurotics.

Some actions of schizoid character neurotics represent a combination of hypervectorial devotion to an abstract cause together with unrestrained aggression. Intrigues, paranoid accusations, litigations, and inciting to violence are common facts of the schizoid existence.

Whereas the schizoid character need not be malicious, he is invariably a constricted personality in search of a morbid outlet for his hypervectorial attitude and his hostility. This strange fusion of hypercathected libido and self-righteous destrudo is the core of the schizoid character neurosis. But this fusion does not necessarily lead to overt hostility. Some schizoid characters refrain from any type of social activity, be it constructive or destructive. These are bitter, hypersensitive, lonely individuals with narrowed interests and apathetic outlooks on life. They are typically moody, depressed, sulky individuals whose libido is faithfully attached to a parental figure and whose destrudo is partially self-directed and partially expressed in a critical, mildly hostile attitude toward the world and its pleasures. Frequently they remain single, leading lonely, flat lives, scornful of everything and everybody, filled with bitterness and cynicism.

Character neurotics deteriorate gradually, their defenses slowly eroding over the years. Often it is someone to whom they have been overly attached who turns on them, thereby precipitating a psychotic break.

Latent Schizophrenia

The emotional life of the latent schizophrenic is cyclic, though the cycles are entirely different from the depression-elation moods of the manic-depressive. Schizophrenic cycles are cycles of positive and negative feeling, dependence and independence, docile self-sacrifice and revengeful rebellion.

Overmobilization of the ego causes a state of almost uninterrupted tension. There is a perpetual striving to perfection in performance, hyperconscientious efforts on the job, over-devotion to daily routine and other compulsive rituals. An overmobilized and tense ego is not conducive to restful sleep; thus insomnia may be regarded as a key signal to an approaching breakdown. The overworked and overmobilized ego fights desperately against the instinctual demands, but it is usually a losing battle. Great parts of the ego are already submerged in the unconscious and, if the erosion continues, a psychotic breakdown is likely.

There are, however, several neurotic-type, ego-protective symptoms in latent schizophrenia. One of them, the feeling of *excessive fatigue*, is actually economical in that it allows for conservation of some emotional energy.

Rigidity, compulsions, phobias, and hypermoralistic attitudes are also ego-protective symptoms because they reduce anxiety and protect the failing ego. Social withdrawal offers avoidance of frustrating and ego-damaging social encounters.

Latent schizophrenia, i.e., the latent psychotic level of hypervectorialism, differs from the neurotic and character neurotic levels by the presence of *ego-deficiency* symptoms, which shall be discussed momentarily. There is no sharp dividing line between the consecutive levels of pathological deterioration, though each consecutive level is characterized by definite personality changes.

Empirically speaking, neurosis and psychosis are two distinct phenomena. In neurosis the ego controls the system with the help of defense mechanisms and at the expense of mental energy.

> The principal injury they [the symptoms] inflict lies in the expense of mental energy they entail and, besides this, in the energy needed to combat them. Where the symptoms are effusively developed these two kinds of effort may exact such a price that the person suffers a very serious impoverishment in available mental energy, which consequently disables him for all the important tasks of life [Fenichel, 1945, p. 214].

Serious failure in reality testing is certainly an ego-deficiency symptom. Paranoid projections, ideas of reference, delusions and hallucinations indicate the failure of the ego to distinguish between inner and outer stimuli. The ego which has been attacked by the hostile-moralistic superego and rebellious id, surrenders to the superego and finds some outlets for the id through externalization of hostility by projection. When hostility is ascribed to others, one can justify his own hostility. Paranoid accusations bestow a vestige of rationality on irrational thinking, the ego thereby exercising partial control over destructive impulses. A schizoid character will utilize neurotic rationalizations to convince himself that he was right in persecuting his alleged enemies. The latent schizophrenic is not as successful in his rationalizations; when he attacks others, his superego is not appeased as is true of schizoid characters, and it mercilessly attacks the ego.

An ego which has lost contact with reality, will perceive the manipulations of the superego as coming from without as a result of externalization and projection. The stronger the superego's pressure, the more estranged the ego from reality, the sooner will ideas of reference set in. In latent schizophrenia the ideas of reference are fleeting and transient, but as soon as they assume frankly delusional proportions it can be assumed that the schizophrenic process has begun.

Hypochondriasis suggests a weakened self-cathexis. The least cathected bodily zones are typically the first to show signs of sickness and send alarm signals. The embattled ego responds to alarms with an increased anxiety. These alarm signals spread throughout the organism creating feelings of emptiness and loss of identity.

Fear of death is prominent in latent schizophrenia. Many latent schizophrenics are dimly aware of their losing battle and actually feel that they "are going crazy." A highly intelligent patient described her feelings as follows: "I know that I am going to pieces. I was reluctant to come to see you, because I feel that as soon as I start to talk about myself, I shall stop existing as myself. I have tried for years to pull myself together, but now I feel I am at the end of my rope. If I go to pieces, will you be able to put me together?"

The loss of identity is related to the loss of ego defenses. In latent schizophrenia the defenses are weak and insufficient. When they collapse, the patient feels that his house has caved in. The unconscious that has already penetrated the conscious and undermined it, now bursts out and floods the conscious.

A psychotic breakdown is usually an escape from self-sacrifice and a relentless hypervectorialism that ultimately lead to disastrous bankruptcy. This escape into a passive, deteriorated mode of existence permits conservation of psychic energy; it is most complete in hebephrenia. The psychotic is in effect saying: "I must survive; if I cannot survive on the conscious level of adulthood, I shall give it up and try to survive as an infant, or an embryo, or an animal. What is the difference after all?"

In the final analysis the psychotic breakdown may be regarded as a victory of life over death, a radical step in the downward adjustment. Thus it is a regression into a state in which survival is still possible.

Manifest Psychosis

The main symptoms of manifest schizophrenia are neglect in personal care, deterioration in intellectual functions, marked decline in self-esteem, depressive moods, social withdrawal, depersonalization, flattened affect, sexual confusion, and inability to control instinctual impulses.

There are four basic schizophrenic syndromes. The first syndrome, *paranoid schizophrenia,* is characterized by the ego's losing contact with reality, leaving the task to the superego. In the second syndrome, *catatonia,* the superego also takes over the motor apparatus. In the *hebephrenic* syndrome the superego is defeated and the id takes over. The *simple deterioration* syndrome is a process of losing life itself.

These four syndromes are descriptive categories roughly corresponding to observable patterns or clusters of symptoms and to personality structure. Sometimes the clinical pattern shifts from one syndrome to another.

The Paranoid Syndrome

Hypervectorials fear their own aggressive and incestuous impulses and consequently hate themselves for harboring such thoughts. Impaired reality testing may lead to the suspicion that mother knows their bad intentions and tries to control them. In paranoid schizophrenia this idea becomes externalized and projected onto other people who supposedly "know" how bad the patient is. Thus the paranoid schizophrenic, believing that the world is hostile and out to trap him, sees no alternative but to fight back. The paranoid syndrome serves this purpose well. The patient becomes suspicious of everything and everybody. When people are nice to him, it is because they want to take advantage, and when they talk among themselves, they are talking about him and conspiring against him.

Paranoid ideas of schizophrenics usually reflect their own sexual and destructive impulses. A schizophrenic woman, who was latently homosexual, accused her husband of raping their daughter. A patient who overtly hated his mother accused her of trying to poison his food. Some paranoid schizophrenics commit murder or even mass murder of their alleged enemies.

The Catatonic Syndrome

In catatonic schizophrenia the superego assumes control of the motor apparatus. Rigid passivity and complete submissiveness are imposed on the organism. The main difference between obsessive-compulsive neurosis and catatonic schizophrenia lies in the ego. As long as the ego exercises control, behavior may be regarded as neurotic. Compulsive neurotics repress their rebellious feelings against tyrannical mothers and develop compulsions to ward off their hostile feelings. Catatonic mannerisms however are controlled by the superego. When one is completely passive, repeating what others say (echolalia) or do (echopraxia), he cannot go wrong and be blamed.

Catatonic symptoms are a product of a desperate struggle between the fear of one's own hostility and the breaking through of that hostility. Echolalia, echopraxia, mutism, stupor and other symptoms reflect the patient's desperate efforts to control his hostile impulses. When these regressive defenses fail, a "terror" type of hostility breaks through. It is the furious rage of a wounded animal that attacks everything and everyone. On that level of regression the destrudo is without a focus; there is no contact with reality.

The choice of symptoms in catatonic schizophrenia is determined by the totality of interactional patterns in the individual's life history.

> . . . in cases of catatonia . . . the parents not only have imposed their will . . . but have also prevented the children from developing the capacity to will, and therefore, to a certain extent, the capacity to act according to their own wishes . . . If these patients make their own decisions, they feel that the mother will be angry, or that the action will turn out to be wrong, and they will feel responsible for the failure . . . One of the frequent methods by which they try to solve their difficulties is by giving up their will and putting themselves completely at the dependency of another person, a symbolic omnipotent mother . . .
>
> If these solutions cannot be found . . . the patients will try to protect themselves from anxiety in any possible way; one frequent method . . . is to resort to compulsive rituals . . . If the ritual is not enough to eliminate anxiety, catatonia will occur and will abolish action [Arieti, 1955, pp. 125–126].

The Hebephrenic Syndrome

In hebephrenia the ego undertakes no activity for self-defense. Rather, overwhelmed by insurmountable conflicts, it "lets itself go." If the present is unpleasant, the ego regresses to the past; if newer types of adaptation fail, it takes refuge in infantilisms, sometimes going as far back as to intrauterine modes of existence.

In paranoid and catatonic syndromes the ego surrenders to the superego; in hebephrenia, the ego surrenders to the id. In hebephrenic regression, infantile elements are strangely intertwined with adult experiences acquired by maturation, conditioning, and cathexis.

The hebephrenic personality resembles a house which has been hit by a bomb, where equipment and furniture belonging to the different floors and apartments are all mixed up. In the hebephrenic, the various developmental stages and deteriorative levels are confused. Hebephrenics, although lacking such ego-protective symptoms as the partial reality testing of paranoid schizophrenics and the stuporous defenses of catatonics, can be just as suspicious or as violent, and can be easily provoked into uncontrolled outbursts of rage directed against themselves or others. Hebephrenics will publicly masturbate or try to make love when sexually aroused. They are frightened neither by homosexuality nor by impulses of an incestuous nature. Many of them are talkative, abusive, hostile, and sexually aggressive. Apparently they have lost all shame and guilt.

The Simple Deterioration Syndrome

The "simple deterioration" type is frequently referred to as "simple" and, as such, erroneously believed to be only mildly disturbed. The onset is usually insidious, gradual and slow. Most simple deterioration cases have a long history of maladjustment, social withdrawal and daydreaming. In their earliest years they displayed autistic features, shyness, inability to do things on their own, lack of interest, lack of initiative, depressed and irritated moods, and a peculiar type of docile, passive, overdependent behavior, with occasional crying spells.

In many cases "neurasthenic" symptoms develop; such pre-psychotic children may have dreamt of greatness, planning to protect their parents and all those who suffer, but obviously lacked the initiative, courage and endurance for any persistent action.

In simple deterioration cases the object-hypercathexis is

excessive and the libidinal resources depleted to a dangerous point. Although the simple deterioration syndrome is less dramatic than the three other schizophrenic syndromes, it is far more self-destructive in that the ego gives up the fight for survival.

On the prepsychotic level, the lives of these patients was a series of defeats. No matter how hard they tried, they found neither peace, protection, nor safety in their homes. One patient would miss classes in high school, sometimes for whole weeks, in order to help his "poor," overworked mother with the household chores; he also worked at night to support his gambling father. Whenever his parents quarrelled (and they did so whenever they were together) he pleaded with them, desperately trying to appease them, or would hide in his room sobbing in despair. His thoughts became more and more confused, his behavior more bizarre, his depression deeper and deeper. Gradually he lost all interest in life and could only lie in bed, sobbing.

This renunciation of one's own narcissistic pleasures and total sacrifice for the parents, is perhaps the purest form of *vectoriasis praecox.* In all other forms of schizophrenia there is still an inner fight going on between the normal self-preservation drive and the desire to protect the protectors. In the simple deterioration syndrome, there is very little, if any, inner fight. The ego gives up its main task of protecting life; the patient gives away all his libido, there being nothing left to sustain him. The profound decline of sensitivity to pain makes them less capable of survival and less inclined to avoid injuries.

The Dementive Level

Schizophrenia is not to be regarded as a static entity or defect. It is a process, a series of changes, the nature of which depends largely upon with whom the schizophrenic interacts. Each success, each friendly interaction with friendly and giving individuals provides courage and helps the schizophrenic, provided it is not too late, to make some headway in the direction of normality. Each defeat or disappointment increases the regressive tendency and promotes further disorganization. Schizophrenics are not always schizophrenic; they have their ups and downs, fluctuating between losing and regaining contact with reality.

Being locked up in a large and impersonal custodial facility, where there is little if any treatment or personal care, is in itself a powerful schizogenic factor. It could be argued that hospital life makes the schizophrenic more schizophrenic than he was before he was admitted. Those observing schizophrenics after years of hospitalization must not forget that their severe deterioration is to a great extent a product of isolation, neglect and hospital routine. One cannot help but wonder what would have happened to an average individual incarcerated for life in a neglected ward of an understaffed, custodial type mental hospital.

It would appear that the deterioration process in schizophrenia is related to the nature of human contacts. Those schizophrenics who attracted the attention of doctors, nurses and attendants, or those who had friendly and considerate visitors from outside the hospital usually deteriorate less. In fact, as early as 1911 E. Bleuler noticed that the visit of an affectionate friend or relative is strangely related to what was called "spontaneous recovery." When no one cares for him, a schizophrenic cares little for himself and gives up whatever civilized behavioral patterns he has acquired in the course of his lifetime.

Dementive schizophrenics show little sensitivity to temperature, pain or taste. They swallow inedible food, hurt themselves badly, and expose themselves carelessly to freezing and boiling temperatures. One who has worked with dementive schizophrenics in the "back wards" of a mental hospital will undoubtedly experience the uncanny feeling of a subhuman environment. The ego and superego are no longer operative; there is no more striving. Repetitive movements, aimless or senseless activity, passivity, lack of bowel and bladder control all remind one of severe mental defectives. Yet dementive schizophrenics are not mentally defective; on the contrary, many of them have good minds which they are unable to use.

⚘ 8 ⚘

Innocent Criminals

Antisocial Behavior

Not all antisocial behavior is a product of the instrumental-narcissistic personality structure and its peculiar dysbalance of libido and destrudo cathexes. Antisocial and aggressive behavior can be caused by a variety of organic, social and psychological factors. The present volume does not deal with brain injuries, tumors, epilepsies and the organic mental disorders; it must, however, be clearly stated that antisocial and violent behavior can be produced by organic causes as well.

Hostility is not limited to the narcissistic-instrumental type. Hostile behavior, which is a given of human nature, starts with the object-directed destrudo in infancy. Actually, from a phylogenetic and ontogenetic point of view, hostility begins prior to the development of object-directed libido (see first three chapters) and represents the fundamental method of struggle for survival. There are, however, distinct developmental stages in the cathexes of libido and destrudo (see Chapter Five).

Adjustment to one's society is one of the most important determinants of mental health. In that society cannot tolerate unrestricted aggression, civilized cultures permit the use of force in self-defense only, and this in a way prescribed by their respective legal systems. Well-adjusted individuals keep their hostile, Aretic impulses under the rational control imposed by the ego and superego. Whether they compete or cooperate, love or hate, they are not carried away by their impulses. Neither saints nor sinners, they act reasonably, in instrumental, mutual and vectorial ways depending on the circumstances. They are not afraid to bear hostility against those who hurt them. In such situations they defend their rights within socially approved limits.

Infantile hostility is irrational as is the hostile behavior of all mentally disturbed individuals. Moreover, the three personality types we have outlined display three distinct patterns of hostile feelings and actions. The schizoid-hypervectorial's Aretic behavior is primarily inspired by the superego and directed inward in self-accusations generally having to do with failure to give adequate love and support to parents or parental figures. When the ego-protective defense mechanisms fail, the destrudo pours out in a wild and indiscriminate violence. The depressive-dysmutual hates those who do not love him or do not love him enough. The narcissistic-hyperinstrumental is not so much concerned with hate as with satisfaction of his own needs regardless of the cost. The destrudo of such individuals is primitive id-anchored, and infantile. In milder forms of the disorder, the ego exercises some degree of self-control in fear of retaliation; severely disturbed hyperinstrumentals (i.e., psychopaths or sociopaths) are unable to control their sexual and aggressive impulses and become a menace to the society. Driven by the id-governed pleasure principle they demand immediate gratification at the expense of other people.

The psychopath is a narcissistic person, "unable to tolerate delay or frustration, has little sense of responsibility, lacks self-control and is anti-socially oriented. He tries to use the other person because of his fear of being used by him" (Schmidberg, 1961, p. 734). Exploitative, narcissistic hyperinstrumental psychopathy has been described by Cleckley (1950) as sociopathic personality disorder. Sociopaths lack insight and compassion, are unable to assume responsibility, to accept blame, to feel guilty, and to have concern for anyone but themselves. Similar behavioral patterns have been described by McCord and McCord (1956) in their study of the narcissistic psychopath, whom they found to be antisocial, impulsive, aggressive individuals, unable to develop feelings of love or guilt.

In my studies of narcissistic disorders I found five levels of deterioration similar to the schizovectorial and depressive-dysmutual types, in contradistinction to the classic psychoanalytic interpretations (see Fenichel, 1945). In narcissistic neurosis and character neurosis, to be described below, the ego struggles for control over the id impulses. Because the libido is self-hypercathected in narcissistic individuals, they are oversensitive to pain and injury (Greenacre, 1945). Thus, they are notoriously hypochondriacal, constantly worry about their health, subscribe to popular health magazines and cheap medical encyclopedias, and eagerly attend doctors' offices. Almost all psychopaths I have treated in private practice were hypochondriacs referred to me by physicians who could not discover organic reasons for their health complaints.

Etiologic Studies

Etiologic studies have been hampered by the apparent confusion between delinquency and psychopathy. Halleck (1967) suggested that only irrational forms of crime or delinquency be labeled as pathological, but the criterion of irrationality is not always clearly definable. Reasonably adjusted people may commit a crime for a variety of reasons, and to complicate matters further, narcissistic hyperinstrumental psychopaths may refrain from violating the law when law enforcement is severe and immediate and penalties are harsh.

As stated above, the antisocial behavior of hyperinstrumentals is a result of their overconcern with themselves and lack of concern for everyone else. Such a persistent behavior pattern has given rise to the belief that there is something fundamentally wrong with the organic constitution of these individuals. Pritchard (1835), Lombroso (1876), Koch (1891), Kraepelin (1904) and many others advocated the genetic and organic origin of psychopathic behavior. Similar ideas were promoted by Sheldon (1949), Glueck and Glueck (1956), Meerloo (1962) and, to some degree, Eysenck (1964). Mc-Learn (1964), in a thorough review of the literature, has shown, however, that there is no evidence for an overall genetic origin of antisocial behavior, though certain types of aggression are definitely related to innate neurological pathology (Polani, 1967).

The question is whether this holds true for the hyperinstrumental-narcissistic types who in extreme cases end up as psychopathic psychotics. The studies of Aichhorn (1935), Banay (1948), Bowlby (1951), Chwast (1958), Eissler (1949), Anna Freud (1949), Karpman (1950, 1951, 1959), Lindner (1944), Lippman (1951; 1959), Spitz (1950), Wolberg (1944) and others have stressed the importance of early emotional deprivation in the development of narcissistic, psychopathic personality traits. It would appear that this for the most part represents a consensus of opinion, though McCord and McCord (1956) maintain that while severe parental rejection is the main cause of antisocial behavior, brain damage must not be excluded as a possible second cause.

Bowlby (1951) related antisocial behavior to separation from the mother, but this hypothesis, promoted by several research workers, could not be completely corroborated (Yarrow, 1964). However, the deprivation of maternal love and care stressed by Bowlby would seem to play the most important role in the etiology of the narcissistic type of mental disorders.

There is a growing body of evidence to suggest that a prolonged neglect and an absence of a significant mothering person in a child's early life may be the crucial factor in the development of the narcissistic-instrumental type, psychopath and delinquent (Halleck, 1971; Kohut, 1966; 1968; Nagera, 1964; Wolman, 1966c). Parental rejection fosters extreme narcissism. Thus "it is the narcissism, resulting from rejection, which accounts for the inability of the child to form an object relation to his mother in the first year of life, to his father and his siblings later, and to those in the external world with whom he comes in contact" (Lippman, 1951, p. 226).

Most psychoanalytic studies indicate the lack of maternal love as the main determinant in the development of a self-centered, narcissistic personality. Friedlander (1945) observed that a child who failed to receive maternal love withdraws interest from objects and remains fixated in a primitive personality structure. Failing to develop a superego, he is thus unable to experience guilt feeling for his antisocial behavior.

In terms of interindividual cathexis, an inadequate supply of interindividual cathexes of libido from without forces withdrawal of libidinal cathexes from objects and overcathexis on oneself. This results in a hyperinstrumental narcissistic intraindividual dysbalance of cathexes (Wolman, 1966d). The consequences for personality dynamics will be explained later.

Also, Lampl-de Groot (1949) saw antisocial behavior as a product of inadequate internalization of parental images and shaky identifications. According to Karpman (1959), "psychopathic development for the most part indicated a clearcut psychogenic relationship with inadequate opportunity in the first years for the establishment of a meaningful primary mother relationship of cathexis . . . the absence of accepting parents who . . . provide the child with the capacity or wish to become socialized" (pp. 143–144).

A weak or defective superego is regarded by Eissler (1949) and Johnson and Szurek (1952) to be the product of parental misguidance or the lack of guidance. Mother's self-contradictory, unpredictable, and shifting emotional attitudes, or frequent substitutions of maternal figures all interfere with healthy identification and formation of an adequate superego. The presence of an inadequate superego explains the fact that psychopathic children appear to experience very little anxiety (Spitz, 1950). Superego deficit together with extreme hypercathexis of the self are not conducive to internalization of fear, which is the basis of anxiety. Should a hyperinstrumental ever feel guilty, his guilt feeling is immediately projected and the blame is placed on the allegedly hostile environment (Lowrey, 1951).

Levy (1943, 1951) distinguished between the "deprived" and "indulged" psychopath. The emotionally deprived child is unable to identify with his parents or parental substitutes. He develops a weak superego and is unable to exercise moral self-control. The child who was allowed to do as he pleased and grew up without any restraint is similarly unable to control his impulses and is likely to become aggressive and antisocial. The identification with his indulging mother is responsible for the overpermissive superego which does not act as an inhibitory factor.

My own clinical observations and analysis of the personality dynamics of the narcissistic-hyperinstrumental type of behavior disorders follow.

To Exploit or to Be Exploited

The patient, a 35-year-old businessman was married, well-dressed and well-mannered. He complained about his wife whom he had married because she had a wealthy father who gave him money to start his own business. From the story he told me I gathered that his business practices have been rather dubious. His need for further financial backing prevented him from obtaining a divorce. Among his many complaints were the following: Does marriage mean chastity?

Must married men become slaves to their spouses? Can't they retain their freedom, sexual and otherwise? Must they renounce their "civil rights," "civil liberties," and "friends" because they are married? Why does his wife demand love, affection and all that nonsense? Isn't she selfish?

The patient sought my help for several reasons. He had been experiencing financial problems and needed more money from his father-in-law. He was afraid of his business associates whom he had apparently cheated. To avoid responsibility he developed "heart attacks," which his family physician diagnosed as psychosomatic in origin, consequently referring him to me. He complained bitterly of his overdemanding wife, her stingy father, his exacting business associates and life in general. It was his belief that he was a nice, friendly, innocent person surrounded by selfish people who tried to take advantage of him.

He did not have much praise for his own parents either. According to his story, his father was an extremely selfish man who did not care for his family. Enjoying drink, he squandered his money on liquor and women. The father was rarely home; the mother had had an affair with a neighbor.

Thus early in life this patient arrived at the conclusion that no one cared for anyone and, unless he could protect himself he would be taken advantage of. This would explain his callous use of others.

My studies of families of narcissistic patients (hyperinstrumentals) revealed a peculiar lack of warmth and even a lack of contact between the parent and the child who is destined to become a psychopath. Such a child grows up in an essentially isolated environment. From his earliest years he is forced to take care of himself, never to experience the security which comes of having human friendship, sympathy and affections.

Psychopaths have never had a stable social relationship in childhood. Their life histories, whether they were reared in splendor or in squalor, resemble the lives of wayward children. They have developed no attachment to anyone, because there were no trustworthy, stable and friendly figures with whom to identify.

In several cases the mother was severely disturbed and unable to care properly for the child: in many instances the psychopathic child exploited and ridiculed his sick mother. Hyperinstrumentals are never proud of their parents; tender feelings toward them are virtually nonexistent.

O'Neal and his associates (1962) found that sociopathic personality in offspring is positively related to parental desertion, lack of support, and failure to supervise. My studies of juvenile delinquency and of acculturation indicate that psychopathic features are closely related to decline in parental authority and to loosening of family bonds caused by migration and acculturation (Wolman, 1949).

Hyperinstrumentals believe that they are poor, innocent, hungry, lonely and mistreated creatures. Given to cowardice, they fear confrontations with equals but do not hesitate to attack those who appear defenseless. Whether or not a hyperinstrumental will become an overt criminal depends largely on circumstances. He is a criminal at heart who will or will not commit a crime depending on the weakness of his victim and the danger involved in attack. Most hyperinstrumentals avoid antisocial acts for which they may be punished: when they are caught, they regret not the crime but the punishment. They are Eichmanns, but not Raskolnikovs.

The outstanding trait of the hyperinstrumental is his extreme narcissism. The dysmutual manic-depressive, having failed in his attempts to give love, tries to get love by alternating his love and hate toward himself and others. The hyperinstrumental is concerned neither with giving nor receiving love. He wants food, whether it is given with or without love; he wants sex, with or without affection; what he wants most are material possessions, comforts and power. The hypervectorial is exceedingly grateful for any human kindness that comes his way; the dysmutual is grateful up to a certain point; the hyperinstrumental is never grateful. Although Clara Thompson (1950) criticized Freud's assumption that a narcissistic person is "richer" than a giving one, it is probably true that hyperinstrumentals have the highest degree of vitality while hypervectorials have the lowest. When hypervectorials reach the lowest level of deterioration, they die, but severely deteriorated hyperinstrumentals kill others. Whatever exists, exists in a certain quantity, and when too much libido is given away, it cannot be reclaimed. Similarly, when no libido is given away, it is all self-cathected to the point where it becomes impossible for any redirection outward.

A hyperinstrumental treats people as if they were tools to be used or food to be eaten. He is less friendly to strong and friendly individuals than to strong and hostile ones, because he himself could never be friendly toward weak ones; friendliness on the part of the strong ones makes him suspicious. Psychopathic patients typically do not trust the friendly attitude of their own therapists. One patient suspected that the psychotherapist was better disposed toward wealthy patients, and another therapist who acted in a friendly manner toward all his patients was believed to be stupid. Hyperinstrumentals do not believe that anyone can be genuinely friendly, honest or self-sacrificing. They are convinced that the world is a jungle full of shrewd, selfish and greedy beasts. In such a world everyone must look out for himself, selfishness and greed being condoned as necessary self-defense.

Destrudo

The hyperinstrumental's use of violence is not only for tangible gains. His deeply rooted inferiority feeling, combined with lack of object cathexis, motivates him to hurt others not only for money or other gains, but also for a show of power. Hyperinstrumentals may kill even after they have robbed the victim; they often torture and mutilate in robbery and rape, because cruelty enhances their feeling of power. When the ego operating on the reality principle loses its grip, a hyperinstrumental psychopath deteriorates, turns psychotic, and attacks, tortures, and murders, displaying inhuman cruelty and deriving great human pleasure from it (Cleckley, 1950; Critchley, 1951).

Psychopaths do not experience genuine feelings of guilt. They know neither of regret nor of self-accusation on moral grounds, though they may hate themselves for being weak or for not being shrewd enough in escaping punishment. Feelings of depression in hyperinstrumentals can originate in a loss of support or loss of property, failure in business or school, loss of a job, fear, feelings of weakness and inadequacy in the face of danger, inability to cope with a job, failure to escape penalty, and so on. It is usually a combination of destructive impulses directed toward oneself and toward others. A hyperinstrumental hates the world that refuses to satisfy his needs and blames it for his frustrations. When he is in a depressed mood, he complains, "How stupid I am; how inadequate, how weak and poor I am. I have to live the life of an underdog." Lacking in remorse or repentance, psychopathic depression does not resemble the self-torturing accusations of the hypervectorial or dysmutual. The hyperinstrumental, convinced of his innocence rarely if ever feels that he deserves punishment.

Sex

In most hyperinstrumentals, there is some overlap between Eros and Ares. Eros is most often subservient to Ares; consequently sex may be combined with aggressive or violent behavior toward the partner. The hyperinstrumental personality structure precludes normal development of a higher organization of sexuality. Thus most hyperinstrumentals remain fixated on infantile sexual levels. For the most part, their inner conflicts originate in fear of others. Having no moral standards, they are guided by a desire to avoid disapproval; this fear is the only inhibitory factor that prevents psychopaths from acting out their impulses. The pleasure principle, that is, the principle of immediate gratification of needs, is the main motive in the life of psychopaths.

A 40-year-old male patient practiced sex with animals, children, men, women, whatever sex objects were available. He knew society condemned his behavior, but he himself did not feel that he was wrong. His only fear was that of being caught; therefore he neither raped nor killed. He did maintain however that if he could get away with murder, "he certainly would commit it." A psychopathic woman, married, 28 years old, was having, as she put it, "occasional" affairs with men. She was not interested in sex; in fact, she was essentially frigid, but when men were "nice" to her, flattered her, bought her little gifts or just impressed her, she saw no reason for being faithful. "As long as my husband did not know," she said, "he was not hurt."

Conscious and Unconscious

The dreams of psychopaths bear witness to their main conflict, which is the wish to devour the world and the fear of being devoured. Whereas the dreams of hypervectorials are frequently nightmares that convey a terrorizing fear that their unconscious wishes may come true, in the dreams of hyperinstrumentals the forbidden wish, be it incestuous, homosexual or murderous, does come through without causing much panic. Hyperinstrumentals dream in a rather unsophisticated manner, yet their dreams use the same pictorial symbols as is the case in the two other types.

Furthermore, when the hypervectorial mind is flooded by primary unconscious process, the resulting confusion is largely confined to the emotional or affectual spheres. Thus even a disturbed schizophrenic may retain some degree of objective thinking and continue his studies or occupation. In hyperinstrumentals, unconscious processes do affect their understanding of the outer world and intellectual functioning.

The Weak Ego

From a comparative point of view, the psychopathic hyperinstrumental has the best chance to prevent serious deterioration of the ego while the schizoid hypervectorial has the least. The emotional disbalance (cathexis of libido) peculiar to each type, explains this difference. That is, as explained earlier the hypervectorial ego is depleted of libidinal investment and consequently most likely to collapse under stress. The impoverishment of the ego also explains the phenomenon of depersonalization in schizophrenics, who are often uncertain as to who they are and suffer delusions and hallucinations, while even severely deteriorated psychopaths somehow preserve their identity.

In all hypervectorials, from obsessive-compulsive neurotics to overt schizophrenics the superego is overgrown, rigid and dictatorial. Their behavior is typically guided not by realistic considerations of the ego, but by moralistic dictates of the superego. In the dysmutual type, the ego inconsistently takes its cues from the id or the superego. In the hyperinstrumental type the ego yields to momentary impulses of the id.

Superego and Morality

An inadequate development of the superego is related to the lack of opportunity for identifying oneself with parental figures. One of my patients was brought up in an institution that preached religious devotion while practicing the law of the jungle. The officers and counselors of this Children's Home ate very well; the children went hungry. As a consequence of their kitchen chores, the children were in a position to compare their own strictly rationed and meager food with the luxurious meals of their educators. Shortage of food and lack of educational guidance led to a general practice of thievery; whenever a child did not appear on time at his table, his food was stolen by other children, and woe to the complainer!

The children wore shabby clothes all year round with the exception of days when important visitors were expected; then clean bedspreads, neat tablecloths and special "visitors" clothes were distributed. The counselors frequently took monetary and sexual advantage of the children who dared not complain. The punishments were severe and God was always there on the side of the bigger fists.

A psychopathic child may identify with the strong aggressor and develop a crude and pathological superego. A young patient identified with the "smart tough guys" who knew how to take advantage of other people, but could not identify with his middle-class parents who were unable to provide any guidance whatsoever. This patient tried to abstain from violence because of its dangerous implications, but he would not refrain from cheating, theft, drinking, and sexual license.

Another patient, a middle-aged man, grew up in a peculiarly disorganized Negro family in the Midwest. Both father and mother had "boyfriends" and "girl friends"; they were divorced, remarried and again divorced. They did not part, but lived together in a common law marriage with several children, practicing overt promiscuity. The patient was a classic psychopath, actively engaged in homosexual relations and occasional heterosexual relations with juniors. His superego excused drinking, fighting and sexual perversion, but he refused to steal because stealing was "immoral." Another man forged checks but would only deceive the wealthy. He

refused to steal from poor men, because "it was not right."
His moral standards reflected the norms of his parents' neighborhood where stealing was taboo.

A psychopath can easily become a criminal, although he is
less likely to do so if the moral standards in his society are
strict and violation of the law invites social ostracism and
severe punishment. A psychopath who belongs to a social
group with a clear-cut moral code is less likely to hurt others
because this would jeopardize his social status and be detrimental to his interests. Thus many psychopaths lead the lives
of honest citizens not out of integrity but because it is more
advantageous to stay honest. However, should an opportunity
for getting away with a crime arise they are quick to seize
upon it. The "honest" psychopaths control their selfish impulses in regard to strangers but show a complete lack of
compassion toward members of their immediate family. Obviously, love and fairness to one's own family are not among
the virtues of these psychopaths who are typically church-
goers and seeming paragons of morality. Psychopaths abstain
from dishonesty, unfairness and violence for one reason only:
the fear of retaliation. They practice all kinds of dishonest
deals in hiding or disguise; they are the bookies, shylocks,
dope peddlers, swindlers and extortionists. Some of them
combine crime with respectable and legitimate business.
While they fear being caught and punished, they are incapable of experiencing guilt.

A society that does not have strict moral standards backed
up by a morally consistent public opinion, a society that fails
to exercise its obligation to protect peaceful citizens, is an
ideal environment for psychopaths. In a way, such a society
invites crime. When public opinion does not condemn unfair
and unethical practices and is permissive toward dishonesty;
when movies, television, and other means of public education
wittingly or unwittingly glorify "the tough guy"; when the
protective and penalizing instruments of society are not en-

forceable—when these factors prevail, psychopathic behavior is reinforced.

Hyperinstrumental (Psychopathic) Neurosis

Psychopathic neurotics rarely seek psychotherapy. They come in contact with psychiatrists, clinical psychologists and psychiatric social workers only when something bothers them. As a rule, they stay in treatment only as long as their immediate troubles persist. Psychopaths do not come for treatment because they are displeased with themselves and wish to be changed; the only thing they desire is to be relieved from physical pain or social hardship.

Psychopathic neurotics are selfish, dishonest, exploitative individuals who feel cheated and exploited by others. They resent the fact that the world is not as nice to them as they would like it to be. Most of them are continuously dissatisfied; they doubt their own abilities, feel insecure and threatened and develop a great variety of symptoms frequently diagnosed as anxiety neurosis, depressive reaction, excessive fatigue, chronic dissatisfaction, apprehension, fear of being attacked, fear of failure, fear of being deprived and abandoned and a variety of psychosomatic symptoms. These ego-protective symptoms reflect an "escape into illness." The hyperinstrumental psychopathic neurotic alleviates his feelings of inadequacy and gains privileges through his pathological symptoms.

The typical elements of neurotic conflict are present in psychopathic neurosis. In all neuroses the ego tries to ward off unconscious impulses. This process takes place in hyperinstrumental neurosis as well but the rationale of the inner struggle is idiosyncratic. In hypervectorial neurosis the ego tries to overcontrol the unconscious hostile impulses because they may threaten love objects. Thus the dysmutuals try to control their hostility only when it may undermine their self-esteem or respect by others. The sole reason for the psychopath's self-control is the fear that acting out his hostile impulses will invite retaliation and he will be hurt. The world is seen by psychopathic neurotics as a hostile place where everyone is left to his own fate. Paranoid mechanisms of blaming others and suspecting them are typical ego-protective mechanisms in psychopathic neurosis.

Some of the so-called traumatic and war neuroses are actually psychopathic disturbances on a neurotic level. When a hyperinstrumental neurotic is called in to active service for his country, he resents being called to do something that does not directly serve his own interests. He likes to fight only when victory is sure and looting is safe. When exposed to danger, he will most likely develop psychosomatic symptoms and regress to an infantile level where his cowardice and shirking of responsibility will be excused and rewarded by medical or psychological care.

Hyperinstrumental Character Neurosis

Hyperinstrumental character neurosis reflects, as do all other character neuroses, the acceptance of neurotic symptoms as a protective shell. As is true of other character neurotics, the hyperinstrumentals glorify their shortcomings and mistake faults for virtues. In the hyperinstrumental character neurosis, the gains are immediate and tangible, and neurotic symptoms are designed to procure definite benefits. One patient used psychosomatic symptoms to be excused from household chores, another exploited his alleged physical illness for gaining of food privileges at home; another female patient obtained concessions from her co-workers in terms of working hours and efficiency, expecting consideration and special privileges because she was a disturbed person.

One patient, a refugee, utilized his symptoms to promote a flourishing business. Whereas his shipmates had all married, had children and assumed adult responsibilities, he deliberately perpetuated his refugee status. He came to consult me after being in this country for 15 years. At the time he was 42 years old, single, unemployed, wandering from one agency to another, and extorting money from his friends by threatening a hunger strike in their homes. He was seeing one psychotherapist after another, requesting them to state in writing that he needed mental treatment but could not afford it. He used these written statements for further extortions, absolutely convinced that there was nothing wrong in his actions.

The Russian writer, Ilya Ehrenburg, told the following story about German prisoners of World War II: when asked whether their invasion of Poland, Holland, Belgium, Denmark, Norway and France was right, they said that all the invasions were justified. They admitted, however, that the invasion of Russia was morally wrong, because in this instance Germany had failed. The First World War was not a blunder, but a betrayal: the moderate Treaty of Versailles was an injustice perpetrated on the poor Germans who deserved to conquer the world and turn it into one huge concentration camp.

The Nazi mentality was indeed psychopathic. The guards of concentration camps felt pity for their pet animals, but had nothing but contempt for the Jewish infants. Some Nazi guards took pleasure in murdering their victims while listening to sentimental music.

Latent Hyperinstrumental Psychosis

The latent psychotic psychopath is frequently aware of his murderous impulses, and fears he may lose control and be severely punished. Latent psychotic hyperinstrumentals are humorless, irritable, quarrelsome, hostile, greedy and suspicious. They are either overtly hostile or passive and apathetic, regressing into a parasitic pattern of vegetation. "I am either a tiger or a vegetable," said a latent psychotic hyperinstrumental.

Latent psychotic psychopaths are realistic enough to fear being caught while they rape or practice exhibitionism, sadism or homosexuality. They will often develop paranoid fears and suspect that they are being watched or persecuted. Their paranoid delusions are less persistent than those of hypervectorials and less elaborate and systematized than the paranoid delusions of the dysmutuals.

A latent hyperinstrumental psychotic in panic may turn manifestly psychotic showing patterns of an aggressive-sadistic type. A psychopath caught in theft or robbery may attack maliciously and torture his victims. However, when left undisturbed in his criminal activities or when victims show cooperation, he may abstain from violence and retain his latent psychotic level of behavior. He acts as if he were saying: "As long as the world recognizes my rights to use others, to loot their possessions, and to enslave them, I shall try to control my savage impulses. But when the world becomes a threat by denying me my rights I will no longer be able to control myself and all my evil impulses may break loose."

A 32-year-old man, married, and a father of an infant, was arraigned as a criminal in a mental hospital because he attacked his wife with a heavy hammer until she fell unconscious, bleeding profusely. The patient maintained that he had been "nice" to his wife, but when she "abused" his patience by snooping in his desk, he could not control his anger. He showed no remorse, for he said, his wife "deserved the punishment."

The weak inhibitions and self-control of hyperinstrumental latent psychotics fail under the impact of anger, sexual urge, alcohol, disappointment or fatigue. As is the case with latent psychotics of the two other types (hypervectorial and dysmutual) latent psychotic hyperinstrumentals live on the edge of a volcano that may erupt at the slightest provocation.

Manifest Psychosis

A manifest hyperinstrumental psychotic has no aims, no plans, no goals, no aspirations, no ideals, no clear conception of reality, no self-control. Blindly following his needs, whims and impulses, he seeks an immediate gratification of his wishes with no consideration for future consequences.

One can distinguish two syndromes in psychotic psychopaths: the *aggressive-sadistic* and the *passive-parasitic*. When the aggressive type has no money, he will cheat, steal or rob, depending on circumstances. A catatonic may, indiscriminately, attack everyone, but a psychopath attacks only those who seem to be weak and easy prey. Exercising poor judgment, a psychopath may underestimate the danger of being caught and commit crimes in a carefree manner, but as a rule, he is too selfish to attack people who are stronger than himself.

A neurotic psychopath does not rape a woman when there are people nearby. A psychotic psychopath becomes less cautious, more impulsive and more dangerous, and may attack, rape or torture a lonely girl, an aging woman, or a cripple. "Moral insanity" is indeed the right name for the aggressive-sadistic psychopath who ripped away the abdomen of one woman and bit off a part of another woman's breast (Critchley, 1951).

Fear is perhaps the only contact with reality in aggressive-sadistic psychopaths who fear policemen only when they see them alert and well-armed. Psychotic psychopaths display poor judgment, an inadequate perception of reality and no understanding of the potential consequences of their deeds. They often torture their victims and derive pleasure from inflicting pain. They usually rob their victims, although robbery itself does not give them adequate pleasure. Additional pleasure will be from beating, stabbing and other forms of torture.

The second syndrome is the parasitic-exploitative. Psychopathic psychotics avoid actual work and typically exist within a parasitic structure. On the neurotic level the psychopathic ego provides the person with the knowledge that he can't escape legitimate employment. On the character-neurotic level such individuals often turn racketeers, extortionists and nonviolent criminals. On the manifest psychotic level they cannot concentrate and are unable to hold a job. They drift around as drunkards and addicts, beggars, and bums. Their existence is aimless.

Dementive Level

Dementive psychopathic psychotics usually end up in jails and in mental hospitals. Psychopathic dementia is a state of deep regression to subhuman life. Dementive psychopaths feel sorry for themselves and resent "unfair treatment" in jail, although they have no sympathy for anyone else. Their mental horizons shrink to the most primitive functions, perception is severely disturbed and memory functions are practically nonexistent.

Subhuman standards and bestiality are perhaps most characteristic of dementive hyperinstrumentals. They sink below the level of cave-men both mentally and morally. Their concerns have only to do with the intake of food, elimination, sleep and sex. Their universe has shrunk to food, dish, toilet bowl, berth and anything that can serve for sexual gratification. There is no shame, no faith, no inhibition, in short no civilization. Hyperinstrumental psychotics cannot perceive, think, or reason; their personality has been reduced to their stomach and intestines, bowels and bladder, penis or vagina. Their minds stop existing; their ego and superego fall apart; what is left is just an animalistic id.

Yet, unlike the hypervectorials, they survive. In hunger or emergency, severely regressed psychopaths will resort to cannibalism. They have lost their human traits.

❈ 9 ❈
Doctor Jekyll
and Mister Hyde

Depression as a Symptom

The term depression has at least three distinct connotations. Depression is a feeling of sadness that follows defeat, frustration and loss. If the depression corresponds to actual events, if it is appropriate, proportionate, and adjustive, it does not signal poor mental health (Jacobson, 1957). When one fails in his efforts or loses a loved one or an important possession, he is likely to experience feelings of sadness, defeat, emptiness and a loss of self-confidence. Such a depression, linked to an actual defeat, is exogenous and normal (see Chapter Six).

In terms of power and acceptance, depression is a reaction to one's awareness of weakness. Achievement and victory make one feel strong and create an elated mood, for the stronger one is (strength here defined as the ability to satisfy needs), the better are his chances for survival. In normal, exogenous depression, one tries to overcome the obstacles to compensate for defeat, and to work toward a more successful behavior, in the hopes that these negative feelings will yield ground to constructive efforts.

Decrease in self-esteem, or the low estimate of one's power, is the common denominator of all depressive states. The less realistic is this estimate, the more pathological is the depression.

In extreme cases depression is totally unrelated to actual loss of power. This intrapsychic depression is referred to as endogenous. People who are given to this kind of depression feel defeated, lack self-confidence, blame themselves, feel isolated and forsaken, have a pessimistic outlook on life, lack initiative, feel perpetually exhausted or agitated and unable to sleep, overeat or undereat, and dwell on past events, unable to take constructive steps.

Endogenous depression is a symptom of mental disorders. The outstanding features of such pathological depressions are (1) their endogenous origins, unrelated and disproportionate to real events; (2) self-accusation, totally unjustified and flying in the face of truths; (3) a tendency to perpetuate the depression instead of seeking a way out. All three characteristics are clearly irrational, often leading to even less rational confessions of uncommitted sins and wishes to be punished.

Endogenous depression may be associated with a variety of psychosociogenic as well as organic mental disorders. Thus one must draw a clear line between a depressed epileptic and a schizophrenic, where depression serves as a symptom, and depression as a clinical entity that can manifest itself on a neurotic and character neurotic level leading to a full-blown depressive psychosis, often called melancholia, manic-depressive or affect psychosis.

Interpretations of Depression

Abraham (1911, 1916, 1924) was the first psychoanalyst to interpret the manic-depressive disorder. Abraham proposed a most interesting hypothesis that unfortunately failed to attract very much attention. At that time Freud maintained that repressed sexuality leads to anxiety; Abraham hypothesized that repressed hostility leads to depression (Abraham, 1911, p. 151ff).

Abraham's essay, with its emphasis on hostility, has stimulated my thought in the direction to be presented in detail in the following pages. Depression is self-directed aggression;

hatred which has been directed inward is the main theme of all levels of the dysmutual-depressive type, from hysteria to manifest psychosis. My major hypothesis concerning the depressive disorders is that they are dominated by Aretic drives, stimulated by a particularly inconsistent and inadequate supply of libidinal cathexes from without—to be explained later on.

In the paper "Mourning and Melancholia" Freud (1917) compared melancholia with normal grief. According to Freud, melancholia resembles mourning insofar as it occurs after the loss of the loved person; however, unlike mourning, melancholia occurs only in individuals who are already disturbed. The melancholic need not have lost his loved object in reality but might have lost it intrapsychically. According to Freud melancholia is a regression from mature object relations to the earliest way of relating to objects, namely to narcissistic identification, in which the object is not distinguished from the ego and in which all the libido is withdrawn from objects and reinvested, as in the earliest phase of development, in the ego.

Freud's (1917) theory of object loss is actually a *particular case* of lack of supply of libidinal cathexes from without. It is one thing to be without a love object, quite another to be in perpetual mourning for the return of one which has been lost. Those who never received love may live without it and develop narcissistic-instrumental behavior disorders such as those described in Chapter Eight. Those who at one time did receive love but lost it may develop "love addiction," "affection hunger," and what is most symptomatic, hatred for those who do not love them and contempt for themselves as being unworthy of love and deserving abandonment.

Psychoanalytic thinking has been particularly concerned with object loss, stressing the mechanism of introjection and identification (Berliner, 1966; Rado, 1928; Gero, 1936; Weiss, 1932; Fenichel, 1945) instead of seeing in introjection a particular, though very important, mechanism related to depression, which I shall attempt to explain later on.

In the 1950 and 1951 Symposia of the American Psychoanalytic Association emphasis was placed on object loss in depression (Greenacre, 1953). Greenacre stressed "identification of the subject with the object loss." Pathogenic depression is characterized by its "intensity, excessive duration and dominance of the organism." Physical symptoms such as decreased "motor activity" and visceral disorder bear witness to the overall involvement in depression which is caused by a failure in the oral-narcissistic supplies.

Bibring (1953) maintained that the basic "mechanism of depression" is the decrease in "self-esteem" due to one's real or imaginary partial or total helplessness. Depression is a reaction to feelings of inferiority and guilt.

Bibring described the "attempts at restoration" aimed at bringing about "restitution from depression." These attempts include efforts at regaining the object goal, and the recovery of self-esteem.

Most participants of the Panels stressed the role of love deprivation in early childhood. There was however no agreement as to whether aggression plays a central or secondary role in depression, nor could it be determined whether aggression is an innate primary function or appears only secondarily in reaction to frustration. As for orality in depression, it has been pointed out that depressives do have oral fantasies and are inclined to seek oral gratification,

Etiologic Studies

There has been a good deal of evidence that lack of maternal love causes severe depressive mood and "affect hunger" (Levy, 1937; Freud and Burlingham, 1944; Spitz, 1945; Bowlby, 1951, 1960a, 1960b, 1961, 1963; and many others).

According to Alfred Adler, the rejected child may try to

win love by intentional suffering and escape into illness. "The discouraged child who finds that he can tyrannize best by tears will be a cry-baby, and a direct line of development leads from the cry-baby to the adult depressed patient," wrote Kurt Adler (1967, p. 332).

Frieda Fromm-Reichmann (1950, 1959) found that most manic-depressives come from large families where no one is genuinely interested in the child's welfare. As a result of lack of a true and meaningful relationship in childhood, the manic-depressive suffers from feelings of insecurity and rejection. Therefore he seeks and quickly forms superficial relationships and tends to be clinging and exploitative.

Munro (1969) critically examined the research data concerning the relationship between parental deprivation and depressive disorders. Malmquist (1971), in a thorough analysis of the literature, demonstrated that although maternal deprivation is generally believed to affect the child's mental health adversely, a specificity of outcome of maternal deprivation has not been established. It will be the task of the present chapter to establish the terms of intrafamilial interaction that produce various degrees of depression in the offspring.

My studies have led me to establish a link between the various degrees of depression viewed as a nosological entity on a continuum of neurotic symptoms (hysterias, etc.) through hysteroid character neurosis, latent psychosis, and full-blown psychotic depression. As will be explained in the following pages, the shifting moods of elation and depression are reflections of dynamic shifts in the balance of libidinal cathexes from self-love to object love, from self-hate to object hate, from love to hate, and vice versa. Under such circumstances normal mutual relationships are rendered impossible. I have called this group of disorders dysmutual depressive, because mutual relationships are disturbed and the underlying dynamic is that of self-depreciation, self-accusation and

self-destruction. I have included paranoia in the depressive
type of disorders because paranoia is an effort to externalize
and project the self-directed hostility of the dysmutual-
depressive disorder.

Beat Me but Love Me

Some people are willing to accept an inordinate amount of
suffering provided they are loved. "Beat me but love me," a
boy requested of his mother. He was 10 years old when his
younger sister was born. His mother never loved him; she
called him ugly duckling, pest and monster. She told him
that she hated him almost as intensely as she hated his father.

When his little sister was born, the mother put him and his
father in a small bedroom, keeping the master bedroom for
herself and her "little princess." The father meekly protested,
but characteristically, surrendered to the iron will of his wife.
The boy took the rejection badly; he felt that his world had
collapsed, for from now on he could no longer cling to the
apron strings of his beloved and rejecting mother, who ordered the maid to serve meals for the boy and his father. The
two rejected males ate their meals silently, daydreaming
about their lost paradise and resenting each other's presence.

The little boy developed headaches but they proved of no
avail in his mother's concern or attention. The maid, acting
on the mother's orders, gave him bufferin. On one occasion,
when the child regurgitated, the indignant maid called his
mother who, filled with fury, beat the boy mercilessly and
put him to bed.

Thus the pattern was set. The boy had intensely cathected
his mother to the point where he even obtained gratification
from the pain she dispensed. A few weeks later he developed
frequent diarrhea and incontinence. His classmates called the
teacher's attention to the foul-smelling child who was subsequently sent home. The maid refused to wash him and the

desperate mother had no choice but to throw him in a bath-
tub, clothes, feces and all. She washed and hit him, soaped
and hit, rubbed and hit.

These were the most delightful and victorious moments in
his life. The new "method" *forced* his mother to take care of
him. The mother was compelled to leave the "little princess"
and minister to his needs. His little body was covered with
black and blue marks, but the soapy water and, alas, his
mother's hands were warm and exciting.

As he grew older, he learned the lesson of winning love by
self-defeat and extorting sympathy by self-inflicted misery.
He became a morose, sulking young man who hated all who
did not love him and hated himself because he was not loved.
He loved to be loved and, whenever people showed some lik-
ing for him, he was joyful, elated, and overly grateful. As
with other hysterics and dysmutuals, he was prone to exaggerate and responded with great love and exulted gratitude
to any sign of mild affection.

His moods oscillated. Most of the time he was irritable and
depressed, full of hatred for others and for himself. However,
as soon as someone showed interest in him, his hatred turned
into love and depression was transformed into elation. Sometimes the change took place without an outside stimulus.
When he reached the bottom of depression, that is, when his
ego lay prostrate at the feet of the superego, his superego,
like his mother, embraced the ego, and his self-pity was
transformed into an ecstatic, manic self-love.

The Cinderella Complex

Despite extensive research, there is no evidence that
manic-depressive psychosis is inherited. (1) The fact that it
often runs in families may prove that parental rejection is
perpetuated from generation to generation. Parental rejection need not be associated with pathological hostility; an
infant may feel rejected whenever his mother is sick, hospi-

talized or unable to take care of him; when she is pregnant with another child; when she works outside her home; or even when she is overburdened with a large family, and is unable to pay enough attention to each child. The most severe rejection is mother's death. (2) Mothers of manic-depressives are neither kind, considerate nor warm persons. Some are psychopathic, concerned about no one but themselves, resenting the burdens of motherhood and often given to abusive language, violent tempers and brutality. The child who is to become a depressive psychotic is treated by his mother with frank rejection, sometimes with hate, and in many cases, he has to compete, unsuccessfully against a more privileged sibling. The future manic-depressive is the "Cinderella" of a family usually composed of a hostile mother, a disinterested or hostile father, and siblings favored by the mother. Such a child is the forgotten "Ugly Duckling," albeit without the prospects of future swandom. In some cases, the entire family—the mother, father and siblings—join in rejection and ridicule.

In contradistinction to the neglected child who turns psychopathic, the future manic-depressive is treated with outright dislike, except when he is seriously ill or in grave danger. The child who becomes schizophrenic has been exposed to excessive demands and unfair criticism for not meeting maternal demands. Thus a child who becomes manic-depressive is made to feel that he is bad or stupid or ugly. He is the unwanted, unloved and forgotten member of the family, treated like a burden and a handicap, except on those rare occasions when his sad condition forces his parents into a position of caring. In most cases, adequate maternal care is given to the infant in his first few months of life, the rejection coming somewhat later. Thus manic-depressives have a tendency to regress to infancy and even to prenatal intrauterine life. Regression does not go back to the point of frustration or rejection, but below that *point*, to the true or imaginary era of the "lost paradise" of safety and love. In milder, neurotic cases of the dysmutual disorder (hysterias and depressive neuroses), the regression is usually to the oral stage.

The symptomatic core of the dysmutual disorder is the "Cinderella Complex," the main objective of which is *to win love*. Whatever behavioral and psychosomatic symptoms develop, all are geared to this goal. Whereas the hypervectorial (schizophrenic type) fears he may lose his mother, the dysmutual (manic-depressive) directs all his energies to gaining her love.

Fusion of Libido and Destrudo

The outstanding feature of dysmutual disorders is the "ever-hungry libido." One may hypothesize that the neonate is endowed with a certain quantity of self-cathected libido and readily mobilized destrudo. A continuous and friendly gratification of the infant's needs gradually introduces changes in the balance of cathexes. The infant receives milk with love from the vectorial parents who give him their nondemanding love. The more love the infant receives, the better he will be prepared for giving it to others in his later life. Whatever and whoever gives satisfaction elicits love; the infant begins "to love" milk, breasts, the good mother, the friendly father, the smiling neighbor. Part of his libido, originally invested in himself, is invested in others (i.e., object-cathected). In normal emotional development the infant grows to love himself because his parents love him. Consequently he begins to love the world, in an instrumental fashion, which gradually becomes mutual. Later on in adulthood, he will love his own children in a vectorial way, and will be able to empathize with the less fortunate members of his community.

However, when milk is withheld from a hungry child or when it is given in an unfriendly manner or accompanied by threatening gestures, the infant is unable to develop proper social relations. Forever uncertain that his needs will be satisfied, the infant feels permanently hungry. Thus manic-depressive patients will consume gross quantities of food, indicative of their oral-cannibalistic fixations.

When a dysmutual feels accepted, that is, when love is given to him, he is full of self- as well as object-love. External supplies make him feel powerful and rich, in love with his own personality and benevolent to others. He is filled with energy and extends himself in being pleasant and friendly to whomever he meets, radiating love and overflowing with kindness. He cannot remain "mutual" in terms of a balanced give-and-take relationship. He demands too much from others and gives too much when in a giving mood.

A dysmutual is unable to love unless he is loved. The less love he gets, the more he needs. Feelings of being loved are usually short-lived. Sooner or later he will experience the pangs of a new emotional hunger which preclude his enjoyment of his current victories. Dysmutuals are *insatiable*, in love, sex, friendship, glory, status or possessions. They perpetually require new supplies, new victories, and are in constant pursuit of "greener pastures." Thus, while they believe themselves to be strong and friendly, others see them as weak (trying too hard to please, overdoing in friendliness) and hostile (demanding what others are not willing to give to them).

Dysmutuals seem to demand remuneration for their love with a Shylock's interest. They say, "You must love me all the time, no matter what I do; if you refuse, you are as mean as my mother was, and I hate you." Their friends, parents, husbands, wives or children are in eternal debt owing them neverending love and gratitude; when such demonstrations are not forthcoming the great love of a dysmutual easily turns into a malicious hate. Small wonder that dysmutual parents often have schizophrenic children, for the overdemanding attitude and emotional exploitation of the child is conducive to the development of a hypervectorial process in their offspring.

Dysmutuals are overconcerned with the attitude of others towards themselves and are exceedingly sensitive even to the slightest sign of rejection or disrespect. Being notoriously tactless, they frequently alienate even those who are friendly toward them. In addition, their self-love (self-cathected libido) is inconsistent. A dysmutual believes that he is good-looking, smart and strong only when he is told so by another person or when he is in a manic bliss and is told so by his own superego. On a neurotic level (hysteria) he depends more on others; on a psychotic level the inner voice suffices. On the neurotic level his elated mood depends mostly on supplies from without; on the psychotic level the contact with reality is tenuous, if anything, and the superego is the sole dictator of his moods.

Being overly dependent on the opinions of others, the dysmutual cannot be consistent in his self-conception. When rejected (unless accepted on his own impossible terms of unconditional admiration, he feels rejected), the dysmutual perceives himself as he is seen by others, that is, as weak and hostile. As one patient put it, "My mother, my father, my brother, my teachers, everyone hated me. So I realized that I am an ugly, stupid little boy."

Dr. Jekyll and Mr. Hyde

The feeling of being rejected is almost constant in dysmutal neurotics and psychotics. They are perpetually depressed and always on the defensive. Pleasant and friendly moods are like rays of sunshine that break through the clouds, but cannot disperse them. Friends and relatives of manic-depressive patients often compare the rapidly changing attitudes to the turning off and on of hot and cold water faucets. The soft-spoken, kind, affectionate Dr. Jekyll turns into a Mr. Hyde whenever his loving attitude is not fully appreciated and repaid with high interest.

Hysterics, manic depressives, and other dysmutuals do not

convey sincerity in their shifting attitudes. Hence it is not surprising that they are typically mistrusted. When in a loving mood, the volatile dysmutual makes exaggerated statements and promises about his great love and unlimited desire to be of help, but at the slightest disappointment he forgets what he said a short while ago, behaving in a highly aggressive manner against those whom he professed to love forever.

The dysmutual himself believes in the sincerity of his feelings. He is not a calculated liar as he may seem to be and as the hyperinstrumental psychopaths are. He exaggerates in mutuality (hence the name "dysmutual"), wanting too much and giving too much. He is easily carried away by his momentary feelings; he says things that bear witness to his poor sense of reality, making promises he cannot possibly fulfill.

Most probably, libido and destrudo are two forms of the same mental energy, destrudo being the more primitive one. The rapid shifts from love to hate in dysmutuals could be explained by a primitive organization of their personality, with libido and destrudo inadequately separated. Thus their destrudo is thrown into the open, and its sublimation, neutralization, and aim-inhibition is rendered impossible.

Self-Defeat and Depression

Dysmutuals will work hard toward a goal, but upon nearing victory they tend to defeat themselves. Thus they repeat the childhood pattern where success brought parental rejection and despair was rewarded.

Depressive moods are long-lasting and painful, yet dysmutuals do little to overcome their feelings of being unworthy, inadequate, inferior, or mean (that is, weak and hostile). They tend to brood and perpetuate the feeling that they themselves are guilty for all their misery. Often they recall past and insignificant mistakes as if trying to hurt themselves intentionally. Many of them are accident-prone. They are exceedingly sensitive and vulnerable to criticism, yet they seem

to agree with their persecutors and blame themselves for that
which their enemies blame them, as if hoping to win the
sympathy of the hostile mother by accepting punishment
willingly.

The desire to suffer or to inflict harm on oneself, called
masochism, often serves as a protection against even greater
pain or harm. Thus the dysmutual was a child who preferred
pain to rejection and hoped to win sympathy by suffering.

The manic-depressive patient described at the beginning of
the chapter is a case in point. He was dry and clean for
years, but when his mother gave birth to a little girl, he regressed to incontinence. His mother never cared properly for
him, but presently she neglected him completely and devoted all her attention and affection to the new sibling. The
patient, feeling utterly rejected, became incontinent and was
the target of ridicule in school. However, his incontinence
forced the teacher to send him home, which ultimately resulted in eliciting maternal attentions, albeit sadistic ones.

Dysmutuals are not pure masochists; they are actually *sa-
domasochists*, who wish to suffer but wish others to suffer as
well. Their suicidal attempts are sadomasochistic, as will be
explained below. Psychopaths (hyperinstrumentals) are
purely sadistic, their aim being to inflict pain on others.

The ego of the dysmutual, as will be explained later, does
not exercise sound judgment nor adequate self-control. Such
individuals act impulsively, their unconscious impulses being
guided by the "win love through suffering" mechanism. Although they are not willing to die, they flee into illness as a
method of engaging the mother's sympathies. Hysterics
whose ego is still intact make spectacular suicide attempts,
yet somehow manage to stay alive. Manic-depressives are
more reckless in their suicidal attempts.

The most dangerous hours for suicidal attempts are in the
early morning when everyone else is asleep. The agitated
manic-depressive psychotic falls asleep easily, but he gets up

early. There is nothing to do in the wee hours, and there is
no one who cares. At such moments the dysmutual psychotic
often acts under the desire to punish himself and those who
do not love him. Manic-depressive patients whose lives have
been saved, report that they hated everyone and hoped that
their suicide would inspire tears and sorrow from their relatives and friends. They imagined themselves listening to the
sobbings of the survivors, believing that their death would
win the love they failed to receive. They almost heard themselves saying to mother or another person who was supposed
to love them, "It's all because you didn't love me. Now you
love me, but it is too late." Some patients could actually
imagine themselves being alive, lying in the coffin and smiling to themselves with a feeling of victory. The basic *wish is
to regress,* to be asleep while mother watches over them; they
desire to sleep in mother's womb, to be united with her and
bathed in her love.

Unfortunately, their impulsive suicidal attempts are all too
often successful. Any sign of rejection may motivate a
manic-depressive patient to attempt suicide. A wife whose
husband went to a party and left her home alone; a man
whose partner broke off the partnership; a mother whose son
told her he didn't need her; a daughter scolded by
mother—all of them impulsively decided to "put an end to
their sufferings." Whenever there was anyone to dissuade the
patient, the tragedy was prevented. Actually, none of them
really wanted to die; all they desired was to be nurtured.

The dysmutual disorders are cyclic: love turns to hate, hate
into love, self-love into object love, object hate into self-hate,
and vice versa. Any loss of love, friendship or support throws
the dysmutual into pangs of depression, reviving his memories of lack of support in childhood.

A hypervectorial in a depressive mood tries to calm himself down, but a dysmutual tends to perpetuate his bad
mood. The more he hates himself, the more he feels love and

pity for himself. Neurotic dysmutuals (hysterics) will drama-
tize their situation and talk to themselves. "You poor soul,
see what happened. Everyone hates you, because you deserve
it, poor chap." The more they feel sorry for themselves, the
quicker will their depression lift.

Sex

The fusion of libido and destrudo is apparent in sexual life.
Certain sexual problems are common to all dysmutuals, and
some are specific to the respective levels and syndromes.

The dysmutual is incapable of resolving his Oedipus complex through proper identification with the parent of the
same sex. Maternal aggressiveness prevents normal resolution
of the family drama. Overdependency on and incestuous attachments to the parents continue throughout their lives and
strong defense mechanisms of reaction-formation make them
hostile to the parent to whom they are most attracted. They
are typically attracted to the most hostile parent.

In practically all cases of male dysmutualism there is an
excessive dependence on the mother. The patient never renounces her as a love object and seeks out her image in all
women. He repeats the pattern of his childhood, forever
trying to induce women to love him. As long as he is involved in pursuit he is submissive and overaffectionate, but
when his courtship has been accepted, he rejects the woman
and looks for another mother-substitute who will love him
more.

Male hysterics and other dysmutuals typically have numerous sexual difficulties. Some of them fear women whom they
desire, a recreation of their attitude to the mother. Sexual
impotence and premature ejaculation are common symptoms
of hysteric men, who often boast about their sexual victories.
In point of fact they do not run after women but away from
them. A similar pattern has been observed in females. A frigid dysmutual female tries to attract as many men as she can

in a neverending desire to be loved by everyone, but she is unable to develop a lasting relationship with anyone. In more severe cases, where maternal rejection has been exceedingly harsh, the boy may turn to the father for love; the image of the punishing and rejecting mother is introjected, and the identification with her leads to a negative Oedipus complex and homosexual desires. Male dysmutuals experience frightening dreams of the "spider-mother" who castrates. Many such patients report dreams in which the threat of castration comes from a female representing the mother, with the father as the love object.

The combination of an absent or weak father and an aggressive mother is conducive to a tendency towards femininity in male offspring. A young man reported that he could not tolerate his father's advances to girls nor his frivolous language. Now 30 years old, he had never had sexual relations with a woman. Whenever the situation was conducive to sexual intercourse, he lost erection and fled. His excuse was "I cannot *hurt* a girl," as if intercourse were a hurting act and he were the girl who might be hurt. In psychotherapeutic work, his female identification was brought into the open. He feared and wished to be raped by his father, and the constant quarreling reflected his reaction-formation.

Unable to engage in more normal sexual practices, dysmutuals often prefer the passive role with the female fondling them. Fellatio permits this role, in which the penis has assumed the role of the breast. Since the sex of the partner in fellatio is of secondary importance, one can see in it a compromise between heterosexuality and homosexuality.

Dysmutual patients cannot renounce mother as a love object nor identify with the father. Their libido and destrudo are vehement and fused with each other. On a neurotic level, the ego builds defense mechanisms against the impulses; psychosis begins when these mechanisms have failed.

The dysmutual perceives all women as potential lovers and

all men as potential enemies. He may identify with women, seek their company and try to win over as many as possible. He easily "falls in love," but actually he is in a continuous search for the good, ideal, understanding mother. Dysmutual men feel ill at ease with other men in whom they see punishing fathers or potential homosexual partners.

The Superego

The superego incorporates the parental rejecting figures and is the primary source of self-directed hostility. The hyperinstrumental psychopaths are severely lacking in superego structures, for they have never identified with parental figures. The hypervectorial schizophrenics have a powerful, dictatorial superego produced by overidentification with the demanding parents. The superego of the dysmutual is highly inconsistent, full of hate yet ready to embrace the ego when it fails. Love and hate are not clearly determined nor separate qualities.

These shifting attitudes are reflected in practically all aspects of the dysmutual's life. A dysmutual can be an idealist and a swindler, cruel and sentimental, religious and atheistic at the same time. Dysmutuals easily shift their moral or political identifications; they have no steady conviction, no persistent philosophy, no guiding rules. They easily identify with whomever they have had contact, as if trying to incorporate new gods. One day they are determined to adhere strictly to the rules of religion; the next day may find them preaching the opposite. Yet they are not practical opportunists as are the hyperinstrumentals. Hyperinstrumentals join the church if it pays to join; dysmutuals join anyone who they believe will accept them. Since they are never content, they abandon their objects as soon as they suspect a diminution of love.

The one area where the dysmutual's superego is fairly consistent is in its attacks on the ego which results in a prevailing endogenous depression.

This kind of superego is like a nagging mother who is always finding fault with her child. Whereas the hypervectorial's superego is demanding, the dysmutual's superego is outright critical and hostile, making the patient feel small, weak, unwanted and rejected.

"I know I am no good. I am a liar, I cheat everybody. Twenty-five years ago I took a quarter without mother's permission. I am just a dishonest person, an outcast, a failure. No one likes me. Why should they? Other people are happy; they have something to show for their lives. What do I have? I am just a disgusting creature," a 38-year-old manic-depressive man kept repeating.

The content of the self-accusations has little to do with the real, present-day happenings. In their depressive moods, dysmutuals recall events that happened years or even decades ago and magnify their significance. It would appear that they are repeating the communication patterns of their mothers: thus, whenever the child broke a saucer, mother used to say, "You broke *all* the dishes. You are a careless, stupid, unreliable child." The superego exaggerates in much the same fashion and with no respect for the truth.

Antidepressive Reactions

There are several possible reactions to depression. Dysmutual depressions are not always self-terminating processes. Certainly the most healthy reaction to depression is its *spontaneous termination.* In the peculiar dysmutual disbalance of cathexes a small supply of libidinal cathexis (affection) from without may terminate the depression. A dysmutual depression may be interrupted by an intake of food or fluid, by rest or play, by praise or achievement. The extreme dependence of the dysmutual on supplies from without places the dysmutual disorder in the realm of *field phenomena:* The dysmutual's symptoms are largely a function of who interacts with him and how.

The neurotic defenses against depression (the *ego-protective* symptoms) include denial, dissociation, fatigue, drowsiness, reaction formation and a galaxy of psychosomatic symptoms, such as headaches, gastrointestinal troubles, etc. The *ego-deficiency* or psychotic symptoms include the manic state, paranoid projections, aggressive-defensive moods and severe regression.

The term "manic-depressive disorder" is perhaps misleading for the manic mood is one of a number of possible reactions to depression. In point of fact, manic-depressive patients are *always depressed*, that is, always incessantly torn by the attacks of the superego (the introjected parental image) against the ego. The manic state is an effort to deny depression and to ward it off. It is a temporary, unstable mood. Manic patients display a flood of words and actions in a desperate attempt to escape the unbearable feelings of guilt and depression. But even at the peak of elation they harbor self-destructive, suicidal thoughts and their depressed feelings never completely disappear.

Manic episodes may come as a reaction to loss and defeat; they can also be triggered by a negligible achievement or by a slight sign of affection from without. Mania is not a good-natured happy mood; it is a state of tension accompanied by a feeling of power. With this feeling of power the manic acts in what appears to be a friendly fashion, indiscriminately talking to and making friends with whomever he meets. However, the slightest oppositon to his overtures or a disagreement with his opinionated statements may trigger an explosion of furious resentment.

Projection, agitated depression, and severe regression are the other possible reactions to depression. A detailed discussion of them will follow after analysis of the ego defenses.

The Ego

The strength of the ego is the main indicator of the *level* of disorder, yet certain deviations in the functioning of the ego

are typical of each *type* of mental disorder. In the hypervectorial type, the ego is subservient to the superego; it is overmobilized, tense and highly attentive, until it collapses in
manifest schizophrenia. In the hyperinstrumental type, the
ego joins forces with the id. The dysmutual's ego shifts from
one alternative to the other, serving either the superego or
the id.

In most cases of dysmutualism the ego is undermobilized,
weak and subservient to the whims of the superego. Manic-
depressives are inattentive and lacking in self-discipline;
unable to withstand superego pressure, the ego withdraws
into the id and merges with it. Contact with reality is tenuous. This is true even with neurotic dysmutuals, i.e., the
hysterics, who are frequently muddled. They show little endurance or perseverance, and even when endowed with excellent intellectual abilities, they are unable to achieve consistently.

The degree of reality testing of the ego corresponds to the
level of disorder. A dysmutual neurotic's ego tries to ward off
superego pressures by rationalizations, reaction-formation,
denial and dissociations. In hypervectorial neuroses the ego
offers a desperate struggle; in hyperinstrumental neuroses it
accepts the easy way out. Dysmutuals rarely lose all contact
with reality as is true of hypervectorials; even on the psychotic level, manic-depressives still preserve some contact
with reality. However, inattention, forgetting, oblivion, distortion of truth to please people or to impress them, exag-
geration, omission of detail, and lack of empathy and understanding for the feelings of others are typical of all
dysmutuals. While the dysmutual is never as alert and attentive as the compulsive neurotic, his ego is never as frag-
mented as that of the schizophrenic.

One of the outstanding features of dysmutualism is the
shifting self-image. At one moment dysmutuals see them-

selves as weak and despondent, but a few minutes later they
may believe that they are giants and heroes. They display a
far-reaching ambition and a short-lived endurance, great enthusiasm and little perseverance. When they feel strong,
they underestimate obstacles. In the elated state dysmutuals
are notoriously overoptimistic and grandiose about their own
material and intellectual resources, seeing the world as a
good mother who is willing to give her breast to her wonderful child.

The motor functions of dysmutuals are usually erratic.
When they are in a depressed mood they are sluggish, pro-
crastinating, indecisive and drowsy, but when their spirits are
better, they are hyperactive, excited, impatient and careless.
The hypo- or hyperactivity of manic-depressives doesn't resemble the catatonic pattern, for they do not exercise rigid
self-control, nor do they experience a complete loss of control. The ego of the manic-depressive is, as it were, pushed
aside or even asleep, but it is never as badly shattered as the
ego of the schizophrenic. One can compare the schizophrenic
ego to an army decimated in combat, while the ego of the
manic-depressive may be likened to an army of deserters,
demoralized and disarmed, but not annihilated.

As a rule, dysmutuals have extremely low self-esteem. The
feeling of their own weakness is at the core of depression,
whether precipitated by external or internal pressures. The
dysmutual tries to overcome his low self-esteem in many
ways, one of which is through extreme ambition. Some dysmutuals, in milder stages of the disorder, rather than escape
into manic moods, try to compensate for their feelings of inferiority by excessive work, long working hours and an overall drive for supremacy.

Success in their endeavors reduces inner tension if it is
acknowledged by others and brings them love and admiration.

Mental Topography

Hypervectorial individuals have, as a rule, an easy access
to their preconscious and unconscious. Thus schizophrenics

often surprise their friends and relatives by recalling, in minute detail, long-forgotten events. On the neurotic level, the overmobilized ego exercises excellent control over preconscious memory traces. When they deteriorate, their memory is not lost but rather mixed up, old and recent events becoming confused.

The dysmutual's control over past memories is hazy. Even gifted hysterics who excel in intellectual areas do not display precision in recalling personal events. If an event was favorable to their self-esteem, they are likely to distort details and magnify its significance, while an embarrassing incident is likely to be repressed. Dysmutuals in depressed moods frequently complain about poor memory.

Repression and amnesia belong to the typical symptom-armamentarium of dysmutual disorders. Breuer's and Freud's (1893–1895) studies on hysteria pointed to amnesia and dissociation as being typical for the hysteric symptom complex.

While the ego of the dysmutual is frequently hazy, half asleep, and subordinate either to the superego or the id, it may surface and represent a realistic point of view in dreams. These "wisdom dreams" have been reported by hysterics, paranoiacs and manic-depressives.

Dysmutual Neurosis

Dysmutual neurotic symptoms include anxiety neurosis, hysteria and depressive reaction. In his fight to win love and to avoid rejection, the patient develops a galaxy of symptoms all aimed at forcing his environment to notice him.

Rorschach test results show that hysterics most often overlook these elements that do not fit—i.e., they block out certain aspects of reality. "Underlying this void is the mechanism of repression or denial" (Wittenborn, 1963, p. 545).

One may distinguish three main neurotic types, namely, the *depressive, dissociative,* and *conversion* (the so-called conversion-hysteria). The mild depressive syndrome, characterized by anxiety states, feelings of inadequacy, and a subservient attitude and desire to please others, signifies a submission of the ego to the superego and continuous effort to alleviate the pressure by a willing acceptance of punishment.

Under stress, the dysmutual seeks relief from the castigating superego whether it be through sleep, fugue, amnesia or splitting. Thus the dissociative syndrome is one where the ego joins forces with the id in the service of escape from guilt.

The third syndrome, hysteria, can imitate a great many physical diseases and produce symptoms resembling most organic disorder although there is no apparent organicity. Hysterical symptomatology includes headaches, nausea, fainting spells, dizziness, heart palpitation, ulcers, vomiting, backache, asthenopia nervosa, paralysis, anorexia, deafness, obstructions of the throat, dysmenorrhea, diarrhea, constipation, aphasia, skin disease, asthma, sexual disorders, etc. Such conditions are referred to as "functional" illness.

Earlier literature reported a variety of hysterical illnesses which are today no longer in evidence, e.g., epileptic-type attacks (grand mal), clonic and choreiform movements, anaesthesia, mutism, and serious gastrointestinal and vasomotor disorders. Although these highly dramatic symptoms have disappeared, Perley and Guze (1962) have been able to enumerate 10 groups of hysterical symptoms.

Manic-depressive patients apparently suffer from a host of hysterical symptoms in their earlier prepsychotic years. As long as these hysterical symptoms prevailed, the patients did not become psychotic; i.e., the symptom defended against the breakthrough of unmanageable psychic material. Depressive neurosis, with its feelings of fatigue, inadequacy, guilt and depression, is probably the most typical pattern of dysmutual neurosis.

Character Neurosis

The dysmutual character neurotic, also called cyclothymic character neurotic, displays a facade of shallow happiness and an optimisitic mood based on professed self-confidence. Typical inferiority feeling and depressions disappear under a mask of self-admiration and glib clichés.

Dysmutual character neurotics are full of tabloid wisdom and express their cliché statements as if they were great and original ideas. They are most eager to teach and preach, to spout pearls of wisdom and world-saving counsel, such as "keep smiling," "don't worry," "let's face it," "c'est la vie," "everyone does it," "it's never too late," offering unsolicited guidance to friends and strangers alike. They are very active, though not necessarily productive. Although quite sociable, they rarely develop profound and lasting human relations. They seem to believe that they are unusual, unique and superior regardless of their success or failure. Their lack of persistence and changing moods often bring defeat which they proceed to glorify. "Stupid people win; smart ones lose. Only crooks and thiefs are successful in these days. An honest man has no chances for success," argued a middle-aged patient. To prove his point, he described his business transactions in which apparent neglect, inconsistency, carelessness and self-defeating actions have been combined with genuine efforts, initiative, and hard work. The patient was a "fallen hero," a man who "sacrificed himself for his family," who "did not give up," but was defeated because of his virtues. He turned his defeat into a sort of "moral victory." He could not blame himself for his failure, for he believed that his behavior was beyond reproach; he worked hard, displayed energy and initiative, honesty and fair play, but he had had "bad luck."

He accepted his defeat with an air of martyrdom and spoke about his "heroic efforts that led nowhere." Repeatedly but not truthfully, he described his failures as if trying to prove how good he was. The basic dysmutual mechanism of craving love was displayed through acceptance of defeat and compensatory superiority feelings. The ego of dysmutual character neurotics renounces those parts of reality that are damaging to self-esteem.

A 50-year-old man eloped with his secretary after losing his business. When rejected by her, he returned to his wife and became a taxi driver. He subsequently blamed his business failure on his wife, his secretary, his business associates, bad luck, competition, and finally the whole world. He believed that he was a brilliant businessman, a great lover, a man of high moral standards, and an overall genius who still waited for a Messiah (preferably a maternal figure) to embrace him and help him to prove his greatness. Meanwhile he smoked big cigars, was a boy-scout troop leader, and maintained that he was a great civic leader, next in status to the town mayor. His tips were unusually generous, especially on dates with college girls or secretaries.

Megalomania is a defense against feelings of inferiority; it is a distortion of reality testing aimed at self-aggrandizement. A high school teacher who failed in practically everything, told his students highly exaggerated stories of his allegedly great deeds and influential friends. An underpaid manager of a small office tried to impress the receptionist by telling her of his great sufferings and great abilities, not yet recognized by the business community and society at large.

Latent Depressive Psychosis

The dysmutual latent psychotic level, as with all other latent psychotic levels, represents the last stop before a manifest psychotic breakdown. The transition from the latent to the manifest psychotic level is usually less dramatic in dysmutuals than in hypervectorials.

Most frequently this transition is not an eruption but an erosion. In latent psychosis, the dysmutual denial of reality goes so far as to deny any setback, failure or defeat. The ego, severely pressed by the superego, abandons reality. Occasionally, latent dysmutual psychotics feel that they are failures, that they have never done anything sensible, that their lives have been a complete waste and that no one respects them. Usually they try to pretend that they are happy and successful individuals. Hypomanic, mild euphoric moods are typical for this stage. Depressed moods, usually occurring in the early morning hours, are signs of deterioration and failure of the ego-protective symptoms. A latent dysmutual psychotic desperately fights depression, as if trying to make the last stand before plunging down into the depressive psychotic mood of "giving up."

A latent psychotic may engage in a great many useless and energy-consuming activities aimed at warding off an oncoming depression. One patient, a musician, decided to become a physicist, mathematician, philosopher, art historian and anthropologist in addition to being a soloist, composer, conductor and an impressario. A female patient was "collecting men" by getting herself involved with scores of casual acquaintances and even total strangers. Another patient started half a dozen projects, contracted scores of people, made hundreds of appointments and kept adding to a repertoire of activities which he never completed.

The term "vacationing ego" describes the mentality of latent dysmutual psychotics. It would appear that all functions of the ego have shrunk to one task, the warding off of the superego's assaults. A latent dysmutual psychotic exercises poor judgment—he tends to accept commitment he can never meet, assumes responsibilities above his capacities, overdoes in friendship and submissiveness, undersells his own services, exaggerates in emotion, overspends his money, and acts in a peculiarly senseless way whenever his notion of "impressing people" is at stake.

A dysmutual latent psychotic overspends his emotional resources but rarely invests them in a continuous and successful effort. He may devote years to building a flourishing business enterprise or career, and in no time destroy what he has built. He may turn against those who faithfully assist him, but he cannot take criticism or hostility. He may win love and social status but cannot preserve them. He must destroy that which he has built, as if his ultimate happiness can only be attained through self-defeat.

General passivity, decline of sexual desire, remorse and brooding, accident-proneness, and neglect of physical appearance indicate that the ego is losing the battle and a psychotic decline may be imminent.

Latent dysmutual psychotics represent a combination of neurotic symptoms such as the happy façade of self-admiration, joviality and hyperactivity, combined with self-accusations and hatred directed toward the world, fear of the future and a profound feeling of hopelessness. The manifest phase comes gradually; when the ego's defenses can no longer halt the superego-induced feelings of rejection and worthlessness, a bleak psychotic depression starts.

Manifest Psychosis

In manifest dysmutual psychosis, that is, psychotic depression, there is regression to a pre-ego developmental phase.

In hypervectorial regression the ego fights and suffers smashing defeat and damage, but in the dysmutual disorders, the ego does not put up much of a fight; it surrenders easily, regresses, and renounces its conscious control over the id and the superego.

On the Rorschach inkblot test, whereas the hypervectorial is afraid to overlook minute detail, the dysmutual doesn't pay attention to detail at all. Whereas hypervectorials overcalculate, dysmutuals act on impulse. The hypervectorial's ego is overmobilized; the dysmutual's ego is undermobilized and drowsy.

The submerged ego may re-emerge in surprisingly intact form. The shock of an attempted but unsuccessful suicide may restore the manic-depressive to an almost normal and realistic assessment of the situation that made him cut his wrists a short while ago.

A strong external stimulus, especially a threat to life, may instantly bring the manic-depressive back to reality. The psychotic course is temporarily abandoned and in this state of remission, the patient functions reasonably well.

One can distinguish four clinical patterns in dysmutual psychosis. These four syndromes, analogous to the syndromes of manifest schizophrenia are not closed clinical entities. They are descriptive categories, related to observable symptoms and personality structure. Shifts from one clinical pattern to another are common.

The first syndrome is *depression* which is the basic state of dysmutual psychosis. However, when the ego and the superego merge, a state of blissful elation or mania begins.

The second syndrome is *paranoia,* the dynamics of which will be explained below. Paranoia occurs when the failing ego externalizes superego pressures, perceiving the world as the rejecting, punishing mother who will eventually be forced to accept the suffering child.

The third syndrome is *agitated-depression.* This syndrome manifests itself when the ego is crushed between the cruel superego and the savage id. There are no elated moods, no escape mechanisms, no respite from severe depression. Danger of suicide runs high in this syndrome.

The final and most regressive syndrome is *simple deterioration,* which occurs when both ego and superego are defeated by the triumphant id. There is some analogy between these four syndromes and the four syndromes of schizophrenic psychosis, especially with regard to the simple deterioration syndromes in both types of mental disorder.

The Manic Syndrome

The manic syndrome does not bring genuine joy and happiness. It is an escape, a desperate reaction to an unbearable feeling of depression. The dynamics of this syndrome represent the surrender of the ego to the superego. When the pressure of the superego becomes unbearable, the ego renounces further resistance, and turns away from reality, as if refusing to deal with it. In a manic mood the self-righteous superego determines what is true and false: thus the manic patients may express dogmatic and self-assured opinions about matters they have not considered heretofore. They become omniscient sages and judges who know everything and have the final say on all problems.

The manic mood may be precipitated by a severe blow to one's self-esteem, a loss of a close relative or friend, the loss of status or property. In reaction to these events, the dysmutual hates those who have let him down; he blames even those who were thoughtless enough to desert him by death. This hate is then taken up by his superego and turned on the self.

Introjection of the image of the rejecting or deceased parent, most often the one of the opposite sex, is typical for the dysmutual disorders. This introjected "love object" functions in a manner analogous to that of the rejecting parent; namely it is hostile and cruel, but only up to a certain point. The despairing ego tries to reach this point by accepting defeat, by magnifying it, and by making life look more horrible than it is. Then it turns to the superego as if to say, "see how miserable I am! You are right, I deserve to be punished. So beat me, but love me."

In some, but not all cases of dysmutual psychosis, the superego accepts the surrender. When the ego gives up in despair, the superego accepts the defeat, embracing the wounded ego as would the bad mother who suddenly felt sorry for her suffering infant.

Once the dysmutual turns self-hate into self-pity, his mood changes radically. The ego, loved by the superego, is full of love and friendship. A manic patient becomes everyone's friend: Thus, a married woman in a manic state invited strange men she met on the street to share her bed; a manic man offered help and distributed money to whomever he met.

The ego that surrendered its prerogatives to the superego does not exercise proper jurisdiction over emotion and motility. The superego is self-righteous; so are the word and deeds of a manic, who believes that his wishes cannot be questioned and his whims are the law.

In elation there is no delay, no reality principle, no planning nor caution. Whatever the manic feels like doing, he will do immediately, here and now. If he is sexually aroused, he may proposition the first girl he meets and become furious if she turns him down. If he is highly aroused he is likely to rape her. He cannot take the slightest frustration.

The manic-depressive wants to be absorbed by his mother. His delusions and hallucinations have to do with martyrdom, with being lost and found, with being Cinderella saved by a Good Fairy or a slave led by a Messiah toward the lost paradise. A typical fantasy is of a disaster that will force mother to love them.

Schizophrenics wish to be God or the Messiah. Since their parents have been weak and unreliable individuals, they must fill the void by becoming the omnipotent, omniscient, benevolent or destructive God-Father, who saves, protects or punishes his parents. Thus, whereas the schizophrenic rescues, the manic-depressive wants to be rescued. In the manic phase, he can be joined with the powerful parents and thereby acquire omnipotence and immortality.

However, even in a manic mood there is an underlying fear of losing the newly regained paradise. Manic patients avoid facing real issues out of a fear that the sharp pin of reality may prick the balloon of their blissful illusion. Thus no real planning or practical steps are taken for fear that the implementation of an idea may bring hardships and disappointment.

The slightest disappointment, true or imaginary, will elicit a severe depression. One dysmutual psychotic patient rambled about his grandiose literary plans. He was writing, at one and the same time, a play, a novel, a philosophical essay, a study of the American economy, a survey of contemporary literature, and a textbook in industrial psychology, all of which were to be finished within the next three months and hopefully win him immortal glory. A few days later he was in the throes of despair and self-accusation. He sat on an armchair in my office, crying and accusing himself of being a complete failure. He blamed himself for the loss of a wallet with a few dollars and recalled, in tears, sad events that had occurred in the distant past: 10 years ago he had lost something, and 15 years ago, it had been something else. "I am a loser; I always lose things. I have never done anything right," he bemoaned. He contemplated suicide and blamed his wife (apparently a mother substitute) for not loving him enough.

Agitated Depression

Not all dysmutual psychotics are capable of manic denial. In some cases, there is no escape from the assaults of the superego. The patient may feel happier if he has had the opportunity to outshine others and bask in the glory of his achievements, but since no human being can always be victorious and constantly admired by others, the short-lived moods of good feeling yield to severe depression.

Agitated depression is loaded with hostility and fraught with suicidal danger. Agitated-depressed patients feel gloomy and angry, rejected and despised, hated and hateful. One patient described his feelings in the following way: "I feel like jumping out of my skin. Doctor, please lock me up before I strangle my wife and my child . . . I cannot stand them. I hate them and hate myself. The best thing would be to put an end to everything." Another agitated-depressed patient who felt tortured by an unbearable state of depression, hospitalized herself voluntarily and felt better on the ward where "she took care of all those crazy characters." She became the leading figure on the ward, an assistant and advisor to doctors and nurses. However, when she was discharged, she felt stranded and her life became senseless and bleak. In that her adult children (she was a widow) were too busy with their own activities to pay attention to her, she grew to hate them, as well as herself, with a vehemence.

Destructiveness and self-destructiveness are the outstanding features of agitated-depression. In that the defeated ego is incapable of reality testing, casual approval by a nurse seemed to offer the patient a reason for living, while her son's lack of interest in her precipitated a violent destructive and self-destructive reaction. Thus, a slight sign of rejection or hate may unleash in dysmutual psychotics uncontrollable outbursts of object and self-directed destrudo.

Paranoia: A Dysmutual Syndrome

One psychotic reaction to depression is full-blown paranoia. A way of defending against the self-directed destrudo (i.e., hate of the superego toward the ego) is to *project* the hate, as if saying, "I do not hate myself, but *they* hate me."

This projective-paranoid mechanism may be used by the ego on many occasions. It takes place *whenever the ego is attacked by the superego and the ego is no longer capable of engaging in adequate reality testing.*

In schizophrenia, when the ego is exposed to intolerable accusations from the superego, it develops paranoid accusations. In psychopathic disorders, when the patient's aggressiveness evokes hostile reactions, the patient denies that he was ever hostile; he believes himself to be an innocent sheep surrounded by a pack of wolves.

In dysmutual disorders, projections become systematized, reproducing the Cinderella story of a persecuted child finally rewarded for his sweetness and goodness. Every paranoid is a martyr, persecuted by a bad mother (stepmother) who is expected to become a good godmother.

Projection

When one feels painfully rejected, he may deny the rejection and pretend that he is greatly loved, or he may come to believe that he is a victim of a conspiracy. In either case he employs the mechanism of projection. In the first case he projects his love for the rejecting love object; in the second, he projects his hatred for the love object, whom he hates for turning down his love. Dysmutual patients tend to exaggerate and advertise their feelings. They often take signs of friendliness or even simple kindness as evidence of great love, and proceed to fall in love accordingly. Sometimes they are carried away by their own wishful thinking and imagine that other people are madly in love with them. A repeated pattern of this nature can assume the proportions of paranoia.

Periodically, depressive neurotic dysmutuals become overwhelmed with the feeling that the world is full of belligerent, noxious, hateful people. One of my patients, despite her high degree, good intelligence and competence in her field, frequently lost jobs because of her paranoid hostility directed against her coworkers, whom she blamed for being hostile toward her. Her mother, a hateful woman, showed love for her daughter only when the latter was severely ill. My patient was a hysteroid (dysmutual) character neurotic who sincerely believed that there was a city-wide conspiracy to get her out of her gainful employment.

In the deteriorated stages of the dysmutual-depressive disorders, projections become more lasting, more severe, more rigid, and less influenced by reality. These swinging moods of projected love and hate become systematized into seemingly logical delusions, forming what has been traditionally called *paranoia*. A paranoiac is a deeply depressed individual who struggles with torturous feelings of depression and worthlessness by either denying their existence or blaming them on the outer world. In the first case, in utter disregard for the truth, he assumes that everyone feels sorry for him and loves him as his mother loved him in those rare moments when he reached rock-bottom misery. In the other case, he believes that the whole world is against him as his mother was.

Prior to the onset of acute paranoia, a 35-year-old patient of mine had been a latent manic-depressive. He was mildly depressed and persistently self-defeating in his college studies, his job and in relationships. He lived with his parents, always struggling to win the favor of his mother, who obviously preferred his brother and sister. The mother was aggressive, hostile and selfish. Only when the patient was severely ill did his mother care for him and show some affection.

The patient's moods oscillated between depression and elation. His had been a passive, inefficient, unproductive life despite his burning ambition to become rich and famous. He was afraid of women. In rare sexual relations, usually initiated by girls, he performed poorly. In his dreams he identified with the powerful mother ("ship") and felt sorry for the father whose penis ("airplane") was doomed to crash. His latent homosexual tendencies never came into the open, but he feared that his lonely life would give rise to the suspicion that he was a homosexual.

To be a communist was less threatening to him than to be a homosexual. When rebuffed on his job, he went to a policeman and tearfully confessed that he was a communist, which, in point of fact, he was not. This admission was an attempt to invite true punishment in order to avoid an imaginary and more severe rejection. In a way, he acted similarly to the earlier reported manic-depressive, who lost bowel control in order to win his mother's attention. In both cases self-induced misery aimed at winning sympathy.

A policeman took the self-accusing man to a mental hospital. There he displayed a full-blown paranoid system, in which F.B.I. agents were thought to be in pursuit of him, the innocent victim of a slander. He imagined that scores of F.B.I. agents were watching his moves, following him on trips, trying to involve him and implicate him in a variety of crimes. Some of the agents, he believed, felt sorry for him.

Another patient escaped from the army during World War II because he believed that two men in his platoon had conspired to kill him. He claimed that all soldiers were cowards who fought only when forced to, whereas he was a military genius who could smash Germany with one gigantic blow. He went to the colonel to report on his military inventions, but the "envious colonel would not let [him] get all the glory" and turned his proposals down. Then, the colonel apparently gave orders to shoot him and to steal his plans. He repeated this story in the mental hospital.

Outside the specific area of paranoid projections, in both patients there was comparatively good judgment and reasonable behavior. Paranoid symptoms and projections occur in several mental disorders, in hypervectorial and hyperinstrumental alike. Yet their aim and structure is not the same in the three types of disorder. Paranoia in dysmutuals is a sort of elation, a denial of depression. It represents the martyr-hero complex, the improperly recognized genius and inventor, or the "good child" rejected by his mother. The dream of "persecuted innocence" and "greatness in defeat" is the Cinderella dream. All good men are persecuted, but some day their greatness will be recognized and innocence rewarded.

Classic paranoia has been linked to the manic-depressive psychosis by several authors. According to Kanzer (1952), guilt feeling leads to a fantasy of magic omnipotence and/or submission to the imaginary persecutor. Internalization of the parental figure (the rejecting mother) is an indispensible element in this mechanism. Salzman (1960) observed that the paranoid megalomania is an effort to deny one's low self-esteem but is little related if at all to the sexuality and the manic state which is closely related to the paranoid state. In classic paranoia the break with reality is limited to a particular set of events. This is also true with all other syndromes of manic-depressive (dysmutual) psychosis. As early as 1924 E. Bleuler spoke of the wish for grandiosity and excessive ambition in manic-depressives which is counterbalanced by feelings of persecution which serve as a detour to the desired goal.

The Simple Deterioration Syndrome

The most regressive syndrome in dysmutual psychosis is the "I don't care," the "hobo" or "Bowery bum" pattern. In simple deteriorative depression, the individual regresses to a sort of intrauterine existence. They seem to hope that somehow, sometime, somebody will take care of them. They themselves surrender all attempts to lead a normal life, finding it too difficult to work and earn a living. If they are given a job they refuse to work. When a simple deteriorated patient was offered a menial job in a mailroom, he found a hidden corner where he could hide in sweet slumber. As soon as his hideout was discovered, he was fired. His reaction was, "I knew that this was going to happen. They are unfair and don't allow a minute of respite; oh, these slavedrivers! It was just too hard for me!"

Everything is too hard for the dysmutual simple deteriorated psychotic who refuses to exert himself. His sleepy ego merges with the id, leaving him in a state of volitional bankruptcy. There is no longer any reality principle, and no longer any attempts at delay, modification or sublimation of primitive drives. In short, the person is at the mercy of the archaic law of the *pleasure principle*. Instant goal gratification is the guiding rule of their behavior. All attempts at personal hygiene and appearance are abandoned. Employment is out of the question.

It was stated earlier that the simple deterioration syndrome in schizophrenia represents hypervectorialism at its purest. The same applies to the dysmutual disorders. The simple deterioration syndrome represents a psychotic surrender of the ego. The individual gives up all efforts and renounces any struggle. It is deep regression to a prehuman level.

The simple deterioration syndrome in the hypervectorial type represents a renunciation of the struggle for self-control and protection of others. The individual accepts defeat and life no longer makes sense to him. The parallel syndrome in dysmutual disorders is a renunciation of the desire to love and to be loved. When life becomes unendurable he may put an end to it, the way the hero in *Sister Carrie* did. Tired, beaten down, rejected by everyone, forgotten by all, the simple deterioration dysmutual psychotic has lost the battle for survival.

The Dementive Level

Yet many dysmutual psychotics survive to old age. In jails, mental hospitals, and in old age homes it is not uncommon to find aged, severely deteriorated individuals who have been diagnosed as manic-depressive psychotics. Whereas the dementive hypervectorial wishes to die, and the dementive hyperinstrumental wants to kill, the dementive dysmutual desires sleep.

Most of the time he lies half asleep on his bed, getting up only when forced to or when hungry. Nothing interests him, nothing catches his aimlessly wandering mind, nothing with the exception of an immediate need which expresses itself impulsively. Passivity, drowsiness, gloomy looks, fear of people, feelings of hopelessness and personality decay are the overt symptoms of dementia in dysmutual disorders.

10

Tragedies and Diseases

The A.P.A. Classificatory System

The American Psychiatric Association published in 1968 the second edition (DSM II) of its Diagnostic and Statistical Manual of Mental Disorders. This new Manual introduced the following classification system for all mental disorder.

THE DIAGNOSTIC NOMENCLATURE:

List of Mental Disorders and Their Code Numbers

I. MENTAL RETARDATION
Mental retardation (310–315)
310 Borderline mental retardation
311 Mild mental retardation
312 Moderate mental retardation
313 Severe mental retardation
314 Profound mental retardation
315 Unspecified mental retardation

The fourth-digit subdivisions cited below should be used with each of the above categories. The associated physical condition should be specified as an additional diagnosis when known.

.0 Following infection or intoxication
.1 Following trauma or physical agent
.2 With disorders of metabolism, growth or nutrition
.3 Associated with gross brain disease (postnatal)
.4 Associated with diseases and conditions due to (unknown) prenatal influence
.5 With chromosomal abnormality
.6 Associated with prematurity
.7 Following major psychiatric disorder
.8 With psycho-social (environmental) deprivation
.9 With other [and unspecified] condition

II. ORGANIC BRAIN SYNDROMES

(Disorders Caused by or Associated with Impairment of Brain Tissue Function.) In the categories under IIA and IIB the associated physical condition should be specified when known.

II–A. PSYCHOSES ASSOCIATED WITH ORGANIC BRAIN SYNDROMES (290–294)

290 Senile and pre-senile dementia
 .0 Senile dementia
 .1 Pre-senile dementia
291 Alcoholic psychosis
 .0 Delirium tremens
 .1 Korsakov's psychosis (alcoholic)
 .2 Other alcoholic hallucinosis
 .3 Alcohol paranoid state ((Alcoholic paranoia))
 .4 Acute alcohol intoxication
 .5 Alcoholic deterioration
 .6 Pathological intoxication
 .9 Other [and unspecified] alcoholic psychosis
292 Psychosis associated with intracranial infection
 .0 Psychosis with general paralysis
 .1 Psychosis with other syphilis of central nervous system
 .2 Psychosis with epidemic encephalitis
 .3 Psychosis with other and unspecified encephalitis
 .9 Psychosis with other [and unspecified] intracranial infection
293 Psychosis associated with other cerebral condition
 .0 Psychosis with cerebral arteriosclerosis
 .1 Psychosis with other cerebrovascular disturbance
 .2 Psychosis with epilepsy
 .3 Psychosis with intracranial neoplasm
 .4 Psychosis with degenerative disease of the central nervous system
 .5 Psychosis with brain trauma
 .9 Psychosis with other [and unspecified] cerebral condition
294 Psychosis associated with other physical condition
 .0 Psychosis with endocrine disorder
 .1 Psychosis with metabolic or nutritional disorder
 .2 Psychosis with systemic infection
 .3 Psychosis with drug or poison intoxication (other than alcohol)
 .4 Psychosis with childbirth
 .8 Psychosis with other and undiagnosed physical condition
[.9 Psychosis with unspecified physical condition]

II–B NON-PSYCHOTIC ORGANIC BRAIN SYNDROMES (309)
309 Non-psychotic organic brain syndromes ((Mental disorders not specified as psychotic associated with physical conditions))
 .0 Non-psychotic OBS with intracranial infection
[.1 Non-psychotic OBS with drug, poison, or systemic intoxication]
   .13 Non-psychotic OBS with alcohol (simple drunkenness)
   .14 Non-psychotic OBS with other drug, poison, or systemic intoxication
 .2 Non-psychotic OBS with brain trauma
 .3 Non-psychotic OBS with circulatory disturbance
 .4 Non-psychotic OBS with epilepsy
 .5 Non-psychotic OBS with disturbance of metabolism, growth or nutrition
 .6 Non-psychotic OBS with senile or pre-senile brain disease
 .7 Non-psychotic OBS with intracranial neoplasm
 .8 Non-psychotic OBS with degenerative disease of central nervous system
 .9 Non-psychotic OBS with other [and unspecified] physical condition
   [.91 Acute brain syndrome, not otherwise specified]
   [.92 Chronic brain syndrome, not otherwise specified]

III. PSYCHOSES NOT ATTRIBUTED TO PHYSICAL CONDITIONS LISTED PREVIOUSLY (295–298)
295 Schizophrenia
 .0 Schizophrenia, simple type
 .1 Schizophrenia, hebephrenic type
 .2 Schizophrenic, catatonic type
   .23 Schizophrenia, catatonic type, excited
   .24 Schizophrenia, catatonic type, withdrawn
 .3 Schizophrenia, paranoid type
 .4 Acute schizophrenic episode
 .5 Schizophrenia, latent type
 .6 Schizophrenia, residual type
 .7 Schizophrenia, schizo-affective type
   .73 Schizophrenia, schizo-affective type, excited
   .74 Schizophrenia, schizo-affective type, depressed
 .8 Schizophrenia, childhood type
.90 Schizophrenia, chronic undifferentiated type
.99 Schizophrenia, other [and unspecified] types

296 Major affective disorders (Affective psychoses)
  .0 Involutional melancholia
  .1 Manic-depressive illness, manic type (Manic-depressive psychosis, manic type)
  .2 Manic-depressive illness, depressed type (Manic-depressive psychosis, depressed type)
  .3 Manic-depressive illness, circular type (Manic-depressive psychosis, circular type)
    .33 Manic-depressive illness, circular type, manic
    .34 Manic-depressive illness, circular type, depressed
  .8 Other major affective disorder ((Affective psychoses, other))
 [.9 Unspecified major affective disorder]
    [Affective disorder not otherwise specified]
    [Manic-depressive illness not otherwise specified]
297 Paranoid states
  .0 Paranoia
  .1 Involutional paranoid state ((involutional paraphrenia))
  .9 Other paranoid state
298 Other psychoses
  .0 Psychotic depressive reaction ((Reactive depressive psychosis))
 [.1 Reactive excitation]
 [.2 Reactive confusion]
    [Acute or subacute confusional state]
 [.3 Acute paranoid reaction]
 [.9 Reactive psychosis, unspecified]
[299 Unspecified psychosis]
    [Dementia, insanity or psychosis not otherwise specified]

IV. NEUROSES (300)
300 Neuroses
  .0 Anxiety neurosis
  .1 Hysterical neurosis
    .13 Hysterical neurosis, conversion type
    .14 Hysterical neurosis, dissociative type
  .2 Phobic neurosis
  .3 Obsessive compulsive neurosis
  .4 Depressive neurosis
  .5 Neurasthenic neurosis (Neurasthenia)
  .6 Depersonalization neurosis (Depersonalization syndrome)
  .7 Hypochondriacal neurosis
  .8 Other neurosis
 [.9 Unspecified neurosis]

V.   PERSONALITY DISORDERS AND CERTAIN OTHER
       NON-PSYCHOTIC MENTAL DISORDERS (301–304)

301   Personality disorders
 .0   Paranoid personality
 .1   Cyclothymic personality (Affective personality)
 .2   Schizoid personality
 .3   Explosive personality
 .4   Obsessive compulsive personality ((Anankastic personality))
 .5   Hysterical personality
 .6   Asthenic personality
 .7   Antisocial personality
 .81   Passive-aggressive personality
 .82   Inadequate personality
 .89   Other personality disorders of specified types
[.9   Unspecified personality disorder]
302   Sexual deviations
 .0   Homosexuality
 .1   Fetishism
 .2   Pedophilia
 .3   Transvestitism
 .4   Exhibitionism
 .5   Voyeurism
 .6   Sadism
 .7   Masochism
 .8   Other sexual deviation
(.9   Unspecified sexual deviation)
303   Alcoholism
 .0   Episodic excessive drinking
 .1   Habitual excessive drinking
 .2   Alcohol addiction
 .9   Other (and unspecified) alcoholism
304   Drug dependence
 .0   Drug dependence, opium, opium alkaloids and their
       derivatives
 .1   Drug dependence, synthetic analgesics with morphine-like
       effects
 .2   Drug dependence, barbiturates
 .3   Drug dependence, other hypnotics and sedatives or
       "tranquilizers"
 .4   Drug dependence, cocaine
 .5   Drug dependence, Cannabis sativa (hashish, marihuana)

.6 Drug dependence, other psycho-stimulants
.7 Drug dependence, hallucinogens
.8 Other drug dependence
(.9 Unspecified drug dependence)

VI. PSYCHOPHYSIOLOGIC DISORDERS (305)
305 Psychophysiologic disorders (Physical disorders of
     presumably psychogenic origin)
.0 Psychophysiologic skin disorder
.1 Psychophysiologic musculoskeletal disorder
.2 Psychophysiologic respiratory disorder
.3 Psychophysiologic cardiovascular disorder
.4 Psychophysiologic hemic and lymphatic disorder
.5 Psychophysiologic gastro-intestinal disorder
.6 Psychophysiologic genito-urinary disorder
.7 Psychophysiologic endocrine disorder
.8 Psychophysiologic disorder of organ of special sense
.9 Psychophysiologic disorder of other type

VII. SPECIAL SYMPTOMS (306)
306 Special symptoms not elsewhere classified
.0 Speech disturbance
.1 Specific learning disturbance
.2 Tic
.3 Other psychomotor disorder
.4 Disorders of sleep
.5 Feeding disturbance
.6 Enuresis
.7 Encopresis
.8 Cephalalgia
.9 Other special symptom

VIII. TRANSIENT SITUATIONAL DISTURBANCES (307)
307 Transient situational disturbances
.0 Adjustment reaction of infancy
.1 Adjustment reaction of childhood
.2 Adjustment reaction of adolescence
.3 Adjustment reaction of adult life
.4 Adjustment reaction of late life

IX. BEHAVIOR DISORDERS OF CHILDHOOD AND
     ADOLESCENCE (308)
308 Behavior disorders of childhood and adolescence (Behavior
     disorders of childhood)
  .0 Hyperkinetic reaction of childhood (or adolescence)
  .1 Withdrawing reaction of childhood (or adolescence)
  .2 Overanxious reaction of childhood (or adolescence)
  .3 Runaway reaction of childhood (or adolescence)
  .4 Unsocialized aggressive reaction of childhood (or adolescence)
  .5 Group delinquent reaction of childhood (or adolescence)
  .9 Other reaction of childhood (or adolescence)

X.   CONDITIONS WITHOUT MANIFEST PSYCHIATRIC
     DISORDER AND NON-SPECIFIC CONDITIONS
316 Social maladjustments without manifest psychiatric disorder
  .0 Marital maladjustment
  .1 Social maladjustment
  .2 Occupational maladjustment
  .3 Dyssocial behavior
  .9 Other social maladjustment
3.7 Non-specific conditions
318 No mental disorder

XI. NON-DIAGNOSTIC TERMS FOR ADMINISTRATIVE
     USE (319)
319 Non-diagnostic terms for administrative use
  .0 Diagnosis deferred
  .1 Boarder
  .2 Experiment only
  .9 Other

Critique of the A.P.A. System

Classification enables scientists to form general concepts. When objects or events are put together into a class or category on the basis of at least one common denominator, generalizations or statements can be made which pertain to the entire class.

There are two rules with regard to scientific classification, namely *economy* and *usefulness*. A classification is economical when (1) no object within a given system of classification belongs to more than one class and (2) every object belongs to a certain class; e.g., if we divide students in a class according to their height and classify those below five feet as short and above six feet as tall, we leave some cases out. If we classify as short those who are below six feet and everyone above five feet as tall, those between five and six feet belong to both classes and our classification is uneconomical.

Classification of mental disorders based merely on symptomatology is usually uneconomical. Consider autistic patterns of behavior, typical not only of schizophrenic children but also of children who have suffered from encephalitis or anoxia. Hallucinations may accompany a great many disorders, as well as depressions, anxieties, phobias, homosexual impulses, psychosomatic disorders, addictions, antisocial behavior, etc. Most of these symptoms accompany more than one type of mental disorder.

The economical classification of biological species into plants and animals, and animals into vertebrates and invertebrates enables the biologist to make general and truthful statements pertaining to each class. The "Diagnostic and Statistical Manual of Mental Disorders" (1968) of the American Psychiatric Association distinguishes psychophysiologic, autonomic and visceral disorders from psychoneurotic disorders. This is an uneconomical classification because a great many psychoneurotics, as described in the same Manual, display psychophysiologic disorders. Furthermore, the same Manual places mental deficiencies in a separate category not included in either organic or inorganic disorders. The logic of such a classification is questionable.

The business of science is the discovery of truth and the explanation and prediction of the chain of causes and effects. When a chemist or a physicist introduces classificatory systems, he introduces them for the sake of generalization, explanation and prediction.

This applies also to our area of investigation. Mental disorders can be classified in many ways (Zilboorg and Henry, 1941), but a classification is scientifically useful whenever it helps to *explain* the present state (symptoms) by invoking past causes and, when knowing past causes, it helps to *predict* their future outcome. A scientifically useful classification must, therefore, include etiologic factors and help to map therapeutic strategy.

Mental disorders can be originated by deficiencies in the organism, i.e., they can be somatogenic. Organic or somatogenic disorders can be either genosomatogenic if inherited, or ecosomatogenic if acquired.

All mental disorders exclusive of the inherited ones are a product of interaction between organism and environment. If this interaction is physical or chemical, the disorder is ecosomatogenic. If it is neither physical nor chemical, we call it *sociogenic*. There are obviously no other categories; mental disorders are either genosomatogenic, or ecosomatogenic, or sociogenic. The so-called functional or psychogenic mental disorders are a product of interaction with the social environment; they are caused either by *cathexes*, i.e., they are a product of the inherited constitutional factors interacting with the environment, or by *conditioning*, i.e., they are a product of environmental factors that modify the constitutional factors. These factors cause morbid changes in the system of cathexes or they condition morbid behavioral patterns.

Psychosomatic Disorders

Consider the psychophysiologic or psychosomatic disorders. The above-quoted Manual of the American Psychiatric Association (1968) divided all these disorders into 10 categories related to a particular organ affected by "physical disorders of presumably psychogenic origin." It seems that the authors of the Manual preferred localization to etiology, in contradistinction to the psychoanalytic tradition based on a deterministic search for causes and effects (Freud, 1912a, B. Jackson, 1969; Ross, 1960).

This classification is obviously uneconomical. It is a well-known fact that all mental disorders can be accompanied by psychophysiologic symptoms. Psychosomatic disorders do not form a distinct clinical category because they are caused by a variety of mental disorders. The A.P.A. classification according to bodily zones and organs would be useful only if there were evidence of their specificity. Peptic ulcers, for instance, are not a closed entity caused by definite and specific etiologic factors, and there is no evidence whatsoever that peptic ulcers are produced by a simple, well-defined set of clinical causes; in fact, ulcers are associated with a variety of mental disorders.

Hyperinstrumentals often develop psychosomatic symptoms in the service of secondary gain. After World War II, some veterans apparently preferred the effortless, comfortable, parasitic life of the hospital and refused to face the outside world with its inevitable trials and struggle. To effect this end they developed psychosomatic symptoms that enabled them to obtain the privileged "sick role" with its concomitant advantages in the present-day welfare society.

Psychosomatic symptoms in dysmutuals are usually a tactic to win love and sympathy. Although the "dying hero" myth assumes various forms in accordance with peculiar needs, environmental attitudes and cultural background, all dysmutuals, especially the depressive psychotic, wish to suffer in the hope of winning love by self-defeat.

Psychosomatic symptoms in all hypervectorials, especially schizophrenics, are not the cause but rather the effect of the hypervectorial disorder. The disturbances in behavior and activity which characterize the schizophrenic process would also be expected to cause biochemical and metabolic deviations especially in urine volume and concentration, in nitrogen metabolism, and in the size and function of numerous organic systems. The physiological and biochemical state of the patient are a part of the sociopsychosomatic schizophrenic process (Wolman, 1967b).

An insufficient self-love, that is an inadequate libidinal self-cathexis, is, in my opinion, the main cause of psychosomatic disorders. The hypothesis of self-hypocathexis as the main cause of psychosomatic symptoms seems to offer definite advantages over the classic psychoanalytic theory and is more in agreement with observable facts. Whereas the hypercathected organ tends to function in the service of sublimation (consider the narcissistic investment in one's hair or figure; the self-love of a narcissistic tennis player proud of his arms), the hypocathected organ is likely to evoke feelings of inadequacy and failure. The hypocathexis theory explains the general decline in vitality, reduced pain sensitivity, and the tendency for self-mutilation in schizophrenics.

The hypothesis I have proposed concerning psychophysiologic or psychosomatic symptoms is based on the balance of cathexes. This hypothesis reads as follows: (a) A dysbalance in interindividual cathexes (social factors) affects the balance in intraindividual cathexes (personality factors) which, in turn, affects the functions of the organism. (b) The excessive object cathexis of libido affects the self-cathexis of libido, specifically, the hypervectorial, schizotype who hypercathects his love objects, thus hypocathecting himself, and is thus most prone to physical disorders caused by psychological factors.

Studies conducted in hospitals where dietary deficiencies and spread of chronic infections were responsible for infectious hepatitis, amoebiasis, thyroid dysfunctions, and vitamin deficiencies related these conditions to schizophrenia. Competent research on somatic factors in schizophrenia (Bellak, 1958; Benedetti and Müller, 1957; Bleuler, M., 1966; Campbell, 1958; Freeman, 1958; D. Jackson, 1960; Kety, 1960; Richter, 1957) failed to prove that schizophrenia is *caused* by somatic factors. Emotional stress may cause substantial changes in adrenocortical and thyroid secretion as well as in the production of epinephrine and norepinephrine. Such changes are an *effect* of emotional stress.

Freud (1938), Fenichel (1945) and other psychoanalysts regard schizophrenia as a narcissistic disorder. According to Fenichel,

> . . . many schizophrenics begin [with] characteristic hypochondriacal sensations. The beginning of the schizophrenic process is a regression to narcissism. This brings with it an increase in the "libido tonus" of the body (either of the whole body or, depending on the individual history, of certain organs) and this increase makes itself felt in the form of the hypochondriacal sensations [p. 418].

Concern for others to the neglect of oneself is likely to result in some kind of symptomatology. Most schizophrenic patients with whom I have dealt suffered from low vitality and lack of energy. Many of them were particularly vulnerable to respiratory diseases and colds. Skin diseases usually developed in their least cathected organs. A girl who doubted her manual dexterity had a severe skin rash on her hands; another, who believed she was ugly, had a facial rash; still another who doubted her femininity, had a pubic rash. The theory of self-hypocathexis in schizophrenia (first introduced by Federn, 1952), explains the decline in sensitivity to pain, and the generally lowered tonus and passivity in schizophrenia. The schizophrenic tendency for self-mutilation is well explained by the theory of *decline* in self-cathexis.

The hypothesis of somatic symptoms resulting from hypocathexis of bodily organs completes the *sociopsychosomatic* theory. My observations have led me to conclude that noxious environmental (social) factors cause an imbalance in *interindividual cathexes*. This imbalance produces a severe dysbalance in the *intraindividual* cathexes of libido and destrudo; this, in turn, introduces a disorder in the personality structure (psychological factors). The personality disorder results in somatic changes, either through a transformation of deficiency in mental energy into organic deficiencies, or through the process of conditioning.

Research in conditioning (Buck, et al., 1950; Bykov, 1957; Gantt, 1958; Hamburg, 1958; Ivanov-Smolensky, 1954; Lynn, 1963; Malis, 1961; Mednick, 1958, and others) supports this hypothesis. Psychologically induced changes in heart-beat, rate of metabolism, circulation of blood and respiration are not limited to Charcot's hysterical patients. They are common to all human beings including schizophrenics, and can be produced by conditioning or cathexis or both. In schizophrenia these processes follow the direction of a "downward adjustment."

Impulses coming from the cortex may inhibit the activity of an organ. Overworked cortical centers may interfere with the work of other organs. New "connections" are continually being formed, and the inner organs become conditioned to react in an unusual way, even if this is detrimental to the survival of the organism. Insofar as this influence seems to be *inhibitory*, it results in a reduction of vitality. "It may be assumed," wrote Bykov (1957), "that in acting on the functioning cells of the salivary glands, the nervous impulses from the cortex along the efferent nerves reduce the excitation of the salivary glands to a minimum . . . A weak excitation on reaching a slightly functioning gland increased its activity, whereas a strong excitation inhibited it" (p. 140).

Also the rate of the general metabolism can be changed through conditioning by word signals. The sound of the metronome together with the command, "Get ready for the experiment," caused in experimental subjects a marked increase in oxygen consumption and pulmonary ventilation. In one experiment, "a man who remained quietly lying on a couch showed an increase in metabolism when it was suggested that he had just completed some very hard muscular work" (Bykov, 1957, p. 179).

In terms of the sociopsychosomatic theory, schizophrenia is an impoverishment of one's own resources and a struggle for survival caused by a morbid hypervectorialism. This state of mind may correspond to a cerebrospinal hypertension.

Analgesias are another example of the same issue. E. Bleuler wrote in 1911: "Even in well oriented patients one may often observe the presence of a complete *analgesia* which includes the deeper parts of the body as well as the skin. The patients intentionally or unintentionally incur quite serious injuries, pluck out an eye, sit down on a hot stove and receive severe gluteal burns" (p. 57).

Analgesias can be produced by conditioning (Bykov, 1957) and/or by a low self-cathexis. The decline in self-cathexis makes the schizophrenic less capable of loving and protecting himself, but in the face of a real danger, schizophrenics may display a strong self-defensive reaction. Severely deteriorated cases, however, with lowered sensitivity to pain, may fall victim to any danger.

This is the schizophrenic paradox: real life is sacrificed for a pseudo-protection of life. The schizophrenic feels he has to give away his life to protect those upon whom his survival depends. His lavish hypercathexis of his "protectors" leads to his own impoverishment and eventual death (Wolman, 1966a).

Arieti (1955, p. 392) believes that the following four psychosomatic changes take place in the cardiovascular system of schizophrenics: (1) a decrease in the size of the heart, (2) decrease in the volume of blood flow, (3) decrease in systemic blood pressure and (4) an exaggerated tendency to vasoconstriction and resulting diminished blood supply.

Several researchers (e.g., Hoskins, 1946), have implied that schizophrenics suffer from a defect in the vasomotor system or in the nerve control apparatus of this system located in the hypothalamus. Cyanosis or the blueing of hands and feet caused by venous stasis is frequently observed in schizophrenics. This symptom has often been interpreted as a constriction of the small arterioles of the skin. Doust (1952) found a significant degree of anoxemia in simple, catatonic, and hebephrenic schizophrenics. The existence of a cerebral anoxemia could not however be proved. It is possible that the passive behavior of schizophrenics prevents dissipation of heat. Furthermore, the bizarre posture of catatonics "activates antigravity vasoconstrictor mechanisms. Without these mechanisms, edema due to blood stasis would be very frequent" (Arieti, 1955, p. 395). The regulation of heat exchange in the human body is of particular interest in the study of schizophrenia. Many of my own patients chronically complain in winter about inadequate heat; it appears that schizophrenics are more sensitive to cold. Buck, Carscallen and Hobbs (1950) found rectal temperature of schizophrenics significantly lower than that of normal subjects.

Addictions

The so-called "personality disorders" comprise another loose category including such disorders as the schizoid, cyclothymic and paranoid personality, sociopathic personality, addictions, and several ill-defined and probably overlapping syndromes such as explosive and passive-aggressive personality, antisocial and inadequate personality, described in the "Diagnostic and Statistical Manual." Insofar as all mental disorders are personality disorders, it would appear that no useful purpose is served by lumping together a variety of symptoms in a subcategory called "personality disorders."

What the Manual classifies as various personality disturbances, has been related in the present volume to the three distinct clinical types. For instance, the so-called "schizoid personality," probably overlapping if not identical with the "obsessive-compulsive personality," has been renamed "hypervectorial character disorder," representing one of the *levels* of the hypervectorial, that is, schizo-type disorder.

Dependence on drugs has been classified as a separate clinical category and been listed in the Manual as a subdivision of personality disorders. Clinical observations, however, suggest that one can become an addict for a variety of reasons and that drug addicts do not form a distinct pathological class. Depressive dysmutuals, always in search of acceptance and power, may find in the oblivion of the drug state, the bliss of maternal union. In search of pleasure and the avoidance of pain, hyperinstrumentals are most inclined to follow the easy path of alcoholism and drug addiction. Since their lives are guided by an urge for immediate gratification, they will do everything in their power to reduce discomfort and increase pleasurable experiences. Drug addiction is for many the preferred route for avoiding responsibility and escaping into the pleasurable world of unreality (Bier, 1962; Kron and Brown, 1965).

Hypervectorials may also become drug addicts, but for different reasons. As long as the ego exercises rigid control (on the neurotic and character neurotic levels) drugs are avoided. It is rather unusual for an obsessive-compulsive, a phobic or a neurasthenic patient to become an addict unless the defense mechanisms fail.

Addiction, whether to alcohol or to drugs, is not associated with any particular clinical pattern. A drug addict is an individual who is unable to cope with the hardships of life and seeks morbid shortcuts into imaginary happiness. The reason for such an escape from reality is by no means uniform. Addiction may lead to a *toxic* disorder produced by the drug (opiates, barbiturates, and so on.) This additional disorder may become superimposed upon the original disorder that led to the addiction. The nature of this toxic disorder de-

pends on the nature of the drug, whether it is an opium derivative, a barbiturate acid or anything else (Solomon, 1966;
Walton, 1960).

A similar situation pertains to alcohol addiction. People
drink for a variety of reasons. Although many people drink
occasionally, only some become chronic alcoholics. Alcoholism cannot be viewed, therefore, as a matter of conditioning
and habit formation. The desire to escape from reality
reflects deeper personality factors. Drinking leads to toxic
mental disorders, such as delirium tremens, acute alcoholic
hallucinosis, alcoholic pathological intoxication, epileptic
states, Korsakoff psychosis, mental deterioration, Wernicke
encephalopathy, and so on. All these disorders belong to the
toxic type of somatogenic mental disorders.

However, it would be misleading to present the problem
of addiction as an instance of individual pathology. Heavy
drinking is endemic and, in many instances, spreads in certain ethnic groups, geographical areas and neighborhoods, as
does drug addiction. While an individual alcoholic or a drug
addict has become addicted for particular reasons related to
his experiences, the fact remains that drug and alcohol addiction are ecologic rather than individual phenomena.

The mass addiction of our times transgresses the limits of
traditional psychology and psychiatry. Social psychology and
social psychiatry are necessarily entering fields hitherto belonging to the realm of sociology of culture, social philosophy and cultural anthropology (Lindzey and Aronson, 1968).
Addiction can no longer qualify as a disease; it is a *tragedy of
many individuals caught in a catastrophic decline of cultural
values and mass disinhibition.* Civilization cannot exist without inhibition. Some degree of self-restraint is the price we
must pay for civilization (Freud, 1930). Perhaps, from time to
time, there is a neurotic surcharge when the inhibitions are
too frequent or too strict, but today we witness a tendency to
act in a disinhibited way advocated by so many, including

some psychopathic therapists who propagate psychotic acting out.

Sexual Aberrations

Sexuality can be practiced on any level; in lower animals it is a purely physiological act, but on higher evolutionary levels sex is often associated with affection, loyalty and mutual care. Some species of fish, birds and mammals remain together after copulation, defending each other, sharing food and shelter and jointly nurturing their offspring. Their behavior is indicative of loyalty and consideration for one another, and their union undoubtedly extends beyond the sheer physical sexual act (Lorenz, 1964).

The roots of human sexuality are physiological, but sexuality transcends physiology. Normal adults develop meaningful relationships with adult individuals of the opposite sex based on physical attraction, emotional involvement and intellectual understanding. Such a relationship involves two mature individuals who are capable of sharing, giving of themselves, and finding happiness in this bond.

Although purely physical sexual excitability starts very early in life, it takes a good deal of growth and learning to attain psychological maturity sufficient to distinguish deeper feelings toward another person from fleeting physical attractions. It takes years before one realizes that he or she cannot have everything and be involved with everybody and that having lots of transient relationships leaves one empty and dissatisfied, while a lasting and meaningful relationship with one person can become a source of genuine happiness. A permanent relationship based on mutual love, understanding and consideration is the sign and reward of adulthood. Adult people are capable of making rational and lasting decisions. They see in the other person not a narcissistic-instrumental sexual object but a human being to whom they can relate with respect, consideration and love. Mutuality based on re-

ciprocal love, respect and consideration is the prerequisite
for an adult give-and-take relationship.

Marriage is a higher level relationship, and is not just another sexual affair. Although marriage is rooted in sexuality,
it encompasses much more than sexuality. It is a bond between two individuals who desire to live together, caring for
each other and sharing life experiences. It is a combination of
sexual attraction with profound friendship, mutual understanding, unswerving loyalty and responsibility. Marriage is a
social institution, supported by economic and legal sanctions.

Impotence and Frigidity

Impotence in males and frigidity in females is an inability
to perform the sexual act in a manner satisfactory to oneself
and/or to one's partner. Impotence in males encompasses a
gamut of sexual inadequacies, such as lack of interest in sex,
inability to have an erection, inadequate erection, ejaculation
before insertion, ejaculation instantly upon insertion, inability
to reach orgasm, and so on. Frigidity in women includes lack
of interest in or aversion to sexual acts, inability to get
aroused, inability to secrete, contraction of vaginal muscles
that prevents insertion (vaginismus) and inability to reach
orgasm. Homosexuals and other perverts, latent or manifest,
generally cannot perform sexually in normal situations.

Most often sexual difficulties are rooted in unresolved oedipal anxiety and the fear of commiting incest. Even severe
sexual inadequacy, such as lack of sexual interest and premature ejaculation, are curable by psychoanalysis. Psychoanalysis does not deal with symptoms but with the psychological
causes of disturbed behavior.

Regression

The theory that deviant sexual behavior represents a repetition of childhood sexual tendencies was introduced by
Freud. According to his findings on the phenomena of infan-

tile sexuality, the sexual aims of perverts are identical with those of children (Freud, 1905a). Freud observed that perverse tendencies and occasional perverse acts or fantasies occur in the life of *every* individual, the normal as well as the neurotic.

> Perverts are persons with infantile instead of adult sexuality. This may be due either to an arrested development or to a regression. The fact that perversions frequently are developed as a reaction to sexual disappointments points to the effectiveness of regression. The simple formula presents itself: persons who react to sexual frustrations with a regression to infantile sexuality are perverts; persons who react with other defenses or who employ other defenses after the regression, are neurotics [Fenichel, 1945, p. 325].

Freud assumed that human sexuality originates as a diffuse desire for pleasure that evolves through various developmental stages until it develops into adult sexuality, when the "erotogenic zone" is the sexual organs, the "object" is an adult person of the opposite sex, and the "aim" is the union of genitals. A newborn infant is "polymorphous perverse," capable of any aberration or deviation in regard to the zone, object and aim. With maturity the infantile zones, objects, and aims become eliminated or subordinated to the genital zone, object and aim. Some early indications, such as oral pleasure in kissing, become relegated to sexual foreplay and subordinated to normal, adult sexuality.

Abnormal sexual behavior is not a clinical entity. It may be a fixation on one of the infantile developmental phases or a regression connected with some personality malformation. But the so-called normal sexual behavior may contain several infantile elements.

Homosexuality

While some early studies hypothesized an organic origin of homosexuality (Henry and Galbraith, 1954), this hypothesis has met with little support in view of the lack of biochemical and endocrine differences between homosexual and heterosexual individuals (Allen, 1962; Westwood and Schofield, 1960).

A homosexual is an individual who is physically normal but whose sexual behavior is abnormal. His sexual objects are either people of both sexes or of his own sex exclusively. Some homosexuals who choose their objects from both sexes call themselves "bisexual," but bisexuality is a misleading term. Being physically normal, every homosexual, male or female, can also practice sex with people of the opposite sex. Whenever one has sexual relations with a person of the same sex he is being homosexual, whether or not he practices other types of sexuality also.

Psychoanalytic studies point to the abnormal child-parent relationship in the etiology of homosexuality. This is not, however, a one-to-one relationship, homosexuality having multiply-determined origins. In most cases the child identifies with the frustrating parent; in normal oedipal circumstances, father frustrates the son and mother frustrates the daughter (see Chapter 3). When mother is masculine and aggressive and father is meek and indecisive, the male child may identify with the "strong aggressor" and develop a homosexual attachment to his indecisive and weak father. This confusion of sociosexual roles is called the *negative Oedipus complex.*

There are at least two explanations for the confusion in sociosexual roles. Many male homosexuals identify with mother and accept a feminine role in a desire to attract other men. Transvestites dress and make-up to look like the opposite sex and thereby derive sexual pleasure.

Some male homosexuals act in a masculine way and seek effeminate men as sexual partners. The "active" male homosexual plays the role of "husband" and seduces effeminate homosexuals, preferably young and soft-looking boys. This "active" type of homosexual often indulges in heterosexual relations.

Femininity in men, that is, the sexual goal of having the sexual partner introduce something into one's body, usually connected with the fantasy of being a woman, is frequently but not necessarily combined with homosexuality: with the choice of a partner of the same sex. Its basis is an identification with the mother in regard to instinctual aim [Fenichel, 1945, p. 335].

Femininity in men is associated with castration anxiety:

(a) The decisive identification with the mother may arise out of castration fear, connected with the sight of her genitals. Certain men, who are not homosexual at all, exhibit love that is full of features of identification with their sexual partner; the identification serves the purpose of fighting anxiety. A patient who loved women with this type of "identification love" wanted to prove to his girl friends: "See how well I understand you and all your interests; see what a degree of empathy I am capable of, that actually there is no difference between you and me!" A relatively late, traumatic observation of a woman's genitals had disturbed this boy's development. He experienced the sight as something entirely strange. He condensed all his earlier castration fears into a fear of this strange thing, which he perceived as an oral danger. He attempted to master this anxiety by denying that women are different; he assumed the attitude: "Women are exactly the same as I am; there are no frightening discoveries to be made, because I know everything about female matters." He identified himself with the object of his anxiety and became "feminine."

(b) In other cases of femininity in men the following attitude is decisive: "Because I am afraid that men might castrate me, I do not want to have anything to do with them; I prefer to live among women." These persons, of course, are heterosexual though feminine. They have to repress their homosexuality because homosexuality would mean having contact with men. Men of this type are interested rather in feminine homosexuality, they want to be a "girl among girls," and are interested in feminine games and activities. Frequently, this type of "femininity" holds anxiety in check only as long as the fact that women have no penises can be denied by some other means.

Femininity as a protection against the danger of castration may fail entirely if the person cannot deny that "becoming a girl" would mean losing his penis. We find in feminine men manifold attempts to keep

up this denial; they try to stress the fact that they actually have a
penis, while acting as though they were girls; thus there are girls with
penises. A similar frequent unconscious reasoning can be formulated
as follows: "I am afraid that I might be castrated. If I act like a girl,
people will think that it has already been done, and in this way I shall
escape" [Fenichel, 1945, p. 336].

Unconscious homosexual desires that do not manifest themselves in overt behavior are referred to as latent homosexual
tendencies. Latent homosexuals are not conscious of their
problem; doubting their own gender, they try "to prove"
their masculinity (in the case of women, their femininity) by
becoming promiscuous.

Playing the role of a Don Juan, he thinks that he chases
after women, but actually, being afraid of commitment and
responsibility, he is forever running away from them. As soon
as he possesses a woman, he flees, no matter how pleasant
she is. The same applies to women.

As mentioned earlier, one can become a homosexual for a
variety of reasons, the main reason being the negative Oedipus complex. Some authors regard homosexuality as a learned
phenomenon but it is unlikely that this is the case. Many
men and women have had transient, coincidental or forced
homosexual experiences in their early years, but rarely has
anyone ever become an overt homosexual unless he has been
a latent homosexual prior to the homosexual experience. Isolated homosexual experiences do not lead to homosexuality.

*Homosexuality is not a separate clinical entity, but a clus-
ter of symptoms that may accompany many mental disorders.*
Schizophrenics, both manifest and latent, are frequently confused in regard to the sexual identity of themselves and others. Their poorly defined sexual identity may induce them to
become attracted to people of the same sex, especially when
the parent of the same sex was seductive.

Depressives usually form the negative Oedipus complex,
identifying with the most frustrating parent. Female homo-

sexuals of this type are usually aggressive, looking for motherly, soft girls resembling their own mothers.

Psychopaths are usually polymorphous, uninhibited perverts, seeking sexual gratification in every possible way, with men, women, children, occasionally with animals, and whenever it is safe, using force.

The following is the case of a homosexual male:

He was a Jewish boy from the Bronx. His father worked for a travel agency but somehow managed never to travel. At the age of 55 he was still a second-rate clerk, but he introduced himself to his friends and acquaintances as an "executive in the travel industry." The family lived in a tiny three-room apartment, but father had to have a new Buick, for otherwise "people would not respect him." The father was a mild-mannered man with rosy cheeks and greyish hair, affable, talkative, trying to please and impress, and often complaining about his hard luck.

The mother was a good-looking, intelligent, and exceedingly selfish woman. She was too lazy to look for a job, preferring to spend her days in gossip, playing cards and occasional "friendships." She thought very little of her husband and exercised complete control over him. She used to tell him what to eat, how to dress and with whom to associate. She was, however, rather diplomatic in her dictatorship. It was typical for her to make such remarks as: "Darling, don't you think the coffee is too strong for you? Didn't you tell me once that you feel like a *man* whenever you can tell me to cook your favorite soup? Aren't you looking like a *big* executive in this grey suit!" and so on. Her husband was meek and gullible, and she had her little "freedoms" with other men who gave her "little gifts." When her husband observed that she was wearing a new watch, she told him that she had purchased this hundred-dollar watch for eight dollars in a sale in Gimbel's basement.

The son, my patient, resembled his mother. He was bright, good-looking, selfish and lazy. He dropped out of college, and held a variety of jobs only for the time necessary to be eligible for unemployment insurance. He would arrive late, skipped days and provoked the boss to fire him.

He came to my office perplexed by minor psychosomatic troubles

that proved later to be a veneer for his true pathology. Shortly thereafter he opened up and spoke about his dreams, wishes and actions.

He had two idols: the Holy Virgin and Adolf Hitler. A few years
ago, immediately after the Second World War, he went on a pilgrim-
age to Berlin to cry over Hitler's death. During the war he was a
high-school student, but he was determined not to serve in the American Army against the beloved *Führer.* He acquired records of Hitler's
speeches to the dismay of his father (What will the neighbors say?),
but with the approval of his mother. After all, Hitler was "a real
man," mother said. She believed in "equal rights and liberties for all."

The patient had identified with his mother, whom he saw
as an ideal figure, almost like the Holy Virgin. He felt loving
toward father whenever the latter drove the Buick, but otherwise preferred more heroic masculine figures.

My patient believed himself to be a nice, sweet, friendly person. He
dressed in a girlish way, always appearing excessively neat. He never
forgot to send Christmas cards to his acquaintances. He even went out
of his way to buy gifts, provided, naturally, that their gifts were no
less expensive.

He had practiced homosexuality from the time of high school. He
liked older, stronger, aggressive boys who "picked him up," played
with him, and used him. He was in the habit of going to men's rooms
in public places to be picked up.

On rare occasions he had engaged in sex with women, but only
when they were much older and they took the initiative in seducing
him. He preferred oral sex to normal, genital intercourse. In oral sex
he was passive, and the sex of the partner did not mean much
[Wolman, *Faces in Darkness,* Unpublished].

The apparent rise in homosexuality in our times cannot be
attributed solely to the particular life stories of particular
individuals. It is not a sheer coincidence that the increase in
incidence of homosexuality has always been coincident with
the decline of civilization and mass disinhibition, so aptly

described in Petronius' novel and Fellini's film *Satyricon*. Unable to identify with the cultural values of their parents, deprived of social norms and realistic aims in life, morally insecure and culturally wayward individuals drift aimlessly from one meaningless relationship to another.

✖ 11 ✖
Interactional Psychoanalysis

No mental disorder is entirely physical and none is entirely mental. Even those mental disorders that have been caused by interaction with the social environment usually have some psychophysiological aftereffects. Psychological methods of treatment cannot therefore be limited solely to the psychological aspects of mental disorder but must concern themselves with psychosomatic symptoms as well.

Who Needs Help?

Even in prehistoric times people under stress sought the advice of sages, magicians and witch doctors. For centuries, clergymen have offered guidance in practically all matters concerning human life, including marital difficulties, occupational failure and feelings of anxiety, inferiority, guilt and depression. Members of the mental health professions are assuming the duties previously held by father-confessors, spiritual counselors and clergymen. Troubled people usually seek advice and guidance in regard to a particular problem and are generally unaware of the underlying symptomatology.

Wise men can give advice, but advice is not the answer when it comes to mental disturbance. When people are blinded in regard to their personality deficiencies, they believe that all that is needed is a solution of the presenting problem. This is, however, rarely the case. It is the nature of mental illness that the same mistakes are repeated over and over again. Guidance for a particular entanglement is of little help; what is required is a complete reshaping of the personality such that the old self-destructive behavioral patterns are no longer reinforcing.

When people are unable to make rational decisions, they either procrastinate or act impulsively. Some people fear things that represent no real threat while remaining seemingly oblivious to the real consequences of their dangerous actions. Some people don't see things the way they are, but the way they wish or fear them to be. Some people overestimate or underestimate their own talents, fear failure or success, closeness or distance. Some people fight with friends and please enemies, confuse, distort, and mix up things. Some people rebel without cause and submit without reason, feel miserable in success and pleased in defeat. In short, when human behavior is disbalanced, disturbed and irrational, human beings are in need of outside help.

Who Can Help?

Psychological help can be obtained from a wide range of sources. Many religious seminaries and institutions offer programs in psychology and training in pastoral psychiatry. Well-trained ministers of religion are of invaluable help in handling less serious cases; more difficult ones are referred to psychiatrists and clinical psychologists.

There are a great many people trained to help those who have minor problems, which often lead to the uncovering of more serious problems. Scores of counselors, guidance workers, and school psychologists are trained in diagnostic work and remedial services for children and adults. Early disclosure of trouble and corrective action may prevent much more serious complications later on.

Since most problems grow out of the home environment, social workers have become an indispensable part of therapeutic teams in clinics, guidance centers and hospitals. Psychiatric social workers have received training in the treatment of mental disorders; some are trained in the practice of psychoanalysis.

Each of the above-mentioned professions offers considerable help to mentally disturbed individuals. Traditionally *psychiatrists* are expected to carry the main burden in the treatment of mental disorders. By the nature of their training, psychiatrists are especially prepared for the understanding and treatment of organic mental disorders. They spend years studying the human body, after which they undergo postdoctoral training in a mental hospital. They must, however, graduate from a Psychoanalytic Institute to become psychoanalysts. Such training requires several additional years.

The other professionals duly qualified for offering help to mental patients are *clinical psychologists*. Clinical psychologists must obtain a Ph.D. in clinical psychology. They too require several years of postdoctoral study in a psychoanalytic institute to become psychoanalysts.

The present status of academic training in preparation for the practice of psychoanalysis is not a product of conceptual planning. Rather it was largely determined by the fact that Freud himself was a physician and, at that particular time, the treatment of mental disorders was believed to be the province of medicine.

Be that as it may, Freud rebelled against his contemporary medical, organically oriented methods of interpretation and treatment of mental disorder. He was opposed to the reduction of mental phenomena to somatic terms, and developed his method independently of medicine and psychiatry.

Treatment Methods

In the treatment of mental disorders one must take into consideration all three factors—i.e., the organism, personality and the social environment—for all mental disorders depend to a greater or lesser extent on all three determinants. Thus, the question to be asked is not whether to apply physico-chemical or psychological treatments, but which method of treatment or which combination of methods will produce the best results. The answer depends on a variety of factors. In some cases it might be necessary to start with the organism and administer drugs or even perform surgery. The purpose of the chemical and physical therapies is not limited to the chemical and physical aspects or causes of a given disorder. In brain injury or paresis, for instance, physicochemical therapies affect the psychological aspects of the disorder and its effect upon human relations.

Theoretically speaking, treatment could start with any one of the three areas mentioned above. Physicochemical methods, psychological techniques and treatment of environmental factors represent the three main approaches.

It can be stated that no treatment method has proved either infallible, or exclusive. Psychiatrists and clinical psychologists generally claim satisfactory results and tend to be partial to the method of their choice. The problem is, indeed, highly complicated. Suppose a patient suffers severe depressions. He has been diagnosed as a manic-depressive (dysmutual psychotic) and has gone to a psychiatrist who administered several electroshock treatments (ECT). The patient's depression has lifted. There is no doubt that the shock treatment was helpful; a heretofore wretched, suicidal patient has been relieved from his suffering and his symptoms have disappeared.

Needless to say, the symptoms may come back and the patient may again be seriously depressed and harbor suicidal thoughts. Manic-depressive patients whose symptoms have disappeared subsequent to ECT are usually discharged from the hospital with the warning that they are not cured and should seek further psychological help. They are advised to contact a competent psychiatrist or clinical psychologist, preferably a psychoanalyst, for prolonged treatment. Some of them take the advice, but others, feeling good and relieved from depression, see no need for psychotherapy, and are consequently rehospitalized. The same applies to other shock treatment methods. A certain percentage of psychotic patients, for example, respond well to insulin and remain well for long periods of time.

While shock treatment is a common procedure for the psychotic population in mental hospitals, drugs are administered to patients at all levels of mental disorder. Colloquially speaking, all drugs are divided into depressants (tranquilizers), on the one hand, and antidepressants on the other. It is the aim of such drugs to counteract respectively elation and excitation, or depression and despondency.

A study by the late New York State Commissioner of Mental Health, Paul Hoch, conducted in association with James Cattell, has proved that the more potent drugs cause more harmful aftereffects. An indiscriminate use of tranquilizers and stimulants may cause serious harm to physical and mental health. There is abundant evidence that the use of hallucinogenic drugs such as LSD may cause irreparable damage.

Although there is no evidence that chemotherapy, as it stands today, can produce satisfactory and lasting results, there is no doubt that it can substantially alleviate the sufferings of mental patients. Most mental hospitals are overcrowded and understaffed. Intensive chemotherapy permits quick discharge of patients and more room for new cases. However, the use of drugs in private practice is often a sign that the psychotherapist, unable to reach the patient through the conventional methods, is looking for an easier route.

Physicochemical methods have been in vogue for several thousands of years. People suffering "melancholy" or other disorders sought the help of witches who brewed fantastic potions which were reputed to have curative value. Blood letting, leeches, hot and cold packs, hydrotherapy and a pro-liferation of vitamins, hormonal preparations and surgeries have been included in the armamentarium for "treatment" of mental disorders. As late as the end of the nineteenth century, hysterectomy was performed on women suffering from hysteria with dubious results, at least as far as the hysteria was concerned.

Even unsophisticated methods will suspend certain symptoms. Thus, a mother who smears the child's fingers with a disgusting jelly may believe that she has "cured" nailbiting. It is likely that as a consequence, more serious symptoms will crop up in lieu of the nailbiting. Hypnosis is used for symptom removal but its effect is dependent on the duration of the hypnotic spell. Some of the recent innovations in psychotherapy practiced as various brands of "behavior therapy" use simple or complex methods of conditioning, unconditioning, and so on. Most of these methods can remove symptoms, but sometimes old symptoms are replaced by new ones.

Freud's revolutionary ideas have radically changed the approach to the treatment of mental disorders. Instead of struggling against symptoms, psychoanalysis attempts to get at their roots.

Psychoanalysis

I do not intend to describe in detail the various psychological treatment methods. One may refer to all psychological methods as psychotherapy. In the vernacular the term psychotherapy indicates all psychological methods exclusive of psychoanalysis and its modifications.

The classic psychoanalytic technique was developed by Sigmund Freud and his disciples. There are, however, several versions of psychoanalysis, in addition to Freud's. Freud's associates and disciples developed new techniques, but the fundamental Freudian principles have been applied, with some modification, to all of them.

A psychoanalyst does not treat patients the way a physician or a dentist does in that the latter are active while the patient is passive. The reverse is true of the psychoanalytic situation.

In a way, the role of the priest is more like that of the physician insofar as he offers advice and requests obedience to his instructions thus resembling a doctor ordering a diet or prescribing certain drugs or activities. A psychoanalyst does not offer guidance nor does he prescribe courses of action. He is there to help the patient discover who he is.

From the beginning to the end of the psychoanalytic treatment the patient is more active than the psychoanalyst. He is expected to communicate and to express his innermost thoughts and feelings while the psychoanalyst listens attentively and makes sparing, carefully chosen comments. It is the patient who makes all the decisions and, in the course of psychoanalytic treatment, becomes aware of his infantile fixations and personality deformation. Psychoanalysis is not only a process of gaining insight into one's problems. Psychoanalysis is primarily a process of emotional growth and personality development. What went wrong in childhood must be reinterpreted and whatever blocks one's road to maturity must be removed.

There are two crucial factors in psychoanalytic treatment and, for that matter, in practically any psychotherapeutic method. All patients *transfer* their childhood emotions onto the personality of the therapist as their emotional target. They love him and hate him the way they loved and hated their parents or parental substitutes. Repressed feelings and forgotten conflicts are dug out and revived in the transference, and are thus open for a new appraisal and readjustment.

No one likes to have his wounds reopened, even when there is a promise of healing. The same forces that have led to the inhibition of the innermost yet dangerous desires and repressed conflicts, continue their opposition to the unraveling work of psychoanalysis. This unconscious opposition, called *resistance*, presents a formidable stumbling block in the psychoanalytic process. The way in which a psychoanalyst overcomes resistance often indicates the difference between a master and a novice.

Psychoanalytic treatment, Freudian, modified Freudian and non-Freudian is always an *interactional process* between two individuals, the analyst and the patient. Since every human being is different, the course of each analysis is largely determined by the individuals participating. An analyst does not respond in exactly the same way to all his patients. Of course, he is expected to treat all people in the same unbiased and objective way, but being human he cannot help being influenced by his own past experiences and present reactions. Undoubtedly the patient does not relate in exactly the same way to all people, and he is bound to be influenced by relevant and irrelevant aspects of the psychoanalyst's personality. Thus, despite the conscious efforts to act in a uniform way, each analysis is a unique, unrepeatable phenomenon.

Transference

Self-analysis is a dangerous, if not impractical course, because no matter how skilled one is, lack of objectivity and lack of outside support may prove disastrous. The risks of mental collapse are great, and the chances for success are slim. Freud described his self-analysis as follows: "Inwardly, I am deeply impoverished. I have had to demolish all my castles in the air, and I have just plucked up enough courage to start rebuilding them" (Freud, 1887–1902).

Freud's self-analysis took several years. He recorded it in letters to Dr. Fliess (1887–1902) and, in a veiled manner, referred to portions of it in *The Interpretation of Dreams* (1900) as well as in a great many papers. Freud's self-analysis made it clear that one's present-day feelings are often a replica and reexperiencing of early childhood involvements. The reexperiencing of the emotions attached to these old experiences is a fundamental aspect of the therapy.

Reconstruction and interpretation may fail to produce change in the patient's personality. A patient may accept interpretations or he may doubt their credibility. In either case, he may develop a defensively intellectual attitude, and view psychoanalytic interpretation as mere news and commentary. Deep conviction is needed for behavioral change, and such a profound conviction can be procured only through actual experience. The reliving of past emotional experiences offers a good chance for lifting of the repressive veil and resolution of past conflicts.

The psychoanalytic situation provides the necessary conditions for reliving infantile emotions. In that the patient comes asking for help, he is automatically placed in a dependent role vis-a-vis the analyst. The analyst's amiable, yet nonparticipant listening contributes to the patient's feeling of having found a friendly, benevolent omniscient parental substitute. Free associations and the reclining position facilitate emotional regression. The patient lets his defenses down and, in a regressive mood, weaves emotional fantasies around the silent analyst (who represents, as indicated, a parental figure). In the transference, past feelings and conflicts reemerge and are reenacted according to the script of the family drama as it was played in his childhood.

During the analytic process, all the patient's tendencies, including hostile ones, are aroused; they are then turned to account in the service of the analysis by being made conscious, and in this way, the transference is constantly being destroyed. Transference, which seems ordained to be the greatest obstacle to psychoanalysis, thus becomes its most powerful ally, if its presence can be detected each time and explained to the patient (Freud, 1905b, p. 117).

The case of Dora (1905b) and the paper on "The Dynamics of Transference" (1912b) describe the problems of transference. The ultimate conclusion was simple. Freud realized that every emotional conflict was "played out in the phenomena of the transference."

> What are transferences? They are new editions of facsimiles of the impulses and phantasies which are aroused and made conscious during the progress of the analysis; but they have this peculiarity, which is characteristic for their species, that they replace some earlier person by the person of the physician. To put it another way: a whole series of psychological experiences are revived, not as belonging to the past, but as applying to the person of the physician at the present moment. Some of these transferences have a content which differs from that of their model in no respect whatever except for the substitution. These then—to keep to the same metaphor—are merely new impressions or reprints. Others are more ingeniously constructed; their content has been subjected to a moderating influence—to *sublimation,* as I call it—and they may even become conscious, by cleverly taking advantage of some real peculiarity in the physician's person or circumstances and attaching themselves to that. These, then, will no longer be new impressions, but revised editions [Freud, 1905b, p. 116].

Transference is a process of cathexis in a state of regression. If it is a cathexis of libido, it is a "positive" transference; if it is a cathexis of destructive energy, it is a "negative" transference.

Transference becomes a neurosis, i.e., a transference neurosis, in which the patient relives his past conflicts using the analyst as a target for libidinal cathexes and destructive assaults. The patient ascribes to the analyst personality traits actually belonging to the patient's parents. The patient becomes less concerned with his own problems as he becomes involved with his analyst. Love and hate for the analyst may reach considerable intensity and, unless treated properly, may impede the progress of psychoanalysis (Freud, 1915).

The psychoanalyst should neither ignore nor satisfy the transference:

> It is, therefore, just as disastrous for the analysis if the patient's craving for love prevails as if it is suppressed. The way the analyst must take is neither of these; it is one for which there is no prototype in real life. He must guard against ignoring the transference-love, scaring it away or making the patient disgusted with it; and just as resolutely must he withhold any response to it. He must face the transference love boldly but treat it like something unreal, as a condition which must be gone through during the treatment and traced back to its unconscious origins, so that it shall assist in bringing to light all that is most hidden in the development of the patient's erotic life, and help her to learn to control it. . . . The patient, whose sexual repressions are of course not yet removed but merely pushed into the background, will then feel safe enough to allow all her conditions for loving, all the phantasies of her sexual desires, all the individual details of her way of being in love to come to light, and then will herself open up the way back from them to the infantile roots of her love [Freud, 1915, p. 185].

Transference may get out of hand if and when, instead of remaining an emotional experience articulated in the analyst's office, it leads to acting out.

Freud was fully aware of the fact that transference is a prerequisite for any progress in psychoanalytic treatment. The heat of transference, as it were, melts the resistance and enables the patient to reopen wounds suffered in early years. Love, admiration, and adoration on one side, resentment, hatred, and disrespect on the other, dominate the psychoanalytic sessions. The patient acts like an unhappy child, as he articulates his feelings toward the omnipotent, yet permissive parent. The neurosis that brought the patient to the analyst's office recedes into the background, and the "transference neurosis" is played out instead. The interpretation of the transference helps to resolve the underlying infantile conflicts; and the cure of the transference neurosis leads to the cure of the neurosis proper.

Some psychoanalysts believe that the interpretation of the transference is the only true change-producing interpretation because it is related directly to the immediate psychoanalytic situation. That is, the patient sees and experiences that which is being interpreted. Such an interpretation, called *mutative,* is capable of producing substantial alterations in personality (Strachey, 1931).

Transference is a universal phenomenon, in that everyone carries within his memory residues of past feelings and experiences. Transference elements influence one's choice of colors, preferences in music and art and choice of love object. Transference elements color human ambitions and desires, for no one can completely get rid of his past.

Transference becomes morbid when the past beclouds the present to such an extent that the individual acts as if he were still a child. In the psychoanalytic situation, regression to childhood is necessary for the resolution of conflicts rooted in the past.

Since the main neurotic conflict revolves around "the family romance" or the Oedipus complex, its resolution must come about through a reenactment of this romance. During his transference the patient runs the gamut of infantile and, most often, ambivalent feelings toward his parents. Reich (1945, p. 33 ff) maintained that the transference neurosis seems to unfold in a sequence that is the reverse of the arrangement of the true neurosis. He suggested that the analysis of transference accounts for this reverse order. Transference usually starts as a resentment against the analyst who is viewed as a father-substitute, then turns into love for the analyst-father, later becoming an identification with the mother, feminine traits having been ascribed to the analyst. This identification turns into hate for the mother-analyst, to be followed by love for the mother represented by the analyst. Oedipal love, if properly experienced and interpreted, makes it possible to engage in mature love later on.

Transference as Resistance

In accordance with the principle of repetition compulsion, recollection of past emotional involvements brings about a tendency to reenact them. The patient tries to destroy the analyst's authority over him and convert him into a lover. Undue intensification of love and exaggerated readiness for a love affair complicate the psychoanalyst's work if such a transference sets up a resistance (Freud, 1915).

Transference as an Interactional Process

Certain aspects of both transference and resistance involve the here-and-now. Although the patient relates to the analyst partly on the basis of past experiences, he is also responding to the real situation. His demands for instinctual gratification are mainly transference needs in that they represent a reactivation of his past infantile wishes. But it must be borne in mind that the patient is not an infant. He is an adult, who is paying for therapeutic services, and his demands, rational or irrational, are a part of the here-and-now situation.

Thus, whatever goes on between the analyst and his patient is a process of interaction. It is always an *exchange of cathexes*, whether correctly or incorrectly perceived by the patient, and sometimes by the analyst as well. The silent analyst may be perceived by his patients as a taciturn or unfriendly individual, who is, or pretends to be, or tries to give the impression of being, an omnipotent figure. If the analyst really tries to impress, it is his countertransference blunder. But whatever he tries to do, and whatever he says or does, there is always interaction.

I venture to say that transference is always manipulated by the analyst. Not only do I agree with Alexander and French (1946) that transference should be regulated, but I would say that *it is always, wittingly or unwittingly, regulated* by the analyst.

Every psychoanalytic treatment is, as Fenichel put it, "based on the analyst's influence on the patient" (1945, p. 447). I suggest that this influence be made explicit in the theory of psychoanalytic treatment and that the analyst become more *aware* of the nature of his influence, for no matter what his point of view, he is always regulating the transference. He regulates it by imposing the "basic rule," by suggesting the reclining position, by saying or not saying "How are you?" by smiling or not smiling, and so on.

Freud's difficulty with schizophrenics as compared with Federn's success with such patients is a case in point. The Freudian insistence on a reclining position facilitated topographic regression; this regression was further intensified by the "basic rule" of free association; and finally, the analyst's remoteness and silence contributed to schizophrenic tension and withdrawal. No wonder Freud believed that schizophrenia is a nontransference disorder (Freud, 1915–1917; Fenichel, 1945, Chap. 18). But Federn (1952), who admitted schizophrenics to his home, witnessed most profound transferences.

The Dysmutuals

Freud's (1920) description of transference in *Beyond the Pleasure Principle* is actually a report of treatment of a dysmutual type of neurosis.

> Loss of love and failure leave behind them a permanent injury to self-assurance in the form of a narcissistic scar, which . . . contributes more than anything to the "sense of inferiority." The tie of affection,

which binds the child as a rule to the parent of the opposite sex, succumbs to disappointment. . . .

Patients repeat all of these invented situations and painful emotions
in the transference and revive them with the greatest ingenuity. They
seek to bring about the interruption of the treatment while it is still
incomplete; they contrive once more to feel themselves scorned. . . .
None of these things can have produced pleasure in the past . . . But
no lesson has been learned from the old experience of these activities,
having led instead only to unpleasure [p. 21].

Dysmutuals easily swing from positive to negative transference. As long as they imagine that the analyst loves them
they are in a blissful euphoria. Most symptoms disappear and
the analytic hours become, as one of my patients put it, "the
happiest hours in my life." In the transference process, such
patients will go through the love-hate swings of the past experience.

Woe to the analyst who lets himself be drawn into the
treadmill of the emotional ups and downs of a dysmutual; the
detached, objective, matter-of-fact treatment of transference,
combined with an incisive interpretation of resistance (and
transference used as a resistance) is the choice method. Let
us remember that the treatment of dysmutuals has been the
bedrock of classical psychoanalysis.

The Hypervectorials

The peculiar difficulty in working with hypervectorial
neuroses (obsessions, phobias, neurasthenias, etc.) lies in the
patients' excessive resistance. One of the motives of resistance is a strong need for punishment, associated with maso-
chistic wishes. Their unconscious need to be punished corresponds to aggressiveness which has been internalized and
taken over by the superego.

We are in doubt whether we ought to suppose that all aggressiveness that has turned back from the external world is bound by the

superego, and so used against the ego, or whether a part of it carries on its silent sinister activity as a free destructive instinct in the ego and the id. Probably there is a division of this kind but we know nothing further about it. When first the superego is set up, there is no doubt that that function is endowed with that part of the child's aggressiveness against its parents for which it can find no discharge outwards on account of its love fixation and external difficulties; and for this reason, the severity of the superego need not correspond to the severity of its upbringing. . . .

People in whom this unconscious guilt feeling is dominant, distinguish themselves under analytic treatment by exhibiting . . . a negative therapeutic reaction. In normal course of events, if one gives a patient the solution of a symptom, at least the temporary disappearance of the symptom should result; with these patients, on the contrary, the effect is a momentary intensification of the symptom and the suffering that accompanies it. It often needs only a word of praise of their behavior during the cure, the utterance of a few words of hope as to the progress of analysis, to bring about an unmistakable aggravation of their condition. . . . Their behavior will appear as an expression of an unconscious sense of guilt, which favors illness with its attendant suffering and handicaps [Freud, 1932, pp. 150–151].

Freud himself recommended active interpretation and direct influence for such patients. As soon as transference is established, the analyst must induce the phobic patient to modify his overt phobic behavior. This change must occur prior to the resolution of the underlying unconscious motives.

In the process of psychoanalytic treatment of hypervectorials, a passive, detached attitude on the part of the analyst will unduly prolong the treatment and, perhaps, make analysis interminable. The analyst must be vectorial, that is, genuinely friendly. He must not, however, transgress his professional role nor deviate from the ethical and professional rule of abstention or frustrating the patient's instinctual demands. He must never fall into the trap of countertransference, and thus become a copy of the incestuous and seductive or seducible parent. A moderate aim, restrained interest in the patient's well-being, is necessary. Such an attitude of friendliness and respect for the patient will help to increase his self-esteem and improve the intraindividual balance of libidinal cathexes.

The dictatorial, overdemanding, irrational superego of hypervectorials must be reshaped. Its irrationality must be exposed and the ensuing severe guilt feelings interpreted and worked through.

A profound transference may make for an interminable analysis. It is not uncommon for neurasthenic, phobic and obsessive patients to feel in some way obligated toward the analyst, as if he were their "poor mommy or daddy." They may have an unconscious fear that he will die if abandoned. Thus it is prudent to discourage an intense transference, especially in severe hypervectorial cases. The more the analyst is frank and outspoken, the more remote are the possibilities of a profound transference. When a hysteric showers the analyst with personal questions, the analyst chooses either not to respond, or he analyzes the patient's curiosity. But when a frightened obsessive or latent schizophrenic ventures a question, a frank and honest answer, matter-of-factly given, seems to be advisable. Such questions as: "Are you married?" "Do you have children?" should be answered openly. There is no reason to surrender to countertransference and confide in the patient, but a clear-cut answer keeps him close to reality and reduces the danger of too vehement a transference.

The Hyperinstrumentals

Hyperinstrumentals, on all five levels, are not prone to cathecting anyone; thus, their transference, if any, remains rather shallow. Whereas hypervectorial transference should be diluted, the crucial task with hyperinstrumentals is to foster as deep a transference as possible, and to mollify the negative transference. As a rule, hyperinstrumentals hate whoever frustrates their wish for immediate impulse gratification.

Manipulation of the transference reaction in these cases can be a formidable task.

The hyperinstrumental may misinterpret the analyst's silent permissiveness as a sign that he is siding with the id. An expression of disapproval by the analyst may lead to the inclusion of the analyst in the paranoid picture of world conspiracy against the narcissistic-instrumental patient. The analyst must take a stand and help in developing the patient's superego, but this task must wait until the transference has developed adequately.

Treatment of Psychotics

The main modifications in technique are dictated by the relative weakness of the ego. Every analytic treatment involves interaction, be it classic or modified and, as such, must be adjusted to the patient's specific needs. I do not intend to discuss those aspects of technique that are common in all types of patients, such as dream interpretation and working through. In working with overt psychotics dream interpretation is not indicated; with latent psychotics it may be quite dangerous. The removal of defense mechanisms is necessary in the treatment of neurotics; it is the main task in working with character neurotics; with psychotics, however, one may have to support the neurotic defenses (ego-protective symptoms) against the danger of a total collapse of the ego.

In his "Recommendations" Freud (1912c) warned psychoanalysts against being too ambitious, and recommended "tolerance for the patient's weakness." This advice must be emphasized with regard to the treatment of psychotics. Treatment of psychotics is, from the beginning to end, a readaptation of the ego. Supportive therapy is necessary for all three types, but it must be applied differently for each type. Testing reality, manipulating the superego, or even a directive approach may be necessary during the initial phases of treatment of psychosis.

The Concept of Cure

With the introduction of the structural concept, ego therapy became the focal task of psychoanalytic treatment. To transform unconscious into conscious, the topographic goal, was not dismissed but incorporated in the new overall goal. "The business of analysis," Freud (1937) wrote, "is to secure the best possible conditions for the functioning of the ego; when this has been done, analysis has accomplished its task" (p. 250).

Thus, Freud's concept of cure highlights the *struggle of the ego*, its ability to form new sublimations, to put its energies to efficient use, and to apply its resources for optimum success and enjoyment. Facing things as they are and making the best of them is tantamount to mental health.

The removal of symptoms reflects the negative part of the goal. When the patient is cured, the symptoms disappear. Thus, "the removal of symptoms of the illness is not specifically aimed at but it is achieved, as it were, as a byproduct if the analysis is properly carried through" (Freud, 1923).

The degree of "cure" varies from one case to another. Broken teeth are one thing and broken bones another; teeth do not grow back, while in some cases bones can be mended. It is one thing to treat pneumonia and another to treat short-sightedness. The optimum treatment depends on the nature and severity of the sickness, handicap, or disorder. For instance, in the case of a missing limb, a prosthetic device can be the best available solution.

The issue becomes even more complex in the treatment of mental disorders. At one time the removal of symptoms was regarded as tantamount to cure, but as mentioned before, symptoms can reappear or be transformed into another set of symptoms.

The definition of cure must therefore be subject to a relative evaluation. No cure is perfect, nor are all cases of cure identical. Ideally one should strive to the best possible state of realistic perception, emotional balance and social adjustment; but such an optimal state varies from case to case. It is impossible to turn a tulip into a rose, but it is possible to cultivate each type. Every individual is different, but everyone should be allowed to attain an optimum in adjustment.

There are obvious limits as to how far one can go in treating mental disorders. The basic rule is to follow the five *levels* of disorder in reverse order. It can be regarded a therapeutic success to help a demented psychotic to regain the less severe state of manifest psychosis. It is an achievement to turn psychosis to latent psychosis, to character neurosis, to neurosis and finally to removal of neurosis.

But sometimes we cannot go that far and must be satisfied with less spectacular results. Many psychotics are incapable of progress. Even surgeons often confine themselves not to what is desirable but to what is feasible and not too risky. A house with a weak foundation cannot be rebuilt; it can be improved, strengthened and made more comfortable, but the reconstruction must not be pushed too far. There are several factors that determine what can be reasonably expected in treatment. The type of disorder, its level, severity and duration, environmental situation, compensatory factors such as talents, opportunities and friends and a host of other factors affect the prognosis. Last but not least is the person, together with the skill of the therapist in the therapeutic interaction.

Once I treated a very severely disturbed psychotic woman who was suicidal and hallucinatory. Four years after I discharged her, she called me for an appointment. She told me her troubles: her beloved grandmother had died; her mother had suffered a stroke; her husband was unfaithful; and her sister was heading for a nervous breakdown. In reply to my question she told me that she cried after her grandmother's death; she placed her paralyzed mother in a hospital; she told her husband that if his infidelity was an isolated incident, she would forgive him, but she would divorce him unless he would be faithful; and finally she called her sister and told her to go to see me . . .

Not all patients are capable of this kind of adaptation. In some cases the treatment must go on for years, until it becomes superfluous. The aim of all psychological treatment is to make further treatment unnecessary. But as long as the patient needs it, the treatment must go on.

The idea of cure should parallel the concept of mental health. A patient is "cured" when his perception of himself and of the outer world corresponds to reality, when his emotional life is balanced, and when he is socially well-adjusted. One may be tempted to call such a person "normal," if not for the fact that perfectly realistic balanced and well-adjusted persons do not exist. Call no man normal.

Bibliography

Abraham, K. (1911), Notes on the psychoanalytic investigation and treatment of manic-depressive insanity and allied conditions. In: *Selected Papers on Psychoanalysis*. London: Hogarth Press, 1927, pp. 137–156.

—— (1916), The first pregenital stage of the libido. *Selected Papers on Psychoanalysis*. New York: Basic Books, 1953, pp. 248–279.

—— (1924), A short study of the development of the libido, viewed in the light of mental disorders. In: *Selected Papers on Psychoanalysis*. New York: Basic Books, 1953, pp. 418–501.

Ackerman, N. W. (1958), *The Psychodynamics of Family Life*. New York: Basic Books.

Adler, K. A. (1967), Adler's individual psychology. In: *Psychoanalytic Techniques*, ed. B. B. Wolman. New York: Basic Books.

Aichhorn, A. (1935), *Wayward Youth*. New York: Viking.

Alanen, Y. O. (1958), The mothers of schizophrenic patients. *Acta Psychiatrica et Neurologica Scandinavia*, 33:724:

—— (1960), Some thoughts on schizophrenia and ego development in the light of family investigations. *Arch. Gen. Psychiat.*, 3/6: 650–656.

Alexander, F. & French, T. (1946), *Psychoanalytic Therapy*. New York: Ronald Press.

Allen, C. (1962), *A Textbook of Psychosexual Disorders*. London: Oxford University Press.

Allport, G. W. (1954), *The Nature of Prejudice*. Reading, Massachusetts: Addison-Wesley.

American Psychiatric Association (1968), *Diagnostic and Statistical Manual of Mental Disorders* (2nd ed.). Washington, D.C.

Arieti, S. (1955), *Interpretation of Schizophrenia*. New York: Robert Brunner.

Asch, S. (1952), *Social Psychology*. New York: Prentice-Hall.

Banay, R. S. (1948), *Youth in Despair*. New York: Coward-McCann.

Bandura, A. & Walters, R. H. (1962), *Social Learning and Personality Development*. New York: Holt, Rinehart & Winston.

Bateson, G. Jackson, D. D., Haley, J. & Weakland, J. (1956), Toward a theory of schizophrenia. *Behavior. Sci.*, 1:251–264.

Beach, F. A. (1965), *Sex and Behavior.* New York: Wiley.

Beck, A. T. (1967), *Depression: Clinical, Experimental and Theoretical Aspects.* New York: Harper-Hoeber.

Bellak, L. (ed.) (1958), *Schizophrenia: A Review of the Syndrome.* New York: Logos.

—— & Loeb, L. (1969), *The Schizophrenic Syndrome.* New York: Grune & Stratton.

Benedetti, G. & Müller, C. (eds.) (1957), *Symposium Internationale sur la Psychotherapie de la Schizophrenie.* Basel: Karger.

Benedict, R. (1934), *Patterns of Culture.* Boston: Houghton-Mifflin.

Berliner, B. (1966), Psychodynamics of the depressive character. *The Psychoanalytic Forum,* 1:244–264. New York: International Universities Press, 1972.

Bettelheim, B. (1967), *The Empty Fortress.* New York: Free Press.

Bibring, E. (1953), The mechanism of depression. In: *Affective Disorders,* ed. P. Greenacre. New York: International Universities Press.

Bier, C. W. (Eds) (1962), *Problems in Addiction: Alcohol and Drug Addiction.* New York: Fordham University Press.

Bleuler, E. (1911), *Dementia Praecox or the Group of Schizophrenias.* New York: International Universities Press, 1950.

—— (1924), *Textbook of Psychiatry.* New York: Macmillan.

Bleuler, M. (1955), Research and changes in concepts in the study of schizophrenia. *Bull. Isaac Ray Medical Library,* 3:1–132.

—— (1966), Conception of schizophrenia within the last fifty years and today. *Internat. J. Psychiat.,* 1:3–30.

Blos, P. (1962), *On Adolescence.* New York: Macmillan.

Bowen, M. (1960), A family concept of schizophrenia. In: *The Etiology of Schizophrenia,* ed. D. D. Jackson. New York: Basic Books.

Bowlby, J. (1951), *Maternal Care and Mental Health* (monogr. 2). Geneva: World Health Organization.

—— (1960a), Separation anxiety. *Internat. J. Psycho-Anal.,* 41:89–113.

—— (1960b), Grief and mourning in infancy and early childhood. *The Psychoanalytic Study of the Child,* 15:9–52.

—— (1961), Childhood mourning and its implication for psychiatry. *Amer. J. Psychiat.,* 118:481–498.

—— (1963), Pathological mourning and childhood mourning. *J. Amer. Psychoanal. Assn.,* 11:500–541.

Brady, A. & Lind, D. L. (1961), Experimental analysis of hysterical blindness. *Arch. Gen. Psychiat.* 4:331–339.

Breuer, J. & Freud, S. (1893–1895), Studies on hysteria. *Standard Edition,* 2. London: Hogarth Press, 1955.

Brody, S. (1956), *Patterns of Mothering*. New York: International Universities Press.

Bronfenbrenner, U. (1967), Response to pressure from peers versus adults among Soviet and American school children. *Internat. J. Psychol.*, 2:199–207.

Buck, C. W., Carscallen, M. B. & Hobbs, G. E. (1950), Temperature regulation in schizophrenia. *A. M. A. Arch. Neurol. Psychiat.*, 64:828–842.

Bychowski, G. (1952), *Psychotherapy of Psychosis*. New York: Grune & Stratton.

Bykov, K. (1957), *The Cerebral Cortex and the Inner Organs*. New York: Chemical Publishers.

Campbell, F. J. (1958), The schizophrenias—current views: Second International Congress of Psychiatry. *Psychiat. Quart.*, 32:318–334.

Caplan, G. & Lebovici, S. (1969), *Adolescence: Psychosocial Perspectives*. New York: Basic Books

Carmichael, L. (1954), *Manual of Child Psychology*. New York: Wiley.

Cheek, F. E. (1964), The "schizogenic mother" in words and deeds. *Family Process*, 3/1:155–177.

Chwast, J. (1958), Perceived parental attitudes and predelinquency. *J. Crim. Law, Criminol. and Police Sci.*, 49:116–126.

—— (1971), Sociopathic behavior in children. In: *Manual of Child Psychopathology*, ed. B. B. Wolman. New York: McGraw-Hill.

Clausen, J. E. (ed.) (1968), *Socialization and Society*. Boston: Little, Brown & Co.

Cleckley, H. (1950), *The Mask of Sanity*. St. Louis: Mosby.

Critchley, McD. (1951), *The Trial of Neville George Clevely Heath*. London: Hedge.

Davidson, S. (1961), School phobia as a manifestation of a family disturbance: its structure and treatment. *J. Child Psychol. Psychiat.*, 1:270–287.

Davis, D. R. (1961), The family triangle in schizophrenia. *Brit. J. Med. Psychol.*, 34:53–63.

Deutsch, M. (1949), A theory of cooperation and competition. *Human Relations*, 2:129–151.

—— (1965), Psychological aspects of social interaction. In: *Scientific Psychology: Principles and Approaches*, eds. B. B. Wolman & E. Nagel. New York: Basic Books.

—— (1969), Field theory in social psychology. In: *The Handbook of Social Psychology*, Vol. I (2nd Ed.), eds. G. Lindzey & E. Aronson. Reading, Mass.: Addison-Wesley.

Dollard, J., Doob, L., Miller, N. E., Mowrer, O. H. & Sears, R. R. (1939),

Frustration and Aggression. New Haven: Yale University Press.

Doust, J. W. I. (1952), Spectroscopic and photoelectric oximetry in schizophrenic and other psychiatric states. *J. Ment. Sci.*, 98:143–160.

Eaton, J. W. & Weil, R. J. (1954), *Culture and Mental Disorders.* Glencoe: New Press.

Eissler, K. (ed.), (1949), *Searchlights on Delinquency.* New York: International Universities Press.

Erikson, E. (1963), *Childhood and Society* (2nd Ed.). New York: Norton.

Escalona, S. K. (1968), *The Roots of Individuality.* Chicago: Aldine.

Esman, A. H., Koh, M. & Nyman, L. (1959), The family of the schizophrenic child. *Amer. J. Orthopsychiat.*, 29:455–459.

Eysenck, H. J. (1964), *Crime and Personality.* Boston: Houghton, Mifflin.

Farina, A. (1960), Patterns of role dominance and conflict in parents of schizophrenic patients. *J. Abnorm. and Soc. Psychol.*, 61:31–38.

Federn, P. (1952), *Ego Psychology and the Psychoses.* New York: Basic Books.

Fenichel, O. (1945), *The Psychoanalytic Theory of Neurosis.* New York: Norton.

Fleck, S. (1971), Some basic aspects of family pathology. In: *Manual of Child Psychopathology*, ed. B. B. Wolman. New York: McGraw-Hill.

Ford, C. S. & Beach, F. A. (1951), *Patterns of Sexual Behavior.* New York: Hoeber.

Framo, J. L. (1962), The theory and technique of family treatment in schizophrenia. *Family Process*, 1(110):119–131.

Freeman, H. (1958), Physiological studies. In: *Schizophrenia: a Review of the Syndrome*, ed. L. Bellak. New York: Logos.

Freud, A. (1949), Certain types and stages of social maladjustment. In: *Searchlights on Delinquency*, ed. K. R. Eissler. New York: International Universities Press.

—— (1967), Comments. In: *On Rearing Infants and Young Children in Institutions*, ed. H. Witmer. Children's Bureau Research Report, 1:49–55.

—— & Burlingham, D. (1944), *Infants without Families.* New York: International Universities Press.

Freud, S. (1887–1902), *The Origins of Psychoanalysis: Letters to Wilhelm Fliess, Drafts, and Notes: 1887–1902.* New York: Basic Books, 1954.

—— (1894a), The neuropsychoses of defense. *Standard Edition*, 3:45–61. London: Hogarth Press, 1962.

—— (1894b), On the grounds for detaching a particular syndrome from neurasthenia under the description (anxiety neurosis). *Standard Edition*, 3:85–115. London: Hogarth Press, 1962.

—— (1896), Further remarks on the neuropsychoses of defense. *Standard Edition*, 3:162–185. London: Hogarth Press, 1962.

—— (1898), Sexuality in the etiology of the neuroses. *Standard Edition*, 3:263–286. London: Hogarth Press, 1962.

—— (1900), The interpretation of dreams. *Standard Edition*, 4:339–627. London: Hogarth Press and The Institute of Psychoanalysis, 1962.

—— (1905a), Three essays on the theory of sexuality. *Standard Edition*, 7:130–240. London: Hogarth Press, 1962.

—— (1905b), Fragment of an analysis of a case of hysteria. *Standard Edition*, 7:3–122. London: Hogarth Press, 1953.

—— (1912a), Types of onset of neurosis. *Standard Edition*, 12:231-238. London: Hogarth Press, 1962.

—— (1912b), The dynamics of transference. *Standard Edition*, 12:97–108. London: Hogarth Press, 1962.

—— (1912c), Recommendations to physicians practicing psychoanalysis. *Standard Edition*, 12:109–120. London: Hogarth Press, 1962.

—— (1915), Observations of transference-love. *Standard Edition*, 12:157–171. London: Hogarth Press, 1962.

—— (1915–1917), Introductory lectures on psychoanalysis. *Standard Edition*, 15 & 16. London: Hogarth Press, 1963.

—— (1917), Mourning and melancholia. *Standard Edition*, 14:243–258. London: Hogarth Press, 1962.

—— (1920), Beyond the pleasure principle. *Standard Edition*, 18:7–65. London: Hogarth Press, 1962.

—— (1921), Group psychology and the analysis of the ego. *Standard Edition*, 18:67–143. London: Hogarth Press, 1955.

—— (1923), The ego and the id. *Standard Edition*, 19:3–63. London: Hogarth Press, 1962.

—— (1923a), Two encyclopedia articles. *Standard Edition*, 18:235–259. London: Hogarth Press, 1955.

—— (1924), Neurosis and psychosis. *Standard Edition*, 19:149–153. London: Hogarth Press, 1961.

—— (1930), Civilization and its discontents. *Standard Edition*, 21:64–147. London: Hogarth Press, 1962.

—— (1931), Libidinal types. *Standard Edition*, 21:217–220. London: Hogarth Press.

—— (1933 [1932]), New introductory lectures on psychoanalysis. *Standard Edition*, 22:5–182. London: Hogarth Press, 1964.

—— (1937), Analysis terminable and interminable. *Standard Edition*, 23:211–253. London: Hogarth Press, 1962.

—— (1938), *An Outline of Psychoanalysis*. New York: Norton, 1949.

Friedlander, K. (1945), Formation of anti-social character. *The Psychoanalytic Study of the Child*, 1:189–204. New York: International Universities Press.

Fromm, E. (1947), *Man for Himself*. New York: Rinehart.

Fromm-Reichmann, F. (1950), *Principles of Intensive Psychotherapy*. Chicago: University of Chicago Press.

——— (1959), Psychoanalysis and Psychotherapy. Chicago: Chicago University Press.

Gantt, W. H. (1958), *Physiological Basis of Psychiatry*. Springfield, Ill.: Thomas.

G. A. P. (1957), *Diagnostic Process in Child Psychiatry* (Report #38). New York: Group for the Advancement of Psychiatry.

Gero, G. (1936), The construction of depression. *Internat. J. Psycho-Anal.*, 17:423–461.

Gesell, A. (1933), Maturation and the patterning of behavior. In: *Handbook of Child Psychology*, ed. C. Murchism. Worcester, Mass: Clark University Press.

Glover, E. (1955), *The Technique of Psychoanalysis*. New York: International Universities Press.

Glueck, S. & Glueck, E. (1956), *Physique and Delinquency*. New York: Harper & Row.

Goldfarb, W. (1961), *Childhood Schizophrenia*. Cambridge: Harvard University Press.

Greenacre, P. (1945), Conscience in the psychopath. *Amer. J. Orthopsychiat.*, 15:495–509.

——— (ed.) (1953), *Affective Disorders*. New York: International Universities Press.

Grinker, R. R., Miller, J., Sabshin, M., Nunn, R., & Nunnally, J. C. (1961), *The Phenomenon of Depression*. New York: Harper-Hoeber.

Guttmacher, M. (1953), Diagnosis and etiology of psychopathic personalities as perceived in our time. In: *Current Problems in Psychiatric Diagnosis*, eds. P. Hoch & J. Zubin. New York: Grune & Stratton, pp. 139–156.

Haley, J. (1962), Family experiments: a new type of experimentation. *Family Process*, 1:265–294.

Halleck, S. L. (1967), *Psychiatry and the Dilemma of Crime*. New York: Harper-Hoeber.

——— (1971), Delinquency. In: *Manual of Child Psychopathology*, ed. B. B. Wolman, New York: McGraw-Hill.

Hamburg, A. L. (1958), Orientation and defense reaction in simple and paranoid states of schizophrenia. In: *The Orientation Reflex and Orient-*

ing-Inquisitive Behavior, ed. L. G. Voronin. Moscow: Academia Pedagogit-cheskich Nauk.

Hartmann, H. (1937), *Ego Psychology and the Process of Adaptation.* New York: International Universities Press, 1958.

—— (1949), Notes on the theory of aggression. *The Psychoanalytic Study of the Child,* 3/4:9–36. New York: International Universities Press.

—— (1950) Psychoanalysis and developmental psychology. *The Psychoanalytic Study of the Child,* 5:7–17. New York: International Universities Press.

—— (1955), Notes on the theory of sublimation. *The Psychoanalytic Study of the Child,* 10:9–29. New York: International Universities Press.

—— Kris, E., & Loewenstein, R. M. (1946), Comments on the formation of psychic structure. *The Psychoanalytic Study of the Child,* 2:11–38. New York: International Universities Press.

Hastings, D. W. (1944), Psychiatry in the Eighth Air Force. *Air Surgeon Bull.,* 8:4–5.

Henry, G. W. & Galbraith, H. J. (1954), Constitutional factors in homosexuality. *Amer. J. Psychiat.,* 13:1249–1270.

Hill, L. B. (1955), *Psychotherapeutic Intervention in Schizophrenia.* Chicago: University of Chicago Press.

Hollingshead, A. B. & Redlich, F. C. (1958), *Social Class and Mental Illness.* New York: Wiley.

Hopkins, F. (1943), Decrease in admissions to mental observation wards during the war. *Brit. Med. J.,* 1:358–360.

Horney, K. (1937), *The Neurotic Personality of Our Times.* New York: Norton.

—— (1939), *New Ways in Psychoanalysis.* New York: Norton.

Hoskins, R. G. (1946), *The Biology of Schizophrenia.* New York: Norton.

Inkeles, A. & Levinson, D. J. (1969), National Character: The study of model personality and sociocultural systems. In: *The Handbook of Social Psychology,* Vol. 5 (2nd Ed.), eds. G. Lindzey & E. Aronson. Reading, Mass.: Addison-Wesley.

Ivanov-Smolensky, A. G. (1954), *Essays on the Patho-physiology of Higher Nervous Activity.* Moscow: Foreign Language Publishing House.

Jackson, B. (1969), Reflections on DSM-II. *Internat. J. Psychiat.,* 7:385–393.

Jackson, D. D. (ed.) (1960), *The Etiology of Schizophrenia.* New York: Basic Books.

Jacobson, E. (1957), On normal and pathological moods. *The Psychoanalytic Study of the Child,* 12:73–113. New York: International Universities Press.

Johnson, A. & Szurek, S. A. (1952), The genesis of anti-social acting out in children and adults. *Psychoanal. Quart.,* 21:323–343.

Kanner, L. & Eisenberg, L. (1957), Early infantile autism. *Psychiatric Research Reports,* 7:55–66.

Kanzer, M. (1952), Manic-depressive psychosis with paranoid trends. *Internat. J. Psycho-Anal.,* 33:34–42.

Kardiner, A. (1939), *The Individual and His Society.* New York: Columbia University Press.

—— (1945), *The Psychological Frontiers of Society.* New York: Columbia University Press.

—— (1959), The traumatic neuroses of war. In: *American Handbook of Psychiatry,* ed. S. Arieti. New York: Basic Books, pp. 245–257.

Karpman, B. (1950), The psychopathic delinquent child. *Amer. J. Orthopsychiat.,* 20:250–265.

—— (1951), Psychopathic behavior in infants and children: A critical survey of existing concepts. *Amer. J. Orthopsychiat.,* 21:223–224.

—— (ed.) (1959), *Symposia on Child and Juvenile Delinquency.* Washington, D.C.: Psychodynamic Monograph Series.

Kety, S. S. (1960), Recent biochemical theories of schizophrenia. In: *The Etiology of Schizophrenia,* ed. D. D. Jackson. New York: Basic Books.

—— (1969), Biochemical hypotheses and studies. In: *The Schizophrenic Syndrome,* eds. L. Bellak and L. Loeb. New York: Grune & Stratton, pp. 155–171.

—— et al. (1948), Cerebral blood flow and metabolism in schizophrenia. *Amer. J. Psychiat.,* 104:765–770.

Kinsey, A. C., Pomeroy, W. B. & Martin, C. E. (1948), *Sexual Behavior in the Human Male.* Philadelphia: Saunders.

Klebanoff, L. (1959), Parental attitudes of mothers of schizophrenic, brain injured, retarded, and normal children. *Amer. J. Orthopsychiat.,* 29:445–454.

Klein, M. (1932), *Psychoanalysis of Children.* New York: Norton.

Klineberg, S. (1965), Problems in social psychology. In: *Scientific Psychology: Principles and Approaches,* eds. B. B. Wolman and E. Nagel. New York: Basic Books.

Klopfer, B. et al. (1956), *Developments in the Rorschach Technique.* Yonkers, N.Y.: World Book, 2 Vols.

Koch, J. L. (1891), *Die Psychopathischen Minderwertigkeiten.* Ravensburg: Maier.

Kohut, H. (1966), Forms and transformations of narcissism. *J. Amer. Psychoanal. Assn.,* 14:243–272.

—— (1968), The psychoanalytic treatment of personality disorders. *The Psychoanalytic Study of the Child,* 23:86–113. New York: International Universities Press.

Kraepelin, E. (1904), *Lehrbuch der Psychiatrie.* Leipzig: Barth.

Kretschmer, E. (1925), *Physique and Character.* London: Kegan Paul.

Kris, E. (1950), Notes on the development and on some current problems of psychoanalytic child psychology. *The Psychoanalytic Study of the Child,* 5:24–45. New York: International Universities Press.

Kron, Y. & Brown, E. M. (1965), *Mainline to Nowhere: The Making of a Human Addict.* New York: Random House.

Kuo, A. Y. (1930), The genesis of the cat's response to the rat. *J. Compar. Psychol,* 2:1–35.

Lampl-de Groot, J. (1949), Neurotics, delinquents, and ideal formation. In: *Searchlights on Delinquency,* ed. K. R. Eissler. New York: International Universities Press.

Lawson, R. (1965), *Frustration.* New York: Macmillan.

Leighton, A. M., Clausen, J. A., & Wilson, R. N. (1957), *Explorations in Social Psychiatry.* New York: Basic Books.

Levy, D. M. (1937), Primary affect hunger. *Amer. J. Psychiat.,* 94:643–652.

—— (1943), *Maternal Overprotection.* New York: Columbia University Press.

—— (1951), The deprived and indulged forms of psychopathic personality. *Amer. J. Orthopsychiat.,* 21:250–254.

Lewin, B. D. (1950), *The Psychoanalysis of Elation.* New York: Norton.

Lewin, K. (1951), *Field Theory in Social Science.* New York: Harper.

Lidz, T., Fleck, S. & Cornelison, A. (1955), *Schizophrenia and the Family.* New York: International Universities Press.

Lindner, R. M. (1944), A formulation of the psychopathic personality. *Psychiatry,* 7:59–63.

Lindzey, G. & Aronson, E. (1968), *The Handbook of Social Psychology,* 1–5 (2nd Ed.). Reading, Mass.: Addison-Wesley.

Linton, R. (1956), *Culture and Mental Disorders.* Springfield, Ill.: Charles C Thomas.

Lippman, H. S. (1951), Psychopathic reactions in children. *Amer. J. Orthopsychiat.,* 21:227–231.

—— (1959), The "psychopathic personality" in childhood. In: *Symposia on Child and Juvenile Delinquency,* ed. B. Karpman. Washington, D.C.: Psychodynamic Monograph Series.

Lombroso, C. (1876), *Crime, its Causes and Remedies.* Boston: Little Brown & Co., 1911.

Lorenz, K. (1964), Remarks in discussion. In: *The Natural History of Aggression,* eds. J. D. McCarthy & F. J. Ebling. New York: Academic Press.

—— (1964), Ritualized fighting. In: *The Natural History of Aggression,* eds. J. D. McCarthy & F. J. Ebling. New York: Academic Press.

Loewenstein, R. M. (1951), The problem of interpretation. *Psychoanal. Quart.*, 20:1–14.

Lowrey, I. G. (1951), The development of psychopathic reactions. *Amer. J. Orthopsychiat.*, 21:242–249.

Lynn, R. (1963), Russian theory and research in schizophrenia. *Psychol. Bull.*, 60:486–498.

Makarenko, A. S. (1955), *The Road to Life*. Moscow: Foreign Language Publishing House.

Malinowski, B. (1929), *The Sexual Life of Savages in North-Western Melanesia*. New York: Harcourt, Brace, & Jovanovich.

Malis, G. Y. (1961), *Research on the Etiology of Schizophrenia*. New York: Plenum.

Malmquist, C. P. (1971), Depressive phenomena in children. In: *Handbook of Child Psychopathology*, ed. B. B. Wolman. New York: McGraw-Hill.

McCord, W. & McCord, E. (1956), *Psychopathy and Delinquency*. New York: Grune & Stratton.

—— McCord, J. & Lola, I. K. (1959), *Origins of Crime*. New York: Columbia University Press.

McLearn, G. E. (1964), Genetics and behavioral development. In: *Review of Child Development Research*, eds. M. S. Hoffman & L. N. W. Hoffman. New York: Russell Sage Foundation.

Mead, M. (1949), *Male and Female*. New York: William Morrow.

Mednick, S. (1958), A learning theory approach to research in schizophrenia. *Psychol. Bull.*, 55:316–327.

Meerloo, J. A. M. (1962), The concept of psychopathy. *Amer. J. Psychother.*, 16:645–654.

Mendelson, M. (1960), *Psychoanalytic Concepts of Depression*. Springfield, Ill.: Charles C. Thomas.

Monly, J. Hampson, J. G. & Hamspon, J. L. (1957), Imprinting and establishment of the gender role. *Arch. Neurol. & Psychiat.*, 77:333–336.

Munro, A. (1969), How to make parental deprivation seem important in depressive illness. *International Mental Health Research Newsletter*, 11/2:10–14.

Nagel, E. (1961), *The Structure of Science*. New York: Harcourt, Brace.

Nagera, H. (1964), Autoeroticism, autoerotic activities, and ego development. *The Psychoanalytic Study of the Child*, 19:240–255. New York: International Universities Press.

—— (1966), *Early Childhood Disturbances, the Infantile Neurosis, and the Adulthood Disturbances: Problems of a Developmental Psychoanalytic Psychology*. New York: International Universities Press.

Nuffield, E. J. A. (1954), The schizogenic mother. *Med. J. Australia*, 2:282–286.

Odegaard, O. (1954), Incidence of mental disease in Norway during World War II. *Acte. Psychiat. et Neurol. Scand.,* 29:333–353.

O'Neal, P. Robins, L. King, L. J. Schaefer, J. (1962), Parental deviance and the genesis of sociopathic personality. *Amer. J. Psychiat.,* 118:1114–1124.

Opler, M. K. (1959), *Culture and Mental Health.* New York: Macmillan.

—— (1965), Cultural determinants of mental disorders. In: *Handbook of Clinical Psychology,* ed. B. B. Wolman. New York: McGraw-Hill.

Parsons, T. and Bales, R. F. (1955), *Family, Socialization and Interaction Process.* Glencoe: The Free Press.

Pavlov, I. P. (1928), *Lectures on Conditioned Reflexes.* New York: Liveright.

Perley, J. M. and Guze, S. B. (1962), The stability and usefulness of clinical criteria. *New Eng. J. Med.,* 266:421–426.

Piaget, J. (1932), *The Moral Judgment of the Child.* New York: Basic Books, 1948.

—— (1954), *The Construction of Reality in the Child.* New York: Basic Books.

Planck, M. (1933), *Where is Science Going?* New York: Norton.

Polani, P. E. (1967), Occurrence and effect of human chromosome abnormalities. In: *Social and Genetic Influences on Life and Death,* eds. Platt & Parker. New York: Plenum.

Powdermaker, H. (1933), *Life in Lesu.* New York: Viking.

Prichard, J. C. (1835), *Treatise on Insanity.* London: Gilbert & Piper.

Proshansky, H. (1970), *Environmental Psychology.* New York: Holt, Rinehart & Winston.

—— & Seidenberg, B. (eds.) (1965), *Basic Studies in Social Psychology.* New York: Holt, Rinehart & Winston.

Rado, S. (1928), The problem of melancholia. *Internat. J. Psycho-Anal.,* 9:420–438.

—— (1956–1962), *Psychoanalysis of Behavior.* New York: Grune & Stratton, 2 Vols.

Rank, O. (1929), *The Trauma of Birth.* New York, Harcourt, Brace, Jovanovich.

Reich, W. (1945), *Character Analysis* (2nd Ed.). New York: Orgone Institute.

Rheingold, J. C. (1964), The Fear of Being a Woman. New York: Grune & Stratton.

Richter, D. (ed.) (1957), *Schizophrenia: Somatic Aspects.* New York: Macmillan.

Ritvo, S. & Solnit, A. J. (1958), Influences of early mother-child interaction on identification processes. *The Psychoanalytic Study of the Child,* 13:64–85.

Ross, N. (1960), Panel: an examination of nosology according to psychoanalytic concepts. *J. Amer. Psychoanal. Assn.*, 8:535–551.

Salzman, L. (1960), Paranoid states—theory and therapy. *Arch. Gen. Psychiat.*, 2:679–693.

Sander, L. W. (1962), Issues in early mother-child interaction. *J. Amer. Acad. Child Psychiat.*, 7:141–165.

Schmideberg, M. (1961), Psychotherapy of the criminal psychopath. *Arch. Crim. Psychodynam.*, 4:742–755.

Segal, H. (1967), Melanie Klein's technique. In: *Psychoanalytic Techniques: A Handbook for the Practicing Psychoanalyst*, ed. B. B. Wolman. New York: Basic Books.

Segal, H. (1972), Melanie Klein's technique of child analysis. In: *Handbook of Child Psychoanalysis*, ed. B. B. Wolman. New York: Van Nostrand.

Shapiro, D. (1965), *Neurotic Styles*. New York: Basic Books.

Sheldon, W. H. (1949), *Varieties of Delinquent Youth*. New York: Harper.

Sherif, M. & Cantril, H. (1947), *The Psychology of Ego-Involvements*. New York: Wiley.

—— & Sherif, C. W. (1964), *Reference Groups*. New York: Harper & Row.

Solomon, D. (ed) (1966), *The Marijuana Papers*. Indianapolis: Bobbs-Merrill.

Spitz, R. (1945), Hospitalism—an inquiry into the genesis of psychiatric conditions in early childhood. *The Psychoanalytic Study of the Child*, 1:53–74. New York: International Universities Press.

—— (1950), Possible infantile precursors of psychopathy. *Amer. J. Orthopsychiat.*, 20:240–248.

—— (1965), *The First Year of Life*. New York: International Universities Press.

Spranger, O. (1928), *Types of Men*. Halle: Niemyer.

Srole, L., Langner, T. S., Michael, S. T., Opler, M. K. & Rennie, T. A. (1962), *Mental Health in Metropolis*. New York: McGraw-Hill.

Stern, J. A. & McDonald, D. G. (1965), Physiological correlates of mental disease. *Ann. Rev. Psychol.*, 16:225–264.

Stoller, R. J., Garfinkel, H. & Rosen, A. C. (1960), Passing and maintenance of sexual identification in an intersexed patient. *Arch. Gen. Psychiat.*, 2:379–384.

Strachey, J. (1934), The nature of the therapeutic action of psychoanalysis. *Internat. J. Psycho-Anal.*, 15:127–169.

Sullivan, H. S. (1953), *Interpersonal Theory of Psychiatry*. New York: Norton.

Thompson, C. (1950), *Psychoanalysis: Evolution and Development*. New York: Hermitage.

Thorpe, W. H. (1956), *Learning and Instinct in Animals*. Cambridge, Mass.: Harvard University Press.

Tinbergen, N. (1953), *The Study of Instincts*. London: Oxford.

Towne, R. D., Messinger, S. L. & Sampson, H. (1962), Schizophrenia and the marital family: accommodations to symbiosis. *Family Process*, 1:304–318.

Walton, D. (1960), Drug addiction and habit formation. An attempted integration. *J. Ment. Sci.*, 106:1195–1229.

Waring, M. & Ricks, D. (1965), Family patterns of children who become adult schizophrenics. *J. Neurosis and Ment. Dis.*, 140/5:351–364.

Weakland, J. H. (1960), The double-bind hypothesis of schizophrenia and three party interaction. In: *The Etiology of Schizophrenia*, ed. D. D. Jackson, New York: Basic Books.

Weiss, E. (1932), Regression and projection in the superego. *Internat. J. Psycho-Anal.*, 13:449–478.

Westwood, G. & Schofield, M. J. (1960), *A Minority: A Report on the Life of the Male Homosexual in Great Britain*. London: Longmans.

Whiting, J. M. & Child, I. L. (1953), *Child Training and Personality*. New Haven: Yale University Press.

Wittenborn, J. R. (1963), Distinctions within psychotic dimensions: a principal content analysis. *J. Nerv. & Ment. Dis.*, 137:543–547.

—— (1965), Depression. In: *Handbook of Clinical Psychology*, ed. B. B. Wolman. New York: McGraw-Hill.

Wolberg, L. R. (1944), The character structure of the rejected child. *Nervous Child*, 3:74–88.

Wolff, P. H. (1966), *The Causes, Controls and Organization of Behavior in the Neonate* [*Psychological Issues*, Monogr. 17]. New York: International Universities Press.

Wolman, B. B. (1938), Chance: a philosophical study. *Tarbitz, Hebrew Univ. Quart.*, 10:56–80.

—— (1946), *Prolegomena to Sociology*. Jerusalem: Kiryat-Sefer.

—— (1949a), Disturbances in acculturation. *Amer. J. Psychother.*, 3:601–615.

—— (1949b), *Freedom and Discipline in Education*. Tel Aviv: Massadah.

—— (1951), Spontaneous groups in childhood and adolescence. *J. Soc. Psychol.*, 34:171–182.

—— (1953), Sociological analysis of Israel. *M. M. Kaplan Jubilee Volume*, pp. 531–549.

—— (1957), Explorations in latent schizophrenia. *Amer. J. Psychother.*, 11:560–588.

—— (1958), Instrumental, mutual acceptance, and vectorial groups. *Acta Sociologia*, 3:19–28.

—— (1960a), *Contemporary Theories and Systems in Psychology*. New York: Harper & Row.

—— (1960b), The impact of failure on group cohesiveness. *J. Soc. Psychol.*, 51:409–418.

—— (1961), The fathers of schizophrenic patients. *Acta Psychotherapeutica*, 9:193–210.

—— (1965a), *Handbook of Clinical Psychology*. New York: McGraw-Hill.

—— (1965b), Family dynamics and schizophrenia. *J. Health and Human Behav.*, 6:163–169.

—— (1966a), *Vectoriasis Praecox or the Group of Schizophrenias*. Springfield: Charles C. Thomas.

—— (1966b), Dr. Jekyll and Mr. Hyde: A new theory of the manic-depressive disorder. *Proceedings of the New York Academy of Science*, 28:1020–1032.

—— (1966c), Classification of mental disorders. *Psychother. and Psychosomat.*, 14:50–65.

—— (1966d), Transference and countertransference as interindividual cathexis. *Psychoanal. Rev.*, 53:91–101.

—— (1967a), *Psychoanalytic Techniques*. New York: Basic Books.

—— (1967b), The socio-psycho-somatic theory of schizophrenia. *Psychother. and Psychosomat.*, 15:373–387.

—— (1968), Le genre de vie schizophrenique. *Médecine et Hygiène*, 26:1–3.

—— (1969), Interaction group psychotherapy with schizophrenics. *Psychotherapy*, 6:194–198.

—— (1970), *Children without Childhood*. New York: Grune & Stratton.

—— (1971), Dada: A willful escape. *Encounter*, 2:53–63.

—— (1972), *Adolescents in a Changing Society*. (In press.)

Wynne, L. D. & Rychoff, I. M. (1958), Pseudo-mutuality in the family relations in schizophrenia. *Psychiatry*, 21:205–220.

Yarrow, L. J. (1964), Separation from parents in early childhood. In: *Child Development Research*, eds. M. L. Hoffman and L. N. W. Hoffman. New York: Russell Sage Foundation.

Zilboorg, G. & Henry, G. W. (1941), *A History of Medical Psychology*. New York: Norton.

Name Index

323

Subject Index